The Last Word

The Last Word

*An Eyewitness Account of
the Trial of Jeremy Thorpe*

AUBERON WAUGH

LITTLE, BROWN AND COMPANY • BOSTON • TORONTO

FIRST AMERICAN EDITION

LIBRARY OF CONGRESS CATALOGING IN PUBLICATION DATA

Waugh, Auberon.
   The last word, an eyewitness account of the trial of Jeremy Thorpe.

   1. Thorpe, Jeremy. 2. Trials (Murder) — England — London. 3. Trials (Conspiracy) — England — London. I. Title.
KD373.T5W38.   345.42′02523   80–18164
ISBN 0–316–92632–9

BP

PRINTED IN THE UNITED STATES OF AMERICA

For Richard Ingrams, guide, philosopher and friend, one of the few Englishmen who emerges with any credit from the narrative of these events

"Remember, I have the last word."

The Honourable Mr Justice Cantley
Old Bailey, 11 June 1979

Contents

The Last Word

"A Rather Bizarre and Surprising Case"

On Friday 24 October 1975, the Right Honourable Harold Wilson was Prime Minister, the Right Honourable Jeremy Thorpe was leader of the Liberal Party whose support was becoming more and more necessary to keep the Labour Government in power. Thorpe's friend, Antony Armstrong-Jones, Earl of Snowdon, was the husband of Princess Margaret, Countess of Snowdon, the Queen's sister. Thorpe's lawyer was Lord Goodman, an eminent man in public life.

That night a dark-coloured Ford Escort stopped in a lay-by on a stretch of the A39 which runs up Porlock Hill and across the moors to Lynmouth on a wild cliff-top stretch of the Somerset coast. A man got out, and ran round the front of the car as if to change places; a second man got out from the driver's seat, followed by a Great Dane. The second man, later identified as Andrew Gino Newton, an airline pilot, shot the dog through the head, killing it instantly, and then pointed the pistol at the first man, later identified as Norman Scott, a former stable lad and male model. The pistol appeared to jam. Shouting, "Oh fuck it! – I'll get you," Newton got into the car and drove back towards Porlock. Scott was left, sobbing hysterically, beside the corpse of his dog on a dark, wet and windy night on the top of Exmoor.

Later he saw headlights coming over the moor, ran out and flagged down the car. He said, "Oh please. He's shot my dog. He tried to shoot me. It's all because of Jeremy Thorpe."

On Tuesday 16 March 1976 Newton stood trial in Exeter accused of possessing a firearm with intent to endanger life. Scott was the chief prosecution witness. Two days earlier, he had been denounced on the front page of the *Sunday Times* as an incorrigible liar in a signed article by the Right Honourable Jeremy Thorpe, leader of the Liberal Party. On the day the trial opened, Harold Wilson announced his resignation, Princess Margaret and Lord Snowdon announced their separation. Newton was sentenced to two years' imprisonment, serving slightly over one year. On 10 May, Thorpe resigned as Liberal leader.

On Friday 4 August 1978 Thorpe was arrested with his old friend, David Holmes, a former deputy treasurer of the Liberal Party, and two others. They were charged at Minehead police station, Somerset, with conspiracy to murder Norman Scott. Thorpe was also charged with inciting David Holmes to murder him.

At Minehead Magistrates' Court, it was suggested that Scott had become a danger to Thorpe's reputation as the result of a homosexual relationship between the two men in the early 1960s. Committed for trial on 13 December 1978, they were to have appeared at the Central Criminal Court, Old Bailey, on 30 April 1979, but on Mr Thorpe's application to the Lord Chief Justice the trial was postponed until 8 May, so that Thorpe could stand for re-election as Member of Parliament for North Devon. Despite enthusiastic support from many Liberals in the constituency, he lost his seat.

The trial, which started on 8 May, ended on 22 June 1979 with a unanimous verdict of "Not guilty," after the jury had been out for fifty-two hours.

Lord Goodman issued a statement to the press immediately after the verdict was announced: ". . . it would appear to be quite unnecessary for any further statement to be made by me except to reaffirm that there is not a scintilla of truth in any of the allegations that have been aired."

Regina

versus

David Holmes, George Deakin, John Le Mesurier,
John Jeremy Thorpe

Dramatis Personae

The Prosecution Witnesses

NORMAN SCOTT (born Josiffe) The victim, who claimed his homosexual relationship with Thorpe led to a murder attempt. "A hysterical, warped personality, accomplished sponger and very skilful at exciting and exploiting sympathy," said the judge. "At one time he was suspected of stealing silver from a house where he was living free in Dublin, but he has denied this. He is a crook . . . He is a fraud, he is a sponger. He is a whiner. He is a parasite. But, of course, he could still be telling the truth. It is a question of belief . . . I am not expressing any opinion."

ANDREW GINO NEWTON (born Nievedonski) The hit man who said he had been hired to murder Norman Scott. He was "a highly incompetent performer," said the judge. "A chump . . . a conceited bungler . . . I doubt whether he has paid any income tax . . . one has to look at his evidence with great care."

PETER JOSEPH BESSELL Chief prosecution witness. Former Liberal MP for Bodmin and close colleague of Jeremy Thorpe, who said that Thorpe in his presence had incited David Holmes to murder Norman Scott, and requested both of them to join a conspiracy to murder him. "A very intelligent, very articulate man," said the judge. "He must have impressed the electors of Cornwall very much. He was a lay preacher at the same time as being [as he put it] sexually promiscuous. And therefore a humbug . . . You must look at Bessell's evidence with suspicion."

DAVID MILLER Printer. A friend of Newton who introduced him to George Deakin as someone "who would do anything for a laugh or a giggle." Later he taped conversations with two of the accused which were produced as evidence. The judge described him as "the last of the dubious commercial witnesses."

JACK ARNOLD HAYWARD A millionaire who paid large sums of money to Thorpe about this time. The judge described him as "a nice respectable witness."

NADIR DINSHAW A Channel Islands business man of Asian extraction who received sums of money from Mr Hayward on Thorpe's behalf and paid them to David Holmes at Thorpe's request, sometimes in small cash parcels. Another "nice respectable witness."

COLIN LAMBERT An old soldier and former employee of one of the defendants, whom he reported (at Minehead) as saying, "A fool was hired to kill Norman Scott. Someone more like you should have been hired to do the job." The judge said it might be that this defendant was trying to make out he had a bigger part in something than he actually had had.

MICHAEL CHALLES The policeman. Detective Chief Superintendent, Somerset and Avon Constabulary. Twenty-six years a policeman. Described by Deakin, after the verdict, as "a real gentleman." The judge had no comment about him until, prompted by the Crown, he agreed that the police conduct had been "impeccable."

Plus a small supporting cast of experts, extras, uncontested affidavits, et cetera.

The Lawyers

PETER MURRAY TAYLOR QC Leading counsel for the Crown.

GARETH WILLIAMS QC Leading counsel for Mr Deakin. Frequently referred to by his learned friends as "Mr Jones".

JOHN CHARLES MATHEW QC Leading counsel for Mr Holmes. Educated by Jesuits, only son of the late Sir Theobald Mathew, DPP 1944–64.

DENIS COWLEY QC Leading counsel for Mr Le Mesurier. Manx Old Radleian. Wears moustache.

GEORGE ALFRED CARMAN QC   Leading counsel for Mr Thorpe. Educated at St Joseph's College, Blackpool. An Oxford contemporary of Thorpe's.

Plus a huge supporting cast of junior counsel, solicitors, junior solicitors, articled clerks and learned gentlemen with watching briefs.

The Defendants

GEORGE DEAKIN   A Conservative. Described by the judge as being "of unblemished reputation," despite earlier prison sentence. Club owner and trader in gambling machines, South Wales. Married.

DAVID MALCOLM HOLMES   Financial consultant. Former deputy treasurer of the Liberal Party. Old and close friend of Thorpe. A bachelor. Did not give evidence.

JOHN LE MESURIER   Carpet dealer, South Wales. Acquaintance of Deakin, business associate of Holmes. A noisy fellow. Married. Did not give evidence.

THE RIGHT HONOURABLE JOHN JEREMY THORPE   A party politician. Member of Her Majesty's Most Honourable Privy Council, former Member of Parliament and leader of the Liberal Party. Did not give evidence. Described by the judge as "a national figure with a very distinguished public record." The fact that he had not given evidence did not mean that his good character should be ignored, said the judge. Thorpe's letters to Scott indicated an affectionate relationship, but "you must not assume that mere affection necessarily implies buggery."

Others

RINKA   A murdered Great Dane. Did not give evidence. The judge had no comment to make about this animal.

THE HONOURABLE SIR JOSEPH DONALDSON CANTLEY   The judge, aged sixty-eight. A press report describes how, trying a case which involved a bull-dozer accident to a twenty-three-year-old man, the judge was told that his injuries had affected the man's sex life. The judge asked if he was married. "No," replied counsel. "Well, I can't see how it affects his sex life," the judge observed. His lordship was married for the first time at fifty-six to Hilda, widow of a fellow judge, Sir Denis Gerard. Of himself, the judge said, "Remember, I have the last word."

The Charges

George Deakin
David Malcolm Holmes
John Le Mesurier
John Jeremy Thorpe

that on divers days between 1 January 1973 and 18 November 1977 in the county of Devon and elsewhere they conspired together and with others unknown to murder Norman Scott

John Jeremy Thorpe

that between 1 January 1969 and 30 March 1969 he unlawfully incited David Malcolm Holmes to murder Norman Scott

Diary of Number One Court
Central Criminal Court
Old Bailey

Regina
versus
D. M. Holmes, G. Deakin, J. Le Mesurier, J. J. Thorpe
8 May 1979 – 22 June 1979

Day one: 8 May Charges read. Jury sworn. Legal submissions to have Mr Bessell's evidence excluded. Also Mr Scott's and Mr Newton's.

Day two: 9 May Legal submissions end. Mr Taylor opens case for Crown.

Day three: 10 May Crown narrative continues.

Day four: 11 May Mr Taylor concludes his outline and calls Mr Bessell.

Day five: 14 May Bessell's examination-in-chief continued.

Day six: 15 May Bessell cross-examined by Mr Mathew and Mr Carman (for Holmes and Thorpe).

Day seven: 16 May Mr Carman's cross-examination continued.

Day eight: 17 May Mr Carman's cross-examination concluded.

Day nine: 18 May Mr Taylor re-examines Bessell, then calls Norman Scott.

Day ten: 21 May Scott's examination-in-chief continued.

Day eleven: 22 May Scott briefly cross-examined by Mr Williams and Mr Cowley (for Deakin and Le Mesurier), then by Mr Carman. Re-examined by Mr Taylor.

Day twelve: 23 May Various minor witnesses and sworn statements. Then Andrew Gino Newton called.

Day thirteen: 24 May Newton's examination-in-chief continued.

Day fourteen: 25 May Newton cross-examined by Mr Mathew, then by Mr Williams.

Day fifteen: 29 May Newton's cross-examination by Mr Williams concluded. Then Mr Cowley cross-examines, Mr Taylor re-examines. Newton dismissed. Minor witnesses.

Day sixteen: 30 May David Miller called by Crown.

Day seventeen: 31 May Miller cross-examined by Mr Williams and Mr Cowley; re-examined. Minor witnesses, including Mr Colin Lambert.

Day eighteen: 4 June Mr Jack Hayward and Mr Nadir Dinshaw.

Day nineteen: 5 June Written statements. Mr Challes called. Various legal arguments.

Day twenty: 6 June Challes's examination concluded. Crown case concluded. Legal submissions of no case to answer.

Day twenty-one: 7 June The defence. No evidence called for Holmes. Deakin examined and cross-examined. No evidence called for Le Mesurier or Thorpe. Defence ends.

Day twenty-two: 11 June Mr Taylor sums up for Crown.

Day twenty-three: 12 June Mr Taylor continues his case.

Day twenty-four: 13 June Mr Mathew's case for acquitting Holmes.

Day twenty-five: 14 June Mr Williams for Deakin: Mr Cowley for Le Mesurier. Mr Carman for Thorpe.

Day twenty-six: 15 June Mr Carman concluded.

Day twenty-seven: 18 June Judge's summing up.

Day twenty-eight: 19 June Ditto.

Day twenty-nine: 20 June Summing up concluded. Jury out. Defendants' bail withdrawn.

Day thirty: 21 June Jury out all day.

Day thirty-one: 22 June Verdict.

Epilogue: 1 July Service of Thanksgiving for Mr Thorpe's acquittal.

Introduction

On the second day of his closing speech, Mr Thorpe's counsel, Mr George Carman QC, urged the jury to reflect that a not guilty verdict was not a "certificate of innocence" by the jury. In law, he said, it meant that the prosecution had failed to make out the charges – no more and no less than that. In almost the same breath, Mr Carman corrected a suggestion of the previous day when, in a fine burst of oratory, he had declared that, as a result of the evidence, the jury would be aware that a political life and political future were now "irrevocably and irreversibly" denied to his client. "But at his age," said Mr Carman next day, having thought about it overnight and possibly discussed the matter with instructing solicitors, "there may still be a place somewhere in the public life and public service of this country for a man of his talents."

On the first point, at least, Mr Carman is surely wrong. His client, the Right Honourable Jeremy Thorpe, a member of Her Majesty's Most Honourable Privy Council, one-time and possibly future Member of Parliament, leader of the Liberal Party, may not have been given a certificate to prove his innocence of conspiracy and incitement to murder. But he has a cast-iron guarantee that he is innocent, not only in the sense that everybody in Britain is innocent until proved guilty of a crime but in the more particular sense that he can never be charged with this alleged conspiracy or this alleged incitement again. If, in the course of this book, I seem to emphasise the Crown evidence, which was heard in an unsuccessful attempt to prove that Mr Thorpe *did* conspire with others to murder the male model with whom he enjoyed at one time a "close, even affectionate relationship," and that he *did* incite his friend, David Holmes to murder him, this is for a very simple reason. No evidence to the contrary was ever offered. Mr Carman did not call any witnesses in his client's defence, nor did Mr Thorpe offer any evidence himself. Only one of the defendants gave evidence – George Deakin – and his evidence was chiefly concerned to establish that the conspiracy (in which he agreed he had a part) was one to frighten not to murder Norman Scott. Mr Thorpe, by contrast, had explicitly denied to the police that he had a part in any conspiracy to frighten.

It is not possible for me – nor is it any part of a chronicler's job – to guess what Mr Thorpe's defence might have been had he chosen to offer any. As the judge was at pains to remind the jury in the course of his summing up, it is the Crown's duty to establish a charge, not the defence's duty to refute it; if the jury had any doubts they should acquit.

So it is inevitable, under the circumstances, that any account of the Thorpe trial should read as a catalogue of reasons for believing that the defendants were guilty, modified only by defence counsel's efforts to cast doubt on these reasons. By the end, of course, after we have had four eloquent speeches by the four defence QCs, reinforced by the judge's tirade against the three chief Crown witnesses, we shall be able to understand the verdict rather better. But it is as well at this stage to emphasise, in a way Mr Carman was apparently reluctant to emphasise, that the jury have effectively given Mr Thorpe a certificate of innocence and nothing whatever must be allowed to impugn it. Mr Thorpe is innocent. That is not a question of opinion or belief or interpretation but a matter of historical fact, and nothing in these pages must be interpreted as calling it into question. The fact of Mr Thorpe's innocence is beyond question and beyond discussion.

On one view of the trial, its results were reassuring enough. As Mr Carman put it, it was "a matter properly investigated and properly decided." To those who followed the story from its beginning, it will seem·less likely than before that an innocent man of good character, let alone a "national figure with a very distinguished public record," will ever be wrongly convicted. There is no tradition in British political life by which party politicians hire gunmen to murder – or even frighten – members of the public who threaten to embarrass their political careers, and it was reassuring to learn that their presence is not yet established. A few of those who listened to Judge Cantley's summing up may have wondered how such a conspiracy could ever be proved against a man in public life. But then the tremendous respect and deference we all feel towards men in public life may make it hard for us to believe that any such person could ever be guilty of consenting to behaviour of this sort. In any case, the verdict shows that these anxieties, if they exist, belong to the future, not to the present.

A different misgiving was expressed – chiefly in the House of

Commons, but also in other official quarters – about the propriety of the charges having been brought at all. It was pointed out that Mr Thorpe had been put to considerable expense and inconvenience – others described it more luridly, talking about the "agony" of Jeremy Thorpe and his family – to establish his innocence of a charge when the law had always assumed him innocent in the first place. Mr Carman was adamant that no adverse conclusion should be drawn from the fact that his client did not apply for costs at the end of the day, and I am sure that nobody present drew any such conclusions. But the astounding fact remains that a large number of people, including the Director of Public Prosecutions, the Avon and Somerset Police and many others, were prepared to entertain the bizarre notion, at some stage, that Thorpe might be guilty. I have to confess that I was among their number. It was this erroneous idea which explains my early interest in what became known as the Scott affair, and my decision to write this book about the trial. It may be read, if people choose, as a gesture of atonement for ever having entertained the silly idea that a Privy Councillor, an MP, an Old Etonian, a barrister, a friend of prime ministers, archbishops and high officials, a former client of Lord Goodman, could ever be found guilty of conspiring to murder a homosexual male model of lower-middle class background and doubtful record. Equally, it may be read, if people prefer, for the light it throws on the prosecution case, offering a partial explanation why so many people were prepared, at one time, to entertain such a preposterous idea.

No doubt the real reason that many of us were open to such wicked and uncharitable thoughts about an eminent party politician lies much deeper. We must all examine our consciences. For my own part, when I first made Mr Thorpe's acquaintance, I felt uneasy in his presence. Becoming political correspondent of the *Spectator* in 1967 I had the opportunity to watch him at close quarters for some time, both on the floor of the House of Commons and in its lobbies and corridors, and decided that my unease might be explained by the double-breasted waistcoats he affected. It is a curious fact that these unusual and slightly absurd garments were worn by prefects as a badge of office at the public school in Somerset where I boarded. From such irrelevant threads as these our intuitions are woven. Moreover Thorpe, as leader of the Liberal Party, had an unmistakably prefectorial air about him which I mistrusted. It would be absurd to pretend that all prefects at my school were hypocrites, sodomites or criminal psychopaths, but enough of them seemed to have tendencies in one or more of those directions to put me on my guard against anyone who retained the uniform and the mannerisms of a public school prefect in later life. For a long time it struck me as significant that none of those who seemed most convinced of Thorpe's innocence – Harold Wilson, the Prime Minister, Harold Evans, editor of the *Sunday Times*, Robert Edwards, editor of the *Sunday Mirror*, most devastatingly of all, Sir Joseph Cantley, the judge – had ever boarded at an English public school.

Later, when I left the *Spectator* and became, for a time, political correspondent of the satirical scandal sheet *Private Eye*, I was not at all surprised to learn of a number of stories at the *Eye* alleging homosexual tendencies in Thorpe at some time in the past. Such tendencies seemed perfectly in keeping with his flamboyant, histrionic manner, his double-breasted waistcoats and general air of a public school show-off.

These stories, as I say, occasioned neither surprise nor shock. So far as they were of any interest to a newspaper like *Private Eye*, it was for their joke value. The source for many of them was Tom Driberg, the slightly sinister left-wing Labour MP for Barking who, shortly before his death, was created Lord Bradwell. Among what I feel may have been his many and various undercover activities, Tom composed an indecent crossword for *Private Eye*, and acted as unpaid informant on the homosexual establishment in Westminster and Whitehall. Few of his stories ever got into print, partly because they were defamatory and unprovable, partly because they were unreliable. Tom suffered from an illusion which is common among homosexuals, that all men would be homosexual if they were true to their natures, and that many more men are truer to their natures in this way than is generally supposed. Among those denounced by Tom Driberg to me as practising homosexuals were statesmen of much greater distinction than Mr Thorpe and who, I am almost sure, are completely innocent of any such behaviour.

Even so, casting a jaundiced eye down the list of members of Her Majesty's Most Honourable Privy Council which appears in *Whitaker's Almanack*, I have no difficulty in finding four, possibly five members who, I am reasonably sure, were practising homosexuals at the time of their appointment to the Privy Council – most of them when it was still illegal. The phenomenon of the crypto-homosexual or "closet queen" has always been a recognised feature of British public life.

So the suggestion that Thorpe might have had homosexual tendencies at one time did not seem particularly remarkable. Kinsey records that thirty-seven per cent of all American males have a significant homosexual experience at some stage in their lives, but among Englishmen who have attended all-male boarding schools, the proportion is almost certainly much higher. Just as distinguished old boys prefer to forget their youthful indiscretions, there is a tendency among Englishmen in public life to cover up for each other. Looking through my files for this period, I can trace only one occasion on which even an oblique reference was made to this tendency of Mr Thorpe. Whatever may be said for or against the British press, it does not regard gossip of this sort as news. When Norman Scott's allegations of a homosexual relationship started arriving in the office of *Private Eye*, either in early 1973 or late 1972, I remember reading them dutifully, but I did not attach any importance to them. As I remember, they arrived – from what source I do not know – as photocopies of a handwritten narrative. Essentially, this described what later became public property as Norman Scott's evidence of alleged events at Mrs Ursula Thorpe's house on the night of 8 November 1961 – his seduction and buggery by Jeremy Thorpe. Nobody in the office of *Private Eye* liked the story much – it was sordid without being particularly funny, its unsolicited appearance had a faint smell of blackmail, it was defamatory, unprovable and, above all, it was more than ten years old. I do not know whether I threw it away or someone else did, but there was no record of its existence when I came to look for it some eighteen months later.

A further reason why *Private Eye* – and, for that matter, the whole of Fleet Street – decided to leave the story alone was that Thorpe had married, fathered a child and been widowed in the meantime and was, in fact, on the point of remarrying. A bachelor might have been fair game, but a reformed homosexual, whose only apparent crime was to have had an unfortunate affair with a neurotic many years earlier, was safe. I stress this point because it seems important. There was not the slightest danger to Thorpe that any newspaper in England was going to print Scott's allegation. Most of them had been given an opportunity to do so, and had declined. Quite apart from the very real dangers of a libel action, the story simply was not news. Before the dog-shooting episode of 24 October 1975, Scott's story had also been presented to the Conservative Party whose chairman, Lord Carrington, had wisely decided to have nothing to do with it. Its outline was well known to the Liberal leadership; the press had had an opportunity to print it under court privilege, when Scott blurted it out at the inquest on his friend, Gwen Parry-Jones, in May 1972. In other words, although

Thorpe may not have realised it and Thorpe's friend David Holmes (who would have pleaded guilty to a charge of conspiracy to frighten Scott) certainly did not, Norman Scott did not present the slightest danger to the Liberal leader when the incident occurred which gave rise to the charge of conspiracy to murder. Scott was simply an embarrassment.

In order to explain and emphasise this point, I will need to recapitulate the narrative of events. In November 1961 when Thorpe met and allegedly seduced Norman Scott (then called Josiffe), he was a foppish Liberal back-bench MP, a bachelor of thirty-two with homosexual tendencies. The affair, if such it was, or the close, even affectionate relationship, as one prefers, was over by the spring of 1963. In 1967 Thorpe was elected leader of the Liberal Party and in 1968, a bachelor of thirty-nine, he decided to marry. His bride, Caroline Allpass, was a pleasant, uncomplicated ambitious girl, who bore him a son next year, in 1969, and was killed in a motor accident soon after the General Election of June 1970. At one time it was fashionable to suggest that she had committed suicide after a call from Scott, and that revenge might be a further motive behind the alleged murder conspiracy, but there is not a shred of evidence to suggest that she committed suicide. Scott spoke to her once on the telephone, some time earlier. Friends who saw her in the two weeks before her death describe her as being garrulous and discussing Scott's allegations freely with people she met, possibly under mild sedation from Valium or some such preparation, as many young women appear to be nowadays. On the day of her death Thorpe decided to take his infant son up with him in the train so that he could be in time for the opening of the new Parliament, leaving Caroline Thorpe to drive from North Devon to London alone. About half-way there, approaching a roundabout, she crashed into a lorry. A witness at the inquest described her a few minutes before the crash as having a dazed appearance. There was nothing wrong with the car. It seems probable that she fell asleep at the wheel, or lost her concentration.

This incident caused a great surge of sympathy for Thorpe. Not one to miss his moment, he built a monument to her memory in a wild corner of Exmoor and arranged for the Archbishop of Canterbury to come down to North Devon by helicopter to bless it. At the time, I wrote a strong piece in the London *Evening Standard* urging him to take it down again on environmental grounds. The best monument to this blameless lady, I urged, would be to leave a little patch of Exmoor unspoiled in her memory. He chose to ignore my advice and the monument to Caroline Thorpe stands to this day on Codden Hill, a permanent source of irritation to those of us who live in the region, and a permanent reminder of the former Liberal Member for North Devon.

After this moment, my comments about the Liberal leader seem to have grown more austere. In 1973 Thorpe married Marion, first wife of Lord Harewood, a cousin of the Queen. This did not quite make him a member of the Royal Family, but the alliance seems to have done him no harm with the non-Conformist Liberal voters of North Devon, who returned him with a much increased majority. Commenting on the overall result of this election at the time, I wrote in *Private Eye* (March 1974) perhaps rather sourly:

"The most disappointing result has been Jeremy Thorpe's success in North Devon. Thorpe was already conceited enough and now threatens to become one of the great embarrassments of politics. Soon I may have to reveal some of the things in my file on this revolting man."

I hope this tiny paragraph tucked away in a corner of *Private Eye* did not alarm him unduly. It was the only fruit of Norman Scott's unrelenting activities throughout this period. By chance my own home in Somerset is only a few miles from Thorpe's constituency of North Devon. Scott had settled in North Devon some time before the February 1974 election, and was to be heard declaiming the account of his relationship with Thorpe in many of the pubs on Exmoor. I never heard him and to this day have never met him but various accounts of his behaviour had reached me. At that stage, it still did not seem a matter to take seriously. Apart from my little remark, the only way to measure the possible result of Scott's presence in North Devon was that Thorpe's majority increased from 369 in June 1970 to 11,072 in February 1974.

Between the two General Elections of 1974, reports about Scott changed emphasis. From being the hunter, Scott had become the prey. There were stories of his being threatened by strong-arm men, beaten up in Barnstaple Market, of helicopters buzzing his cottage on Exmoor. One was not sure how much these stories should be credited – perhaps the Liberals of North Devon were striking back, perhaps some friends of Thorpe were trying to protect him, perhaps there was a more sinister conspiracy or perhaps Scott was imagining things. One awaited developments with some interest but without extravagant feelings of sympathy for either party.

Just before the second General Election of 1974, I find I was advising readers of *Private Eye* to vote Liberal, on the grounds that

Ladbroke, the bookmaker, was offering 150 to one against a Liberal victory:

"If enough of us put our votes where our money is we might make the killing of all time – even if this means having the absurd Jeremy Thorpe with his peculiar tastes and unsavoury habits as Prime Minister for a while."

Possibly as a result of this advice, voters deserted the Liberal Party in droves, and Thorpe found his North Devon majority reduced from 11,072 to 6,721.

Thereafter all interest in Thorpe and his tangled affairs subsided until the night of 24 October 1975 when Scott was found on Porlock Moor in a terrified and hysterical state by a passing motorist, beside the corpse of his Great Dane bitch, Rinka, who had been shot through the head. Scott's story was that he had been the victim of a murder attempt by a man whose gun had jammed.

That was all I knew at the time. I knew nothing of Peter Bessell's testimony, that Thorpe had been planning to kill Scott as long ago as 1969. I had never heard of David Holmes, Thorpe's old friend and best man at Thorpe's first wedding, named by the would-be hit man, Andrew Newton, as the person who had hired him to murder Scott. But it seemed to me that this apparent attempt to murder a man whom the Liberals found politically embarrassing lifted the Scott affair from being of minority, largely satirical interest, to being a matter of genuine public concern. At that time nobody who had followed the story doubted for a moment that Scott had been the victim of a murder attempt. Nobody imagined that anything useful could have been achieved by frightening him, particularly when we all saw the results of his fright on Porlock Moor.

My local newspaper, the *West Somerset Free Press*, carried a fairly full account of what it called the Mystery of the Dog in a Fog. It even mentioned Norman Scott's claim to be a friend of Jeremy Thorpe. But the *West Somerset Free Press*, whose area includes Porlock, is not much read outside Somerset. The *Daily Express* carried a rather cryptic report which nobody who did not know the full background to the case could have understood. I decided the press needed a little nudging, and wrote a paragraph in *Private Eye*, drawing attention to the fact that a man (Newton) had been arrested in connection with this incident. At last, it seemed that the story was going to break, whether the press establishment in London wanted it to or not. This is what I wrote in *Private Eye* for 12 December 1975:

"West Somerset is buzzing with rumours of a most unsavoury description following reports in the *West Somerset Free Press* about an incident which occurred recently on Exmoor. Mr Norman Scott, a thirty-five-year-old writer, of Combe Martin, North Devon, who claims to have been a great friend of Jeremy Thorpe, the Liberal statesman, was found by an AA patrolman weeping beside the body of Rinka, his Great Dane bitch, which had been shot in the head.

"Information about this puzzling incident has since been restricted, on Home Office orders, but a man arrested at London Airport on a firearms charge will be appearing before Minehead magistrates on 19 December, when we may learn more.

"My only hope is that sorrow over his friend's dog will not cause Mr Thorpe's premature retirement from public life."

The one measurable result of all this was a paragraph in the *Sunday Times* for 14 March 1976. This was published two days before Newton's trial in Exeter, on a charge of using a pistol with intent to endanger life. The same issue carried a front-page article by Jeremy Thorpe called "The Lies of Norman Scott." The effect of both pieces was to discredit the testimony of Norman Scott as chief prosecution witness – "a man whose allegations are often demonstrably untrue" – and protect Thorpe – "a man whose word has proved reliable through a long career in public life." The Insight enquiry team seemed to see a conspiracy between *Private Eye* and the *West Somerset Free Press* to blacken Thorpe's name – "The ground had been well prepared by the stories in *Private Eye* and in the *West Somerset Free Press*."

This editorial intrusion by the *Sunday Times* had two results, the first of considerable importance. Peter Bessell read both pieces in California, and decided from that moment to be a witness for the prosecution. Not to put too fine a point on it, he changed sides. Since the case could almost certainly not have been brought without some direct evidence against Thorpe, one might say that the *Sunday Times*'s efforts to protect Thorpe were directly responsible for his arrest and prosecution. Peter Bessell's reasons for changing sides will be obvious to anyone who has read the two articles. In one, Thorpe denies any knowledge of Bessell's payments made on his behalf to Scott, just as he denies any knowledge of Holmes's payment of £2,500 for the Bessell letters. In the other, it is suggested that these payments were made "very possibly in order to suppress information about his [Bessell's] own business operations, not about anyone's sexual peccadilloes."

Some weeks earlier, Holmes had persuaded Bessell to write an untruthful letter claiming to have been blackmailed by Scott. Bessell agreed to do so in order to help Thorpe on the understanding that it would never be published. The idea was that the threat of prosecution for blackmail would inhibit Scott from his customary outburst against Thorpe during the Newton trial. In the event, the contents of the letter were released, leaving Bessell in an extremely delicate position. Somebody, after all, had apparently tried to murder Scott. Bessell withdrew his letter and within a few months was spilling out his story to the journalists Barrie Penrose and Roger Courtiour, as well as to any other journalists who would listen.

The second result of the *Sunday Times*'s intrusion into the course of justice is much less important. It persuaded the author of this book to take a personal interest in the matter and not to let it drop until Scott's allegations against Thorpe had been thoroughly aired and the circumstances of this apparent murder attempt had been fully investigated.

Perhaps I should explain this personal reaction more fully as it must serve in part, also, as my apology for the book. Scott's original allegations of a homosexual relationship with Thorpe struck me as intriguing but no more than that. If true, they could be used to point a moral or adorn a tale, reminding us of the essential frailty of the human condition, the absurdity of public life or whatever. Since they were unproven and possibly untrue, there was no reason why they should be broadcast to the nation; they might indeed, have caused injustice and mischief if they had been. They were of minority interest, to be discussed and weighed among people (like the political correspondent of *Private Eye*) who are constantly assailed by "information" that such-and-such a prime minister is a Soviet agent, such-and-such a member of the Royal Family a violent psychotic, such-and-such a Cabinet minister is a pederast. But as soon as pistols were drawn and bullets started flying, the whole complexion of the matter changed. Previously there might have been honourable reasons for wishing to protect Thorpe. A sexual indiscretion, thirteen years old, is no reason for destroying a man's political career unless one has other oblique.or disreputable reasons for wishing to see it destroyed. And Thorpe, as a party politician, was definitely less objectionable than most. But the intimidation – let alone attempted murder – of someone for political reasons was something entirely different, something new in British politics, and something which there could be no honourable reason for concealing.

One was accustomed, as a journalist, to seeing important matters ignored by the press, sometimes out of laziness, sometimes out of ignorance, most often out of cowardice. Britain's press laws, which require journalists to prove the truth of any disparaging or defamatory statement, are the strictest in the free world, with the result that corruption and incompetence are seldom exposed in our press unless the police decide to prosecute, or unless the information comes out in court or Parliament for some other reason. Even then, the press frequently decides to ignore it.

However, it was a new development, in my experience at any rate, to see newspapers enthusiastically throwing themselves behind a move to restrain further investigations into what looked, at this stage, very much like an attempted murder for political purposes.

Other newspapers had decided that the matter needed further investigation than was permitted at Newton's trial, where Scott was effectively restrained by prosecuting counsel, Mr Lewis Hawser QC. Mr Hawser probably felt Scott's allegations were scurrilous and irrelevant, but I am not in his confidence. I did not meet him until a little later when he was acting for Sir James Goldsmith in Goldsmith's attempts to close down *Private Eye* with a prosecution for criminal libel and sixty-four writs for civil libel. These appeared to have nothing to do with the Thorpe case although Goldsmith, a rich and ambitious grocer who befriended Harold Wilson's personal secretary, Lady Falkender, was later named by the *Sunday Express* as the man who was paying Jeremy Thorpe's legal expenses at the Old Bailey – a report he does not appear to have denied, although given the opportunity to do so. Later versions, which were confirmed by Goldsmith's lawyer, suggested he had paid £5,000 towards the defence costs.

What is certain is that Lady Falkender was a friend and supporter of Mr Thorpe at a time when *Private Eye* was leading the pack against him. At the same time as Sir James Goldsmith (as he became half-way through the case) was trying to close down *Private Eye*, Lady Falkender was involving herself in another equally curious enterprise.

On 12 May 1976, only seven weeks after he mysteriously resigned as Prime Minister and two days after Thorpe's resignation as Liberal leader, Harold Wilson received two BBC journalists, Barrie Penrose and Roger Courtiour in his home in Lord North Street, Westminster, and instructed them to expose a sinister South African plot to discredit Thorpe, with ramifications extending to right-wing elements in MI5, the domestic security service.

On 9 March, only a week before his resignation as Prime Minister, Mr Wilson (as he was then) said in answer to a parliamentary question that he had no doubt at all that there was "strong South African participation in recent activities relating to the leader of the Liberal Party." He suspected "very strong and heavily financed private masterminding of certain political operations." He told the reporters of his suspicions that these same South African agents had been involved with right-wingers in MI5 to smear himself and Lady Falkender as Soviet agents. He suspected that both Downing Street and his home in Great Missenden had been bugged and revealed that he had asked a friend of Lady Falkender, Sir James Goldsmith, to deal with the matter.

Lady Falkender, as recounted in their excellent book *The Pencourt File*, took over the job of keeping in touch with the two reporters, whose investigations, far from implicating South Africans or MI5 right-wingers in a plot to smear Thorpe, eventually turned up what proved to be the skeleton of the prosecution case against Jeremy Thorpe on the charges of conspiracy and incitement to murder. Suggestions that there had been an attempt by MI5 to smear Lady Falkender, and through her Sir Harold Wilson, as Soviet agents remain unexplained to this day. So, to a large extent, do Wilson's reasons for resigning when he did. Lady Falkender, I am happy to say, remains a close friend of the newly-knighted Sir James Goldsmith and was rumoured at one time to be considering an offer of employment in his Cavenham food empire.

At this point the former Prime Minister and his Political Secretary drop out of the narrative. Lady Falkender described her motives to the two reporters as being a simple desire to protect Jeremy Thorpe from public disgrace. "That is why I tended to come to his rescue," she said. "And so did Sir Harold. It was a gut reaction on his part, I am sure."* The two reporters seem to have little doubt that the announcement of Wilson's resignation was engineered by the Palace to coincide with the timing of Princess Margaret's separation from her husband, Lord Snowdon, thus taking the heat off the Royal couple. Whether there was any connexion between the timing of these events and the opening of Newton's trial in Exeter must remain a matter for conjecture.

On 6 April 1977 Newton was released from prison and on 19 October of that year the London *Evening News* printed his allegations of having been hired by a prominent member of the Liberal Party – David Holmes was not named – to murder Scott. The police

* *The Pencourt File*, p. 177.

investigation was reopened. Throughout these police investigations an extraordinarily accurate account of them continued to appear in the magazine *Private Eye*, which had earlier been threatened with a prosecution for criminal libel by Thorpe's lawyers – the editor, Richard Ingrams, printed their threat as a reader's letter. In July 1978, after an article headed "The Ditto Man" which described how Thorpe was refusing to answer any questions, a writ was received. On 4 August, Thorpe, Holmes and two others were formally charged with conspiracy to murder Norman Scott. Thorpe alone was later charged with inciting Holmes to murder him. I immediately started making arrangements to write a book about the trial.

On 20 November 1978 committal proceedings opened in Minehead Magistrates' Court, less than twenty miles from my home in West Somerset, and within the area of the alleged murder attempt on Porlock Hill. Demand for seats at the hearing was enormous, and I was fortunate in securing one by virtue of having applied early. The *Sunday Times* was not so lucky, and had to hire a lawyer to threaten proceedings before it secured a seat. At the time, everybody supposed that reporting would be forbidden, but on the application of one of the defendants, George Deakin (who explained that he had nothing to hide), reporting restrictions were lifted. Thorpe's solicitor, Sir David Napley, later expressed satisfaction at this development, and used the occasion for a memorable performance as Thorpe's advocate. For three weeks, the newspapers were full of lurid accounts of Crown allegations: from Norman Scott, how he had been buggered by Thorpe in Thorpe's mother's house, biting the pillow to prevent himself crying out in pain; from Peter Bessell, how he had been consulted by Thorpe about methods of murdering Scott and disposing of the body; from Andrew Newton, how he had been hired by Holmes to carry out the murder for £10,000; from Jack Hayward, how he had been asked by Thorpe for two sums of £10,000 each and sent them to Thorpe's friend, Nadir Dinshaw, in the Channel Islands; from Mr Dinshaw, how Thorpe had instructed him to send the money to Holmes, and threatened him with exportation if he revealed this to the police.

For most people these details came as a surprise. They knew that Thorpe was charged with attempting to procure the murder of Norman Scott, who claimed a homosexual relationship with him, but no more than that.

No defence evidence is heard at these committal proceedings, whose only purpose is to decide whether the Crown has a *prima facie* case for the defendants to answer. Defence counsel reserve their arguments for the trial, being concerned only to discredit the Crown witnesses and suggest there is no case to answer. They also have an opportunity, in this preliminary cross-examination of Crown witnesses, to discover the weakest points of the Crown case and establish, where possible, inconsistencies between evidence given in the magistrates' court and evidence given later in the Crown Court. Many people expressed the opinion that a fair trial would be impossible now that the prosecution case was so well known in advance, but this had not been the experience of criminal courts, at any rate so far as the defendants' chances of acquittal were concerned. For the general public, this early exposition of the Crown's evidence meant that it had no surprise value when it was heard for the second time in the Old Bailey. At this stage, every-body was expecting a formidable defence to be mounted in the Old Bailey, with witnesses of the greatest eminence testifying to Thorpe's good character and scores of others casting doubt on the reliability of the Crown case, especially the testimonies of Scott, Bessell and Newton. In the event this was not necessary, as the judge took it upon himself to destroy the good character of these three key witnesses without any evidence having been called. But nobody knew this at the time. After the magistrates had decided there was indeed a *prima facie* case for them all to answer, a certain thrill went round the tiny courtroom in Minehead when Thorpe, speaking for the first time since the hearing began, said, "I plead not guilty and will vigorously defend this matter."

This was on 13 December 1978. The trial, after various attempts to delay it, was planned to open on 30 April 1979. Before that date Mr Callaghan's Labour Government was defeated on a vote of confidence and a General Election was called for 3 May. It was authoritatively claimed that Thorpe had promised David Steel, the new Liberal leader, to resign his seat if Scott's allegations became public. In the event, he decided to stay put. It was said that he had also assured Mr Steel that he would not attend the Liberal Party Conference in the autumn of 1978, after being charged, but in the event he attended and monopolised it. Finally, he had promised not to stand for re-election until the case was over, but once again he changed his mind and announced himself the Liberal candidate for his old constituency of North Devon, with enthusiastic support from many Liberals in the area.

First, it was necessary for him to have the trial delayed, since it might seriously cramp his style if, while the other candidates in

North Devon were parading themselves at the hustings, he was confined to the dock at the Old Bailey on charges involving an attempted murder. Moreover, the reporting of the trial might not have helped his chances of re-election. Accordingly, the Lord Chief Justice of England was persuaded to grant him a deferment until 8 May, despite objections from two of his co-defendants.

On 14 April I wrote my weekly article in the *Spectator* complaining about this – it seemed wrong that he should be treated differently from any other alleged criminal – and complaining about the behaviour of certain Liberals in North Devon and at the Liberal Conference in Southport, who had insisted on treating him as a hero ever since he had been accused of conspiracy to murder. It was one thing to observe the principle of English law that a man is innocent until proved guilty, but another principle of English law, on which the whole of our oppressive libel law is founded, insists that a man's reputation suffers in the estimate of right-minded people if he is publicly accused of reprehensible behaviour, let alone a serious crime. The magistrates had decided that a *prima facie* case existed against him, which he had yet to answer, and the cheering Liberals of North Devon and Southport seemed to be showing contempt both for the legal process and for the electoral system by demonstrating that they were not right-minded citizens.

There was a strong undercurrent of morally uninformed opinion at this time which held that even if Thorpe was guilty of conspiring to murder Norman Scott, he was right to do so since the man was a blackmailer. It seemed to me that where this mistaken view threatened to become the consensus, those in a position to do so had a certain duty to resist it, however ineffectually. Although not by nature a political person, I agreed to the suggestion of Mr Richard Ingrams that I should stand in North Devon against Mr Thorpe as *Private Eye*'s candidate in the Dog Lovers' interest. This was plainly a reference to the murdered Great Dane and caused a little ripple of embarrassment among the more enthusiastic supporters of Jeremy Thorpe.

The gesture involved me in one or two unscrupulous political accommodations, like affecting a greater interest in doggies generally, and a greater concern for the endangered doggies of North Devon in particular, than I naturally felt. I remember also speaking to a reporter on *Gay News* who enquired about my attitude to Gay Dogs and assuring him of my compassionate attitude to the problems of homosexuality among dogs, while secretly feeling they ought to be whipped.

Two weeks later, in the *Spectator* of 28 April 1979, I published my adoption meeting address, explaining that it had been composed and delivered in a bathroom at my home in Combe Florey, Somerset. Various copies were sent out to local and national newspapers, but only the *Guardian* printed it. One of the local North Devon newspapers thoughtfully gave its copy to the Liberal agent in North Devon, Mrs Lilian Prowse, who showed it to Mr Thorpe, with results which soon became apparent. Here is the adoption meeting address in full, as it appeared in the *Spectator*:

CITIZENS OF BARNSTAPLE AND
VOTERS OF NORTH DEVON

Unaccustomed as I am to public speaking I offer myself as your Member of Parliament in the General Election on behalf of the nation's dog lovers to protest about the behaviour of the Liberal Party generally and the North Devon Constituency Liberal Association in particular. Their candidate is a man about whose attitude to dogs – not to mention his fellow human beings – little can be said with any certainty at the present time.

But while it is one thing to observe the polite convention that a man is innocent until proven guilty, it is quite another thing to take a man who has been publicly accused of crimes which would bring him to the cordial dislike of all right-minded citizens and dog lovers, and treat him as a hero.

Before Mr Thorpe has had time to establish his innocence of these extremely serious charges, he has been greeted with claps, cheers and yells of acclamation by his admirers in the Liberal Party, both at the National Conference in Southport and here in the constituency. I am sorry but I find this disgusting.

I invite all the electors of North Devon, but especially the more thoughtful Liberals and dog lovers to register their disquiet by voting for me on 3 May and I sincerely hope that at least fifty voters in this city will take the opportunity to do so.

Genesis XVIII 26: And the LORD said If I find in Sodom fifty righteous within the city, then I will spare all the place for their sakes.

1 Samuel XXIV 14: After whom dost thou pursue? after a dead dog, after a flea.

Rinka is NOT forgotten. Rinka lives. Woof, woof. Vote Waugh to give *all* dogs the right to life, liberty and the pursuit of happiness.

No sooner had the *Guardian* article appeared than I received a telephone call from a journalist in London. He congratulated me on a great battle I had just won before the Lord Chief Justice and two other judges in the Queen's Bench Divisional Court. I replied that I knew nothing about it. It seemed that Mr Jeremy Thorpe through his counsel, Mr George Carman QC, had sought an injunction to ban my election address and commit me to prison for contempt of court on the grounds that it might prejudice a jury at Thorpe's subsequent trial. The Lord Chief Justice, in his wisdom, had refused to do anything of the sort. Knowing nothing of this move, I could only conjecture that Thorpe's motives might have been more concerned with the voters of North Devon than with jurors at the Old Bailey. Asked for a comment, I said that the Divisional Court's decision restored my faith in British justice, and suggested that things would have come to a pretty pass if alleged criminals could not only stand for Parliament, but send any opponents to prison who mentioned this circumstance.

I was celebrating this great victory quietly when the telephone rang again, about an hour later. Mr Thorpe had taken the Divisional Court's decision to appeal and been awarded his injunction by Lord Denning, sitting with two appeal judges. Next day Lord Denning listened to arguments hastily put together by counsel on my behalf and dismissed them with contumely, saying he had been reading my column in *Private Eye* and had no doubt that my motives in standing for Parliament were improper. Mr George Carman QC, enlarging on his client's case, said that two points at issue were who shot the dog Rinka and whether or not there had been a homosexual relationship with Norman Scott, both of which were hotly disputed, and both prejudiced by the election address. In point of fact, there was never any doubt about who had shot the dog – Andrew Newton – and when it came to trial Mr Carman conceded that his client was a man of homosexual tendencies at the relevant time, even though he continued to deny that Thorpe had ever exercised these tendencies on Norman Scott, who was not mentioned in the address. Nor did anyone at the trial deny for a moment that the dog was shot – with or without Mr Thorpe's connivance – in order to assist the Liberal cause and Liberal candidate in North Devon. But it is an unattractive and otiose occupation to moan about judicial decisions which have gone against one. Lord Denning, one of the greatest and best judges we have ever had, plainly thought the Dog Lovers' candidature in bad taste, when he said it was as "plain as plain can be" that the election address might prejudice Thorpe's trial, and was not prepared to consider the view that the Liberal's candidature was in even worse taste. The most interesting aspect of this episode, from my own point of view, was not so much that as a parliamentary candidate I now faced the electorate without an election address or any explanation of why I was standing – under the circumstances, it was a great tribute to North Devon Dog Lovers that seventy-nine of them were prepared to abdicate their democratic right of choosing a government by voting for me – but that Thorpe had overcome his handicaps. One began to take the measure of the enormous sympathy for this ex-barrister, ex-Oxford man, among his own kind.

But he did not do so at the election. At half past three in the morning of 4 May 1979 he learned that the seat he had won from the Conservatives in 1959 – the only Conservative loss in that election – was lost on a huge swing away from him. In February 1974, Thorpe received 34,052 votes to give him a majority of 11,072 over his Conservative opponent. By the General Election of October that year, his vote had sunk to 28,209 and his majority to 6,721. In May 1979, he received only 23,338 votes, and his Conservative opponent was elected to Parliament on a majority of 8,473 with 31,811 votes. The rag, tag and bobtail of "fringe" party candidates – Labour, Ecology, National Front, English National, Dog Lovers, Wessex Regionalist and Democratic Monarchist Public Safety White Regionalist, in that order, made no noticeable difference to the result, all of them losing their deposits of £150.

To many, the most remarkable factor in this election result was that 23,338 voters were prepared to cast their votes for a man living under the cloud of a serious criminal charge. One will never know what proportion of that number was demonstrating its belief in his innocence and what proportion was demonstrating its continued support for him whether he was guilty or not. In the first instance the voters would appear to cast doubt on general beliefs about the effect of bad publicity; in the second, one can only draw one's own conclusions about the moral climate in North Devon, and possibly in the country at large.

The most interesting aspect may be that he lost only 5,000 votes as a result of the intense publicity given the committal proceedings in Minehead. There can be no doubt that he had a large personal following in North Devon, but the important point is that it was not quite large enough. His gamble had not paid off.

A few years earlier, Thorpe had been named in a report by Department of Trade inspectors dealing with the collapsed fringe bank London and County Securities, from which he had been drawing £5,000 a year as non-executive director. The post appeared to carry no duties, although £5,000 a year was a substantial salary then, being considerably more than an MP's salary when he joined the bank in 1971. The inspectors suggested that the collapse of the bank

"must remain a cautionary tale for a leading politician. For unless he is properly informed of the affairs of the company he joins, he cannot make his own judgment on the propriety of its transactions; and he is liable to be reminded . . . that his reputation is not only his most marketable, but also his most vulnerable commodity."

Oddly enough, Mr Thorpe's reputation did not seem to have suffered in the least. He remained as leader of the Liberal Party without difficulty, with an ever more important role in the conduct of public affairs as the Labour Government's hold on Parliament grew weaker. It did not prevent the judge at the end of his trial referring to all four defendants as men of "unblemished reputation" even though there had been no evidence on this point in the case of two of them, and one had a prison record. But Thorpe's defeat in North Devon did appear to leave a mark. By whatever rash exercise in optimism he had persuaded himself that he could hold the seat, his failure to do so plainly came as a grave shock. He still wore an air of dazed surprise when he took his seat in the dock of Number One Court at the Old Bailey four days later on Tuesday 8 May 1979 for a trial which was expected to last up to three months and had already been billed as the Trial of the Century.

1

Is it Fair, Right and Just?

Day one: 8 May 1979

"Linda Binns," cried the courts administrator. Or possibly it was an usher, or high sherriff, or Deputy Constable of the Tower of London. A middle-aged woman with grey hair detached herself from the press of potential jurymen standing at the back of the court. In answer to the judge's question, she assured the court that she had never read a book called *The Pencourt File* by Barrie Penrose and Roger Courtiour, or another called *The Thorpe Committal* by Peter Chippindale and David Leigh. Since the abolition of property qualifications for jurors, and apart from being on the voters' list and aged between eighteen and sixty-five, this was the only qualification she required to sit in judgment on her four fellow citizens accused of conspiracy to murder Norman Scott; one of whom, the Right Honourable John Jeremy Thorpe, was also accused of inciting another to murder him. In due course, Linda Binns took her place in the jury box and swore by Almighty God that she would faithfully try the several issues between her Sovereign Lady the Queen and the prisoners at the bar.

The four prisoners at the bar remained standing for twenty minutes while the jury was sworn. Thorpe, having made what was to prove his only contribution to the entire proceedings when he answered "Not guilty" to the question "What say you, Thorpe, are you guilty or not guilty?", watched the jurors closely as, one by one, those who had no objection to serving in such a long trial denied that they had read either of the books in question and took their places in the jury box.

"Debora Stevens."

"David Greenberg."

Suddenly there was a bellow of "Challenge" from Denis Cowley QC, counsel for John Le Mesurier. David Greenberg, a quiet, tidy, bearded man with the studious air of the professional class, stood down. In all, four jurors were objected to – three as inscrutably as Mr Greenberg, a fourth on the probable grounds that he raised objections to trying the case with the judge, who over-ruled them.

"Peter Hattart."

"Alan B. Sturrock."

"Frederick Fee."

"Kevin Neagle."

"Harold Walker."

"Henry Smith."

"Michael J. Window."

"David R. Forrard."

"John M. Haskell."

"Celia Kettle-Williams." (Later chosen as foreman of the jury.)

Twelve anonymous faces. All capable of voting and no doubt holding political opinions – whether those were their real names, or just what their names sounded like, is something we shall never know. No sooner were they sworn than the judge reminded the sixty-nine pressmen in court not to make any contact with them.

"Never ask them questions, interview them or anything else. If I find anyone who has in any way interfered with a member of the jury I'll bring him back here and punish him. Better bring a toothbrush here with you if you are going to do that."

No sooner were the jurors sworn than George Carman QC, for Mr Thorpe, said that he wished to make legal submissions in the jury's absence. They filed out again, being told by the judge that they could take the rest of the day off. Their moment of individual identity had passed and we did not hear from Celia Kettle-Williams again until the last day of the trial, when, like Jeremy Thorpe on the first, she answered "Not guilty" to each of the five questions put to her.

Thorpe was met on his arrival for the first day of the trial by the keeper of the Old Bailey, Mr Jack Gamble, who ushered him and his wife into a lift. Thereafter, he disappeared from view into the various small rooms of the Old Bailey reserved for defence consultations. It was only while he was in the dock of Number One Court that he had to act out the slightly embarrassing charade of being a prisoner at the bar, charged with conspiring to commit a cowardly and contemptible murder in order to protect his reputation as a statesman and national figure. His mother, Mrs Ursula Thorpe, sat in court to give him strength. She never wore a monocle or a bowler hat, as she was rumoured to do, and seemed in many respects a less formidable presence than the tiny, doll-like figure of Thorpe's second wife, Marion. A pianist by calling, Marion Stein had been for many years the friend of Benjamin Britten, the composer, after marrying the Queen's cousin, Lord Harewood, as his first wife in

1949. Her robust championship of her second husband's right not to answer questions about his sex life had silenced a press conference called by Thorpe in October 1977 to discuss this very subject, and her presence had a steady, depressing influence over the press benches throughout the trial.

Before starting on his legal submission, Mr Carman said he was going to request that two journalists be ordered to leave the court, Barrie Penrose and Roger Courtiour. His grounds for this were that "they may be potential witnesses." Mr Taylor, for the Crown, hastened to assure the court that he had no intention of calling them, but Mr Carman stood his ground. In retrospect, since Mr Carman called no witnesses at all for the defence, let alone choosing to subpoena potentially hostile witnesses, this initiative might be mistakenly seen as vindictive, since it was the painstaking research of these two journalists in *The Pencourt File* which revealed the bare bones of the Crown case some considerable time before any of the defendants were arrested. At very least it shows how defence tactics changed during the course of the trial – and this, too, is odd, since the prosecution sprang no surprises and confronted defence counsel with nothing of any importance which they had not already heard and seen in Minehead.

These two gentlemen had been in very close contact with Mr Peter Bessell, the chief Crown witness, and should not be in court while submissions were made about him, said Mr Carman. After various sarcastic comments about how much money they were alleged to have made from their book, they were ordered to leave and this order was later extended to exclude them from listening to the evidence of Bessell, Scott and Newton, although by then reporting restrictions had been lifted and they could read a full account in any newspaper.

But legal submissions, being made in the absence of the jury, were not allowed to be reported, so the British public was unable to learn, at the time, what followed. This proved to be Thorpe's last attempt to exclude the evidence of the Crown's most inconvenient witness, Peter Bessell.

Bessell, it transpired, had signed a contract with the *Sunday Telegraph* for the serialisation of a book he proposed to write. In part, it would deal with the case, and the *Sunday Telegraph* had stipulated that if they were unable to print the book for legal reasons they would pay only half the proposed fee of £50,000 for a series of background articles in its place. This was interpreted as meaning that if Thorpe was acquitted, the libel risks would become too great and Bessell would lose £25,000. In other words, he had a direct financial interest in securing a conviction.

"My lord, there could not be a more scandalous situation," said Mr Carman, than where a witness was hoping to make money out of his evidence. The contract must be seen either as a contempt of court or as a conspiracy to pervert the course of justice, possibly both, and if the judge allowed Bessell to give evidence under these circumstances, he would be endorsing a continuing contempt of court.

One began to feel that Mr Carman was pitching his case a little too high when the judge interrupted, at quite an early stage, to say that if Mr Carman had a contempt of court to report he would have to take it to the Queen's Bench Divisional Court. "I've got enough to try," said the judge.

But Mr Carman ploughed on. An immunity from prosecution given to Mr Bessell in respect of anything which might transpire except his own perjury meant that he was immune from prosecution for either contempt or conspiracy to pervert the course of justice, he claimed.

"I submit that the giving of evidence by Mr Bessell is an abuse of the process of the court. Your lordship's jurisdiction should, if not require, *compel* you to forbid it."

His lordship was beginning to show signs of irritation. Should he exclude in advance the evidence of defence witnesses on similar grounds, he asked, where there was suspicion of a conspiracy to pervert the court of justice? If so, the law would be an ass. Perhaps seeing that the argument was going against him, Mr Carman uttered what can only, in retrospect, be seen as a slightly bizarre threat. If Bessell were allowed to give evidence, he said, he (Mr Carman) planned to keep him in the witness-box for a week while he cross-examined him on this point of his contract with the *Sunday Telegraph*.

Later, with the support of Mr Mathew, for Holmes, and Mr Williams, for Deakin, Mr Carman added that everything he had said about Bessell's evidence applied to Scott and Newton (the witness who would claim to have been hired to murder Scott). At Minehead, said Mr Carman, Newton had told the magistrates that he had no other source of income apart from what he hoped to make by selling his story to newspapers and television. The judge at this point prompted him, saying rather disconcertingly that Newton hoped to milk the case for all it was worth. This interjection reassured those following the case that the judge had read what had been sent up to him from Minehead, but it was also the first indication of what would later emerge as a strong line. The judge disapproved very strongly of anybody making money from the case – apart, of course, from the lawyers, many of whom were making far more money than any witness could possibly hope to make.

It is to Mr Carman's credit that he spotted this tendency on the judge's part at a very early stage. In fact, Mr Carman did not keep Bessell in the witness-box for more than two and a half days. This was only the first of several hints at an elaborate and prolonged defence performance which somehow never materialised. One wondered, at times, whether he was not under some pressure – from instructing solicitors, perhaps, or from Mr Thorpe, who was rumoured to be directing his own defence, or even from Sir James Goldsmith, later rumoured to be paying for it – to shorten the proceedings as much as possible. But no such pressure, one would guess, had been brought to bear at this stage.

Mr Carman was a contemporary of Thorpe at Oxford. His practice was in the Northern circuit, where he had established the reputation of a competent performer in difficult criminal cases. After this sticky beginning, his relations with the judge seems to improve. His greatest strength was not in his set speeches, where he often struck the wrong note, but in his apparently sympathetic cross-examination of Crown witnesses whose credibility he intended to destroy. His manner on these occasions was seldom that of the bully, more that of a friendly doctor with a hopeless psychiatric problem on his hands.

Mr John Mathew, who appeared for Holmes, was the son of a former Director of Public Prosecutions, Sir Theobald Mathew. Educated by the Jesuits at Beaumont, he made his reputation as leading Crown counsel at the criminal bar before branching out into more lucrative private practice. His method of cross-examination – contemptuous, disdainful, vaguely abstracted – seemed more effective at Minehead Magistrates' Court than it was at the Old Bailey, where he had made his reputation. Perhaps the mantle of prosecuting counsel still attached to him. He could never win a jury on grounds of pity. He did not even seem much interested in the appeal to honest doubt. It was essential to his approach that the prosecution witnesses should seem the greater villains. Since he was prepared to acknowledge his client's culpability of conspiracy to frighten – a serious enough criminal charge, carrying penalties less severe only than those for conspiracy to murder – this should be seen as a major feat.

Mr Denis Cowley, for John Le Mesurier, a carpet merchant in

North Wales whose involvement was never fully-established, lacked the opportunity to deploy his fine, loud voice or superior manner to best advantage. Such evidence as there was against his client referred only to events after the incident on Porlock Moor, when the conspiracy, if it ever existed, came to an end. Mr Cowley plainly hoped to get his client off on this ingenious technicality – nobody disputed that Le Mesurier had handed over the money to Newton in payment of the contract – but in the end such subtlety was unnecessary as the jurors plainly decided that they were not sure that a conspiracy to murder had been established.

Mr Gareth Williams for George Deakin, a North Wales club owner who introduced Newton to Holmes, was the most colourful of the four defence counsel. For the moment, he confined himself to suggesting that Bessell and Newton were so tainted that one would normally expect a record of the case to be sent to the Director of Public Prosecutions. Not on this occasion, of course, because of Mr Bessell's immunity. On Mr Williams's thin Welsh lips the word was made to sound like some nauseating upper-class privilege, awarded to the former MP as a means of persecuting his client, a simple working man who had nothing to hide. Mr Williams never tried to disguise his contempt for the manoeuvres of Jeremy Thorpe – his refusal to answer questions at the police investigation, his friendship with Home Secretaries and Prime Ministers, his ultimate refusal to give evidence in his own defence.

Mr Peter Taylor, the leading Crown counsel, now rose to answer the defence submissions. He quoted the £20,000 reward offered for information leading to the conviction of Jack the Ripper. It would be absurd and unjust if a case could not be brought because the evidence had been invalidated by the very means which brought it to light. In any case, the magistrates at Minehead had already heard all these objections and committed the defendants for trial despite them. The judge was being asked to dismantle the entire Crown case, since without these three witnesses there would be no trial. It was a function of the jury, not the judge, to decide whether their evidence was capable of belief or not. Mr Taylor doubted whether the judge had discretion to exclude these witnesses even if he wished to do so.

The suggestion that he might not have discretion appeared to annoy his lordship, and Mr Taylor hastened to add that it was mistaken to suppose that Mr Bessell's immunity covered contempt of court, since the court had its own jurisdiction on the matter. The immunity merely covered police prosecution, which was not necessary where contempt was concerned. The judge appeared mollified, happy that his power to rattle toothbrushes was not threatened, but defence counsel had not wasted this opportunity, in the absence of the jury, to throw dirt at the main prosecution witnesses. One will never know how much this contributed towards the judge's subsequent attitude towards them, or whether he had already made up his mind on this point from his scrutiny of the proceedings at Minehead.

Mr Carman intervened to remind the court that Scott and Newton had both appointed literary agents; these two witnesses, neither of previous literary experience, were now writing books. All three were using the court – Mr Justice Cantley's court – as a vehicle for their commercial success. Newton had said at Minehead, as the judge had already reminded us, "This case is the only source of income I have. I have resolved to milk it as hard as I can." Bessell had said, "I have lied to many people on many occasions. I have a credibility problem." And Bessell, Mr Carman reminded the judge, had a strong financial interest in conviction.

When I heard this admission at Minehead, I judged it to be part of a plea from Mr Bessell that he should be believed on this occasion. Nearly all the lies he had told – apart from a few commercial ones – had been in order to protect his friend and colleague, Jeremy Thorpe. The judge, as subsequent events proved, took any such admission as an invitation to disbelieve him now. As the judge had acerbically remarked earlier, when called upon to take account of the whole course of justice, "I am only trying this case." The course of justice could look after itself. It may be that in his anxiety to do justice to Mr Thorpe and respect the assumption of innocence which all defendants enjoy, he was going to do less than justice to Mr Bessell who was not, of course, on trial.

Perhaps Mr Taylor began to realise at this stage, on the first day of the trial, what an uphill task he would have to convince the judge of his witnesses' credibility. Mr Taylor is a handsome, blunt man, with a fine Roman profile. The son of a doctor, he went to Newcastle Grammar School before being taken on an exhibition to Pembroke College, Cambridge. Well-mannered and moderate in tone, he spoke the beautiful, plain English of an educated man – civilised, humorous, only occasionally indignant. His manner seemed to apologise for the role in which fate had cast him: it was distressing to have to take sides, he would have been happier as a judge. But there was no doubt in his mind of the defendants' guilt, and he confidently expected all right-minded men to share this perception. His witnesses may not, individually, have been very impressive, but he seemed to feel that the cumulative effect of their evidence was unanswerable. The only thing which moved him to indignation was when he described what he saw as Thorpe's attempts to fix the record and muzzle his witnesses. The alleged crime itself did not seem to affront him so much. Certainly he never managed to inspire the judge with an awareness of its gravity, except to the extent that it made Thorpe less likely to have committed it. Perhaps it was his well-mannered approach which persuaded the judge, at the end of the day, that if the jurors were to convict they would do so "sadly." Or perhaps he was merely responding to an obvious reluctance on the part of the judge. Nothing in the judge's previous experience, it would appear, had prepared him to suppose that a public figure of such unblemished character as Mr Thorpe would be capable of such wicked acts.

The court rose while Mr Taylor was still on his feet. Events overnight were to reveal the watchfulness of Thorpe's defence team and their determination not to miss a trick, where any lapses by "the media" were concerned.

Day two: 9 May 1979

Before Mr Taylor could resume his reply to Mr Carman's submission, in the absence of the jury, that the three key witnesses should be excluded, Mr Carman rose to his feet and said that three things had occurred overnight which he wished to draw to the judge's attention.

In the first place, he said, a bulletin on BBC Television's Nine o'clock News had referred to the legal submissions as being intended to exclude prosecution evidence. "That may not be a terrible thing," said Mr Carman, "but . . ."

The judge interrupted: "That is a matter of fact . . . it did occur to me that you might welcome that."

Mr Carman replied that he did not wish to be over-critical. He was merely bringing it to the court's attention to see whether it was desirable.

His next complaint was that on BBC's *Tonight* programme there had been a discussion of various legal matters involved in the case by Professor Michael Zander, of the London School of Economics. In the course of it Professor Zander, mentioning Bessell's immunity, had referred to him as a "key witness." Reminding the judge that he had spent much of the previous day submitting that Mr

Bessell should not be allowed as a witness, Mr Carman said it was "really rather damaging" to have public debate on this matter, adding, no doubt for the especial benefit of the judge, "Questions of law are solely for your lordship."

The judge revealed that he had watched the programme, too, and could see nothing improper in it. "I will tell the jury in due course to take the law from me and not from Professor Zander."

The third complaint was more serious. From a report in the previous day's *Evening News* it appeared that Mr Bessell had been giving a press conference outside the courtroom. Mr Carman handed a copy of the newspaper to the judge. It contained the words, "Outside the court the walnut-faced Mr Peter Bessell held the floor." The judge instructed that Bessell be brought before him. Melodramatically, Mr Carman interposed to say that nobody was to tell Mr Bessell what he was wanted for.

When the walnut-faced former MP arrived – this was the first the judge had seen of him – he was asked to stand in the well of the court and explain himself. Mr Bessell, looking surprisingly self-possessed, replied in his strange, laryngophonous accents, a sort of tinny gurgle, as if he were reading a prepared reply to some parliamentary question:

"Before the proceedings started yesterday morning, my lord, one reporter came to me and asked me whether I still drank as many cups of tea as I used to. I said 'Yes' and that was the extent of the conversation as I recall it."

That, indeed was as much as the newspaper had reported, and the interview took place before the start of the trial. What was surprising was the fierceness with which the judge now warned him against talking to the press or anyone else:

"If I find anything that amounts to tampering with evidence not only would the person that sought to tamper be in danger, you might even be in danger yourself. Be careful."

From his manner, the judge plainly saw Bessell as a threat to the dignity of the court and an obstacle to the course of justice – and this was before the wretched man had given any evidence at all.

In raising the matter, Mr Carman explained his motive: 'I would not like it to be thought in public that Mr Thorpe is in some way anti-press, or opposed to proper reporting of the trial. The constant anxiety is whether there can be interference or impropriety."

Whatever Mr Carman would or would not like to be thought in public, few pressmen present were in any doubt about his reasons for raising these matters. None of the journalists I spoke to afterwards could remember an occasion on which the toothbrushes had been rattled so blatantly.

Submissions resumed

Mr Taylor said he could think of hundreds of reasons why Bessell, Scott and Newton should not be excluded by virtue of inducements they had received from the press. What about common informers? A judge could not stop evidence even if he thought the witness was lying. Now he was being asked to stop evidence even before it was given.

"It is a novel, dangerous and wrong proposition that your lordship has any discretion to do that," Mr. Taylor cried.

At the time, I thought he was making a mistake. Mr Justice Cantley did not strike me as the sort of judge to be browbeaten by any suggestion of *ultra vires*.

When Mr Taylor pointed out that every attempt that could be made, and some that should not have been made, had already been made to prevent Mr Bessell coming to England, the judge snapped at him: "That is prejudicial. It must not be reported."

Mr Taylor was referring to some earlier, unsuccessful attempts by Thorpe's lawyers to have Mr Bessell's evidence excluded by the Divisional Court, and also to attempts by Thorpe himself to persuade Mr Hayward, the Bahamas-based millionaire, to threaten Bessell with bankruptcy proceedings if he returned to England to give evidence. But the judge's interruption was nevertheless a curious one. There was no question of Mr Taylor's remark being reported, as the arguments were being heard in the jury's absence and nothing was being reported.

Listening to Mr Taylor's pleading it seemed inconceivable that any judge would stop the case in this way before it had begun. How could Mr Carman ever have entertained such a fatuous hope? Yet the pleadings continued well into the afternoon of the second day, ending only at 3.30 pm with a three sentence ruling from the judge.

The interlude gave Mr Carman an opportunity to exercise his rhetorical skills in two ways. In the first, he appealed to the judge's sympathy in a manner which might not have been calculated to appeal to the jury's. In a finely modulated Shakespearean actor's voice, he suggested that "because Mr Thorpe has known distinction, honour and fame, the ironic effect of this is that he is at a disadvantage." Because of it, he said, prosecution witnesses were under improper pressure. "We are saying this evidence should not be called because it is unfair and oppressive. Although the scales of justice at the top of this building appear to be evenly balanced, in fact in a criminal case they are not. The court is more concerned to protect the innocent from wrongful conviction than it is to punish the wrongdoer. That is the basis of criminal law," he said, adding that the categories of what might be considered unfair were not closed.

The other function of this interlude, from the defence point of view, was simply to get in a little early dirt on the three main prosecution witnesses. Earlier, referring to a letter from Bessell to Lady Falkender – on the lawyers' benches, we saw Sir Lionel Thompson, with a watching brief for Mr Hayward, Lady Falkender and Sir Harold Wilson suddenly take an interest – Mr Carman had described Bessell as a "combination of Uriah Heep and James Bond." Now he laid into the Crown witness with a vengeance. He could not think of anything more repugnant to justice than that a case should rest on the evidence of two liars and a perjurer, all intent on milking the case. Both Bessell and Scott had admitted to telling lies in the past, and Newton admitted to perjury at his trial in Exeter, when he had pretended to have been blackmailed by Scott over an indecent photograph. For some reason, the judge did not find these references to Minehead prejudicial in the way he had found Mr Taylor's remark about attempts to stop Bessell coming to England.

Mr Carman ended his lengthy, second harangue with two questions to the judge:

"Is your lordship sure that there is no real risk of the course of justice being interfered with or obstructed by the admission of this evidence?

"Is your lordship *sure* it is fair, right and just to admit this evidence?" His lordship decided it was fair: "I have come to the conclusion that it is fair to admit this evidence. I have come to the conclusion that I *have* discretion [to exclude it]. No judgment on the veracity of the evidence is implied."

So the last attempt to prevent the case being heard had failed. But perhaps, in pitching his argument as high as this, Mr Carman had succeeded in intruding the idea into the judge's mind that these three witnesses were only heard by virtue of his own magnanimity in allowing them; that he must take especial responsibility for seeing that they did not abuse this dispensation. I don't know. There may be many explanations for the judge's rough treatment of the witnesses and considerate – not to say deferential – treatment of the defendants. At the time, most of us in court felt that Mr Carman had gone on too long and was wasting his client's money – five QCs and nearly twice that number of junior counsel, not counting solicitors and solicitors' clerks, sat ticking away like taximeters, chalking up their tremendous fees. We had no reason to suspect, at that stage, that Thorpe might be having his expenses paid by Sir James Goldsmith, the Marmite king. Even so, I am not sure in retrospect, that Mr Carman was not putting in some of his most useful work at this point.

The next few minutes, before the jury's return, were taken up with the puzzling episode, already referred to, of Pencourt's exclusion. Mr Carman rose to suggest that the journalists Barrie Penrose and Roger Courtiour should be excluded from the trial – as they had already been excluded from the legal arguments – on the grounds that "they might be potential witnesses."

A barrister hastily summoned by London Weekend Television, for whom they were preparing a documentary film on the case, put in an appearance here. He did not seem to have had time to acquaint himself very thoroughly with his clients' problems. He pointed out that the two journalists had been present throughout the Minehead hearing and he understood that there was no question of the Crown calling them as witnesses. Mr Taylor agreed, assuring the court there was no question of that. Mr Carman said mysteriously, "I did not say I am going to call them. Someone might. I am not speculating."

From the judge's interruptions at an early stage it was plain which side he was going to take, but Pencourt's barrister battled on in the manner of a man determined to justify his fees, citing precedents and other legal examples.

The judge looked mysterious. "I can easily visualise a situation in which they might be called," he said. "They are not ultimately deprived of knowing word for word what is going on. This is a serious matter for the defendants, if not for your clients. It is a bit of a goldmine they have found. I rule that Mr Penrose and Mr Courtiour should remain out of court during the evidence of Bessell, Newton and Scott."

The two journalists who had done more than anyone else to bring Thorpe to trial, with the possible exception of Detective Chief Superintendent Michael Challes of the Somerset and Avon Constabulary, stood up and left the court. Needless to say, nobody ever did call them as witnesses. After the acquittal, London Weekend Television decided against showing any part of their £250,000 documentary. Once again, information about Mr Thorpe, painfully acquired over many months, was consigned to oblivion.

2

Tale of Mr Peter Taylor

In a Nutshell

When the jurors finally took their places in the court, after ten hours of legal argument aimed at aborting the whole trial, it was the sleepy hour of the afternoon. Mr Taylor treated them first to a brilliantly summarised thumb-nail sketch of the prosecution case. I watched them closely throughout, but only five members showed much interest, and only three of these were able to sustain it throughout the ten minutes or so of Mr Taylor's summary, delivered in clear, forceful English, with no rhetorical flourishes.

"Twenty years ago," said Mr Taylor, "in 1959, Mr Jeremy Thorpe was elected Member of Parliament for North Devon. During the early 1960s he had a homosexual relationship with Norman Scott. From then on Mr Scott was a continuing danger to his reputation and career. It was a danger of which Mr Thorpe was constantly reminded by Scott pestering him for help and talking of the relationship with others.

"In 1967 Mr Thorpe was elected leader of the Liberal Party. But the higher he climbed on the political ladder, the greater was the threat to his ambition from Scott.

"His anxiety became an obsession, and his thoughts desperate.

"Early in 1969 at his room in the House of Commons he incited his close friend, David Holmes, to kill Norman Scott. Peter Bessell, a fellow Liberal MP, was present. Holmes and Bessell tried, over a period of time, to dissuade Mr Thorpe from this plan, and to humour him. Other, less dramatic measures, were suggested and tried – seeking to get Scott to America, trying to get him a job, paying him money, purchasing damaging letters from him. But Scott remained a constant and serious threat.

"Shortly before the first of the two General Elections in 1974, Scott went to live in Mr Thorpe's constituency. He had been talking openly about his relationship with Jeremy Thorpe, and he was seeking to publish a book about it.

"The accused, David Holmes, eventually became convinced that, as Mr Thorpe had repeatedly urged, the only way to stop this threat both to Mr Thorpe and to the Liberal Party effectively was to kill Scott.

"Mr Holmes had connections in South Wales. He knew the accused John Le Mesurier, a carpet dealer. Through him he met the accused George Deakin, a dealer in fruit machines, and a plot was hatched to find someone who would kill Scott for reward.

"Mr Deakin recruited Andrew Newton, an airline pilot, as the hired assassin. Mr Deakin met him and briefed him. Mr Holmes also met Newton and briefed him further.

"The reward was to be £10,000. Attempts were made – but failed – to lure Mr Scott to his death, but eventually in October 1975 Mr Newton met him in Devon, gained his confidence and drove him out on to the moors.

"There Newton produced a gun. Scott had brought a dog with him. Newton shot the dog but failed to shoot Mr Scott.

"Mr Newton was arrested, charged and convicted in March 1976. He had been charged with possessing a firearm with intent to endanger life, but at his trial the true history of the shooting did not emerge.

"He was sent to prison and on his release in 1977 he was paid £5,000, half the contract price. The cash was handed over to him by Le Mesurier at a remote spot in South Wales.

"The money to pay for this contract was procured by Jeremy Thorpe. He had persuaded Mr Jack Hayward, a wealthy benefactor, to make substantial contribution to Liberal election funds.

"Mr Thorpe then personally arranged for the money to be delivered by a devious route through the Channel Islands to Holmes, so that payment could be made to Newton.

"In a nutshell, this is what the case is about. It is the Crown's submission that in 1969 Mr Thorpe was guilty of inciting Mr Holmes to murder Scott. That is one of the two charges. It is also the Crown's submission that later all four of these men were guilty of a conspiracy to murder Scott."

That ended the Crown's summary of the case against Thorpe and the other three defendants. Those with an ear for the finer points noticed that although Mr Taylor had referred to the three other defendants, at one time or another, by their surnames, he always spoke of "Mr Thorpe" or, just occasionally, "Jeremy Thorpe," the one being an eminent public figure, the other a familiar and popular name.

At the end of this summary, Mr Taylor reminded the jury that it was up to the Crown to prove the guilt of the accused "so you must be sure before you can convict." He also urged them to consider the case against each defendant individually. Finally, he warned them that the trial would take a long time.

As if to emphasise the point, he now embarked on a much longer outline of the Crown case. What took him only a part of a morning in Minehead was now to take him two full days. Even so, Mr Taylor left out many background details to the case which were already familiar to those who had been following it at Minehead, in *The Pencourt File* and in the newspapers. Nothing which was not strictly relevant to the case was admitted; there was to be no gratuitous dirt, not even any evidence of Thorpe's homosexual inclinations which did not bear on the alleged relationship with Norman Scott.

The story began, said Mr Taylor, as far back as 1961, when Thorpe was a bachelor MP of thirty-two and Scott a bachelor of twenty-one, working in the Oxfordshire stables of someone called Mr Norman Vater. Vater was a friend of Thorpe, who visited him there.

It was in relation to some letters from Thorpe to Vater which Scott stole that Mr Carman later made the admission of Thorpe's homosexual tendencies, but the contents of the letters were never discussed; in fact, the judge was later to interrupt and prevent them from being discussed. This circumstance inevitably leads to speculation about a possible agreement between prosecution and defence, with or without the judge's knowledge, that no evidence of Thorpe's homosexual background would be called provided Thorpe was prepared to acknowledge homosexual tendencies at the relevant time. Without in any way questioning the propriety of such an agreement, if it existed, one can justifiably question whether the prosecution got the better of the deal. Traditionally, evidence of a wider-ranging nature – as to background and character – is permitted in a conspiracy trial though not in other criminal cases. By his gentlemanly reticence, Mr Taylor denied himself the usual benefits of a conspiracy charge, while accepting the disadvantages, and denying the jury any fuller glimpse into the background of a defendant who was to be described by the judge as "a national figure with a very distinguished public record" possessing an "unblemished character." Mr Vater remained a shadowy figure, identified by name alone.

On one such visit, Mr Taylor continued, Thorpe very briefly met Scott, then called Norman Josiffe, sometimes Lianche-Josiffe. Later Scott fell out with his employer and left. After a period in a clinic due to a nervous breakdown, Scott went to see Thorpe at the House of Commons and asked for his help.

The date was 8 November 1961. Later that night, Thorpe took Scott and his Jack Russell terrier called Mrs Tish to the house of Thorpe's mother, Mrs Ursula Thorpe, at Oxted, Surrey, explaining that to make things easier he would introduce him as a member of the camera crew which was to take him abroad next day. At Thorpe's request, said Mr Taylor, Scott (*the name Josiffe was still used in Taylor's account until some time later, but for clarity's sake I will refer to him throughout as Scott*) signed the visitors' book with a false name and address.

That night, said Mr Taylor, Thorpe visited Scott's room on several occasions, on the second of which homosexual relations took place. This was the start of the homosexual affair.

Next day, Thorpe gave Scott some money with which he rented a room at 21 Draycott Place, Chelsea, not far from the House of Commons. On his return from abroad, Thorpe visited Scott frequently at that address and the homosexual relationship continued between them intermittently, certainly until 1963, said Mr Taylor.

Thorpe had proposed to spend Christmas at a Barnstaple hotel. He now arranged for Scott to stay with some people called Collier at a house nearby. Collier was a friend of Thorpe and a prospective Liberal candidate. On one occasion, after lunch with Scott, the Colliers and his mother, Mrs Ursula Thorpe, everybody else went for a walk in the garden while Scott and Thorpe had sexual relations, said Mr Taylor.

Later, there was a second visit to Mrs Thorpe's home at Oxted. On this occasion, Scott was introduced by his proper name (of Josiffe). Mr Taylor asked the jury to look at photocopies of the visitors' book. Experts would reveal how the entries had been altered, he said.

After this second visit, Scott returned to the Colliers. A further incident occurred when Scott was back in Draycott Place. A girl whom Scott met there and became intimate with, later accused him of having stolen her fur coat. Two policemen went to interview Scott about this at Thorpe's office in Bridge Street, opposite the House of Commons. When they arrived, according to Scott, Thorpe was making sexual advances at him.

Mr Taylor pointed out that Thorpe flatly denied having had any homosexual relationship with Scott, but the prosecution did not rely on Scott's word for it. There were also Bessell's evidence of admissions made to him by Thorpe and two letters, the first of which Mr

Taylor proceeded to read. It ended with the famous lines: "Bunnies *can* and *will* go to France, Yours affectionately, Jeremy. I miss you."

"The tone and content of these letters, we submit are entirely consistent with, and tend to confirm, what Scott will tell you about the relationship."

Mr Taylor added that "Bunnies" or "Bunny" was the name Thorpe apparently used for Scott, being a reference to their first night together when Thorpe said Scott looked like a frightened rabbit. He said he did not want the jury to come to any conclusions so early in the case, but at some stage the jury was going to have to ask itself whether this was a letter from a Member of Parliament to someone down on his luck, or whether it had the ring of a much more intimate personal involvement.

Meanwhile Thorpe was trying to sort out Scott's insurance cards, which had been mislaid. At some stage Thorpe moved into a flat in Marsham Court, Westminster. Scott visited him there, sleeping on a camp bed. The sexual connection continued. But at the end of 1962, Scott was in a depressed, almost suicidal state. He was even thinking of killing himself and Jeremy Thorpe.

On 19 December 1962 he went to the Easton Hotel in Victoria where he found, quite by chance, that the receptionist was Mrs Mary Collier, with whom he had been staying in North Devon at the beginning of the year. Another woman was present who knew both him and Thorpe. As a result of Scott's condition and what he said, two policemen came to the hotel. Mr Scott made a statement and handed them the two letters in Thorpe's handwriting which the jury had seen.

"It might be that he also handed them some other documents," said Mr Taylor.

Mr Taylor did not expand on these other documents at the time, and their identity was never much debated subsequently. It seems probable, if they existed, that they were the letters from Thorpe to Norman Vater which Scott had stolen on leaving Vater's employment. If so, of course, they would have been Vater's property and the police would have been under no obligation to return them to Scott when he later took steps to have his own letters returned to him, many years later. The police never produced them nor revealed what they contained, and their nature remained another of those little pools of reticence, dotted around the case like quicksands to trap the unwary commentator. The other lady at the Easton Court Hotel was later named as Caroline Barrington-Ward, another character in the drama identified by name alone. But this police statement of December

*1962, later read to the court, spelled out Scott's accusations against
Thorpe at a time when homosexuality between consenting adults was
still a criminal offence. The police took no action, then or subsequently, and it was not until the second police investigation had
started in October 1977, after Newton claimed he had been hired to
murder Scott by a prominent Liberal, that its existence was
acknowledged.*

The crisis passed, said Mr Taylor, and the story moved to 1963.
At this point the judge adjourned the hearing until the next day,
urging the jury not to discuss the case outside the court, even with
their families. "You are to keep an open mind throughout the trial,"
he said.

Day three: 10 May 1979

The only incident to be recorded in 1963 was a letter from Thorpe
to Gieves of Bond Street, complaining about a bill for a pair of silk
pyjamas which Scott had ordered on Thorpe's account. In
December 1964 Scott was again without a job. Thorpe paid for him
to go to Switzerland and stay with a doctor, but Scott was not happy
abroad and returned to England after a few days, leaving his suitcase behind him. Thorpe was annoyed to be told that Scott had left a
number of incriminating letters in the suitcase, and took steps to
recover the suitcase. Scott, meanwhile, went to Ireland, where he
wrote a long letter to Mrs Ursula Thorpe, complaining of her son's
treatment of him. Thorpe went to Bessell, to whom he had already,
in an earlier conversation, confessed his homosexual tendencies.
Thereafter, said Mr Taylor, Bessell acted as Thorpe's agent in all
matters connected with Scott. First Mr Bessell went to Dublin, saw
Scott and gave him a little money. Next, arrangements were made to
recover the lost suitcase. In June 1965 it was returned from
Switzerland, collected by Bessell's secretary and taken to his office
where, said Mr Taylor, Thorpe went and removed his letters.

"The luggage was then closed up and sent by Aer Lingus to
Dublin where it reached [Scott] in its depleted state."

Since it was plainly Scott's letter to Mrs Ursula Thorpe which had
set the cat among the pigeons, by Mr Taylor's reckoning, I give an
extended summary of it, as read out by Mr Taylor:

"Dear Mrs Thorpe,
    For the last five years, as you probably know, Jeremy and I have
had a homosexual relationship. To go into it too deeply will not help

either of us. When I first came down to Stonewalls, that was when I first met him. Though he told you something about a TV programme and Malta, this was all not so true. What remains is the fact that through my meeting Jeremy that day I gave birth to this vice that lies latent in every man."

The letter traces their relationship, mentioning an occasion when they had lunched together at the Colliers' after a funeral. "I think that was the day I realised that Jeremy did not care for me as a friend but only as a —— Oh, I hate to write that. It upset me terribly and I was rather sick, because you see, I was looking for a friend in the real sense of the word."

Later, Thorpe took him to his new London flat. "When he had satisfied himself he put me to sleep on a hard little camp bed. This was when I realised he did not care for me."

Later, the letter said, he had spent eleven months in a nursing home, unfortunately becoming addicted to drugs. "Homosexually, as I was being kept under sedation, I was cured, but of course when I left there I went straight back to Jeremy."

In Ireland (this is still 1963 on an earlier visit) he managed to buy a riding school. It was a flourishing little business, but lacked capital. He was incapacitated in an accident and bills started coming in.

He thought of Thorpe, the letter said. Perhaps Jeremy could lend him some money to get him on his feet again. But, as the letter described it, things did not turn out like that:

"I was to go to England – to Jeremy – to corruption. Your son offered me £2 after he had satisfied himself. He really is a very splendid person. So of course the business folded up. I was bankrupt."

He was determined never to see Thorpe again. He became very depressed and took an overdose of sleeping tablets. In St George's Hospital, "They asked me why I had done it. Could I tell them? No, I am too loyal, the quality your son fails at miserably . . ." He adds that at this point Thorpe was "terribly embarrassed" by him.

"He gave me £2 for services rendered. I heard of a job in Switzerland. Jeremy was thrilled, now I see why."

When he got there, he found he had lost his luggage, he had to walk over two miles in the snow to the house where he found a loft with no light or water. It was haunted by rats and smelled of horse manure.

He now found himself, wrote Scott, in Dublin, where Thorpe had sent him, with no wages. In desperation he went to a priest and told him everything.

"The priest advised me to ask Jeremy to lend me the money to at least get my luggage back. You see, I have no clothes and life is impossible. I got somebody to ring Jeremy, who was very sweet and said: 'I have spent £30 on Norman and his luggage and phone calls.' This was the last straw. Was our 'love' to be measured in monetary value? £30 is so little. I was so hurt . . .'."

"Jeremy could lend me the money but won't. Perhaps he knows I will never say anything about us to anyone. It is so easy to say 'Norman must start for himself,' " the letter went on. "Mrs Thorpe you are probably shattered by all this. I am so sorry but what can I do? Will you ask Jeremy to please send me at least the money for the luggage.

"I hate asking because I know it may cause friction and I know how close you both are. This is really why I am writing to you. Jeremy owes me nothing, possibly I owe him a lot, although I feel we balance out.

"Now instead of helping a cast-off friend I appeal to his finer feelings as a man to help me who is in real need. I promise I shall repay every penny as soon as I am on my feet – believe me I mean this."

The main part of the letter concluded: "I am in desperate straits or I shouldn't be asking.

"Yours sincerely,
Norman Lianche-Josiffe."

A postscript said that he was to have been married in September but the girl had found out about his relationship with Thorpe – "hence I shall probably remain single." He ended the postscript:

"I now have a real desire because of this tremendous priest, to do what is best for myself. Can you understand any of this, Mrs Thorpe. I am so sorry. Please believe I am so desperate for help."

In introducing this letter, Mr Taylor had sounded the first apologetic note about his witness:

"This letter, you may think, was a very hurtful letter to have written. But Mr Scott will tell you in evidence that although it dealt specifically with their homosexual relationship, he thought Mrs Thorpe was aware of that by this stage, and he was himself desperate at the time he wrote the letter."

A further justification of Mr Taylor's decision to introduce the letter at this stage may have been that whatever else one might say about it, it is not the letter of a blackmailer. It specifically repudiates any suggestion that if Scott did not receive the money he would spill the beans. Nor, in blackmailer's terms, is he asking for much. On the other hand it can reasonably be claimed that this letter, read to a judge and jury who have not yet had the opportunity of seeing Scott, portrays him in his most absurd and odious light. No doubt the judge, no less than the jury, was at pains to preserve an open mind through-out the case, but the evidence of this letter was the first direct im-pression of Scott which the court had been allowed, and it is human nature to build assessments on the foundation of a first impression. At the end of the trial, the judge had this to say to the jury about Mr Scott, whose role in the matter, we must remember, was that of the victim in an alleged murder conspiracy:

"I am sure you remember him very well, his hysterically warped personality, an accomplished sponger, very skilful at exciting and exploiting sympathy. . . . He is a fraud, he is a sponger, he is a whiner, he is a parasite."

One does not know at what stage the judge decided to think of Scott in these terms, but it seems reasonable to suppose that the letter, introduced at this stage, made a powerful impression which was bound to colour reactions to Scott when he eventually appeared. Moreover, Mr Taylor's insistence that Scott under no circumstances could be thought of as a blackmailer did little to add to the murder motive. A jury may well be impatient of such subtleties. While they can be persuaded, with some difficulty, that it is an improper thing to try and murder a blackmailer – this was the point made by the judge at Newton's trial in Exeter – they might be confused if the blackmailer, in such a narrative, denies that he is a blackmailer. Under those circum-stances it might appear that two people were on trial, one for black-mail, the other for conspiracy to murder, as if the jury were required to choose between them. Mr Justice Cantley, at the end of the trial, invited the jury to decide that Scott was, indeed, a blackmailer, but he produced this as further reason for finding against Scott's evidence rather than as further motive for murdering him.

Mr Taylor continued his narrative. In response to this letter, Bessell, whose help had been recruited at a luncheon in the Ritz Hotel, flew to Dublin armed with threats of proceedings being taken for criminal libel.

In 1967 Thorpe became leader of the Liberal Party. When Bessell mentioned his anxieties about Scott, Thorpe said that if it ever became public he would take his life. In August, Bessell began to pay Scott a retainer of between £5 and £7 a week, a large part being reimbursed by Thorpe. Scott was set up as a freelance model, and it was at this point that he changed his name from Josiffe to Scott. In 1968, Thorpe married his first wife, Caroline Allpass, and in December of that year Thorpe made his first suggestion – to Bessell – that Scott should be killed, said Mr Taylor. This suggestion was made in Thorpe's room in the House of Commons, he said, with Thorpe explaining "it is no worse than killing a sick dog." At this meeting, Thorpe suggested that the man to do the murder was David Holmes, an old friend who had been best man at Thorpe's wedding.

This suggestion was put to Holmes, in Bessell's presence, some time in early 1969 – again in Thorpe's room at the House of Commons. Holmes was reluctant to comply. Bessell's account of this meeting was all the evidence on the charge of incitement.

On 13 May 1969 Norman Scott married and their problems seemed to be over. Thorpe was only partially convinced, and thought that the "ultimate solution" might eventually be needed.

Thorpe's misgiving eventually turned out to be right, said Mr Taylor, because Scott soon found himself hard up without his national insurance cards to claim benefit and with a pregnant wife. He threatened to take his story to the Sunday papers. To make matters worst, Scott's marriage was failing – "despite," said Mr Taylor, the birth of a son in November. The Scotts parted in early 1970 and in October the same year Mrs Scott started divorce proceedings.

According to Mr Taylor, Thorpe was worried about what might come out in the divorce proceedings. Bessell put Scott in touch with a solicitor who would represent him and also, the jury might think, keep Thorpe's name out of the proceedings. Thorpe decided that Scott should be killed in America; Bessell and Holmes went through a charade of taking him seriously. The purpose of this was to persuade Thorpe that it was impracticable.

Scott meanwhile formed an association with a widow called Gwen Parry-Jones in North Wales. In May 1971 Scott and she visited London and Scott spoke to leading members of the Liberal Party – Mr Emlyn Hooson, Mr David Steel and Lord Byers, showing them letters which he had received from Bessell to accompany payments of the "retainer." Nothing came of this.

In March 1972 Mrs Parry-Jones died, said Mr Taylor. *He did not add that at her inquest – she may have committed suicide – Scott had blurted out an account of his relationship with Thorpe. No newspaper chose to print it, although they could have done so without risk of a libel action from Thorpe, under the privilege attaching to reports of court proceedings.*

On 21 September 1972 Mrs Scott's divorce went through. *Mr*

Taylor did not feel it necessary to add that no mention of Thorpe's name was made in the course of the proceedings. On 23 April 1973, the divorce fees were paid to Mr Ross by Thorpe.

In 1973 Scott moved to South Molton, Devon, in Thorpe's constituency. He started talking in public houses about his relationship with Thorpe, telling his story to a freelance reporter called Gordon Winter, who made tape recordings and took photocopies of Scott's letters, mostly from Bessell. On 27 February 1974, the eve of polling day in the first General Election that year, he surrendered the letters to Dr Gleadle, a local practitioner who was treating him for depression, in exchange for £2,500. Holmes later admitted this money came from him.

A month later, said Mr Taylor, on 10 April 1974, Thorpe wrote to Jack Hayward, a wealthy benefactor of the Liberal Party, asking, among other things, for £10,000 to be paid to Mr Nadir Dinshaw, godfather of Thorpe's son Rupert. Mr Dinshaw sent a cheque for the whole £10,000 to Holmes, said Mr Taylor.

Mr Bessell had meanwhile gone to live in America, following the collapse of his English companies. According to Mr Taylor, it was at this moment, between the two elections of 1974, that Holmes became converted to the view that Thorpe was right and Scott would have to be killed if the threat of disclosure was to be averted. "Both Thorpe and the Liberal Party were in a position that they had much to lose." At this point, said Mr Taylor, "we move from incitement to conspiracy."

Plans were set in motion to find someone to carry out the killing, said Mr Taylor. Earlier, in about 1973, Mr Le Mesurier introduced Holmes to Mr Deakin for professional advice. On a subsequent occasion when all three were together, Le Mesurier told Deakin that a friend of Holmes was being blackmailed and asked him if he knew anyone who would frighten the man off. Deakin asked Mr David Miller, a friend, the same question, and Miller said he did. The man Miller had in mind was his old friend Andrew Gino Newton, an airline pilot.

Meanwhile, on 4 February 1975, a curious incident occurred in Barnstaple. Two men, one of them saying he was a journalist from *Der Spiegel* called Steiner, tricked Scott into showing them some documents which they then stole. Scott had cautiously left copies of them with his solicitor. Mr Taylor said the two men concerned were Holmes and Deakin and that, later, Holmes admitted as much to Newton.

On 25 February 1975, said Mr Taylor, Miller introduced Newton to Deakin at a Showman's Dinner in Blackpool. Newton said, "Is it true you want someone bumped off?" and proceeded to offer his services, saying, "I'm your man," or words to that effect.

At a later meeting between Deakin and Newton the sum of £10,000 was agreed as a fee for the killing, said Mr Taylor.

After a mix-up over the address – Deakin told Newton that Scott was to be found in Dunstable, instead of Barnstaple – Newton was put in touch with Holmes, who confirmed the fee of £10,000 at a meeting in the Sloane Court Hotel, Chelsea and gave him the correct address in Barnstaple.

On 5 March 1975, said Mr Taylor, Thorpe wrote another letter to Mr Hayward asking, among other things, for a further cheque of £10,000 to be sent to Dinshaw in Jersey. Holmes then spoke to Dinshaw and asked for the money to be paid to him in cash as and when he wanted it. Mr Dinshaw then started paying sums in cash to Holmes over a period.

Newton then made two attempts to fulfil his contract, said Mr Taylor. He tried to get Scott to come to the Royal Garden Hotel in Kensington where he intended to kill him with a chisel. Newton pretended to be interested in hiring Scott for modelling services. Then it was planned to lure Scott to the Holiday Inn at Bristol, where Holmes would pose as a reporter. Again, Scott did not rise to the bait.

"We now proceed to the crucial month of October 1975 when the shooting took place," said Mr Taylor, explaining how Newton hired a car in Blackpool and drove to Devon where he met Scott. They had a long meeting at which Scott told Newton his whole story, and Newton made notes on two pieces of pink paper.

These notes, although Taylor did not say it at the time, were to create an enormous amount of trouble. One of them contained the name of a Person whom Scott, at this stage, claimed to have met in the early days of his association with Thorpe. Crown, defence and judge alike were most anxious that the name of this Person should never be mentioned in court. The satirical magazine, Private Eye, *rushing in as always where angels feared to tread, suggested that Scott was claiming to have met Lord Snowdon, husband of Princess Margaret and brother-in-law of the Queen, at a house in Dulwich on the night of his initial seduction by Thorpe. Scott may have claimed so in his time, but it now seems certain that he never met Snowdon. Under cross-examination Scott disarmingly claimed never to have been told the surname of the man introduced to him as "Tony" on this occasion. Whether Snowdon was named in these notes or not, no sugges-*

tion of impropriety was ever made against him. Yet on several occa-
sions the whole trial was held up while judge and counsel debated
ways of avoiding a mention of this man's name.

A second meeting was arranged between Newton and Scott at the
village of Combe Martin, where Scott was living. This time Newton
brought an old Mauser automatic and some ammunition. He borrowed his girl-friend's car.

"But there was a surprise for Mr Newton," said Mr Taylor.
"Being somewhat apprehensive, Scott brought with him his large
dog, Rinka, a Great Dane." This was not what Newton had
intended, but Scott and the dog got into the car. Newton drove to
Porlock where he stopped at the Castle Hotel. When they drove
back over the moors, Newton pretended to be tired and Scott
offered to drive. Newton stopped the car. The two men got out, and
so did the dog.

Newton pulled out his gun and shot the dog in the head. He then
pointed the gun at Scott and said, "It is your turn now." But the gun
did not fire:

"Whether the gun jammed and thereby saved Scott, or whether
Newton got cold feet – or perhaps already had cold feet before he
set out that evening – you will have to consider."

After tinkering with the gun, Newton drove away to the Cardiff
home of his friend, Mr Miller, where he stripped the gun and got it
working again. Newton would later claim this was play-acting, and
the gun had never really jammed.

On 18 November 1975 Newton and Miller, returning from a
short holiday abroad, were met by the police and Newton was
detained over the dog incident. The gun was recovered by police
and an expert found it had a tendency to jam. Newton was charged
with possessing a gun with intent to endanger life and committed for
trial at Exeter on bail.

Clearly, said Mr Taylor, Newton's trial was fraught with danger to
those involved in the conspiracy. Holmes met Newton a number of
times before the trial to discuss his defence. Newton said he was
going to say that Scott had blackmailed him over a nude photograph; Newton, of his own accord, had taken a gun to frighten him.
Newton made it clear that he expected at least half the contract
figure – £5,000, said Mr Taylor.

Holmes said he was going to the United States to get help for
Newton's defence, and that a letter would be sent supporting the
story that Newton had to tell. Holmes then went to California, told
Bessell what had happened, and persuaded him to write a letter

saying that Scott had been blackmailing him about an affair with his secretary. This would discourage Scott from telling his story about Thorpe at Newton's trial.

Bessell agreed to write the letter, said Mr Taylor, on condition that it was never made public and that he would not be required to testify. Afterwards according to Bessell, Holmes admitted that the airline pilot had been hired to kill Scott.

In the event, his letter was not needed, as Scott blurted out his story of a relationship with Thorpe at a national insurance tribunal in Barnstaple on 29 January 1976, six weeks before the Newton trial was due to start. *This time the British press did not ignore it, and Scott's allegations were printed across every front page.*

Meanwhile, however, the contents of the letter had been "leaked" to the press by Cyril Smith, another Liberal MP, to Bessell's fury. Bessell announced he was going to withdraw the letter, whereupon Thorpe telephoned him on 2 February and begged him not to.

In early February Thorpe was given a vote of confidence by his party, despite Scott's outburst in court, and Bessell decided it was safe to withdraw the letter which he did.

Thorpe next made a statement to the police on 8 February 1976, denying any knowledge of the £2,500 paid by Holmes for Scott's letters, or any knowledge of the dog-shooting incident beyond what he had read in the press. He also wrote a letter to Bessell, dated 19 February, denouncing Cyril Smith as a man who has "opened his mouth too often." Thorpe advised Bessell not to withdraw the letter, adding:

"The press are still being bloody and still trying to destroy me. Harold, on the other hand, is being quite superb."

Mr Taylor explained that "Harold" was a reference to Harold Wilson – now Sir Harold – who was then Prime Minister. The letter ended: "Yours affectionately, Jeremy," and Mr Taylor reminded the jury of reference to "that bastard Bessell" in other letters of Mr Thorpe at this time – his begging letters to Jack Hayward.

Before describing the method by which £5,000 was paid to Newton by Le Mesurier after Newton's release from prison, Mr Taylor gave a series of warnings to the jury.

The first, in the light of press interest in the case, was to put aside anything they may have read about it and concentrate on the evidence they heard.

The second concerned witnesses who had accepted money from the press. "The fact that a witness sells his story to the press does not mean that it is false," said Mr Taylor. "The only question that you will have to decide as each comes to give his evidence is a simple one – is he telling us the truth?"

Both Miller and Newton had made extensive tape recordings of conversations with the main characters in the affair. The jury would hear them, and they were "very revealing and significant." But Miller might be seen as an accomplice to the conspiracy, and so quite clearly was Newton. Mr Taylor warned the jury to take the greatest care in considering the evidence of an accomplice; they should not rely on it unless it was supported by independent testimony.

A few minutes after the warning, Mr Justice Cantley decided it was time to adjourn for the day. The time was 4.15 pm, quarter of an hour after the usual time for adjournment, but Mr Taylor showed no signs of flagging. The judge said it was a natural break and expressed some concern that members of the jury might find their attention wandering after such a long speech. *So the last thought left in the jury's mind at the end of the third day was that they should take the greatest care before accepting the word of those who had supplied so much of Mr Taylor's narrative. Perhaps Mr Taylor had a different conclusion to his day's speech in mind. If so, we shall never know it.*

Day four: 11 May 1979

This, being a Friday, was the end of the first week of the trial. Mr Justice Cantley repeated his now ritualised warning to journalists before the start of the day's hearing. He said he had been asked by one of the "responsible" journalists in court to rule on whether it would be permissible to talk to witnesses for background material which would not be published until after the trial.

The judge had decided to refuse this permission. His reason was that it would create difficulties for him in finding out whether it was a responsible piece of interviewing or a piece of interference.

"It does not arise from any mistrust of the responsible journalists in court," said the judge, "but there is a suggestion of irresponsible journalism, and the presence of *ad hoc* journalists.

"In view of that, and for the administration of justice in this case, I consider it essential that no witness should be interviewed at all."

One could understand his reference to "responsible journalists" as meaning the traditional corps of courtroom reporters, who never offered an opinion on anything they heard, and whose discretionary role was limited to little more than sub-editing their own shorthand notes. The reference to "irresponsible journalism" presumably covered those journalists whose investigative reporting had finally obliged the Director of Public Prosecutions to bring a prosecution – at least one of whom was alleged to have offered large sums to the witness Newton subject to Thorpe's being convicted. The reference to "ad hoc" journalists was more puzzling for anyone who knew of the rigorous scrutiny applied to applications for a press seat in the Old Bailey. Perhaps the judge knew nothing of this background and was just sounding off, as elderly gentlemen have always been privileged to do. I sat in the press benches for six weeks and never saw an "ad hoc" journalist there, unless the judge was referring to Mrs Sybille Bedford, the immensely distinguished novelist and chronicler of court cases whose book on the Bodkin Adams trial, The Best We Can Do, *is a classic of the genre.*

But the simplest explanation was that Mr Justice Cantley was once again rattling his toothbrushes at the press. Part of the defence was that the whole case against Thorpe had been got up by the press – most particularly by the two journalists Penrose and Courtiour. The suggestion, which was never fully developed, was that they had acted as liaison officers between Bessell in California and Newton and Scott in England to produce the amazing similarities in their evidence. By his repeated warnings, Mr Justice Cantley impressed on the jury's mind the idea of the press – or at any rate its less responsible or "ad hoc" members – as a force dedicated to the perversion of justice. Its only motive – or the only one to which he referred – was money. In fact, as every journalist knows, a higher circulation does not necessarily make a newspaper richer, and richer newspapers do not necessarily pay journalists more. Neither professional pride nor the pursuit of excellence were attributable to journalists, only the basest desire for sensationalism. It did not seem to occur to him that elements of the press were chiefly concerned to see that the truth should not be suppressed; or that his impression of them might seem as absurd to journalists as it would seem to him if a journalist suggested that some of his judicial colleagues took bribes.

Tale of Mr Peter Taylor resumed

After some preliminary remarks re-stating the involvement of the three other defendants in the alleged conspiracy, Mr Taylor returned to the attack on Thorpe in the last day of his opening speech, emphasising in particular Thorpe's last-minute attempts to protect himself by tampering with witnesses, as Mr Taylor put it.

Over lunch at Boulestin's restaurant in Covent Garden on 10 November 1977 – some time after police enquiries had been resumed – Thorpe suggested to Mr Nadir Dinshaw he should say that the money paid to Holmes had come from Mr Dinshaw himself, said Mr Taylor. Thorpe suggested he could say he got the money from Mr Hayward as part of a business deal. Mr Dinshaw refused, and said he would tell the truth.

On 4 April 1978 the police started a series of interviews with defendants. On the same day, Thorpe arranged to meet Mr Hayward and asked him to put pressure on Mr Bessell to keep him out of England. If Bessell could be made bankrupt, he would be unable to return to the United States. Mr Hayward declined to do so.

A few days later, by Mr Taylor's account, Thorpe made another attempt to tamper with Mr Dinshaw's evidence. He said that if the truth came out, Mr Dinshaw, a Pakistani, might be asked to leave the country.

Mr Taylor went on to describe an interview, also on 4 April 1978, between Detective Chief Superintendant Michael Challes, of Somerset and Avon Police, the officer in charge of the enquiry, and David Holmes, the defendant alleged to have hired Newton to do the killing on Thorpe's behalf. When asked whether he knew Newton, Holmes replied, "No comment."

Mr Taylor then produced Thorpe's written statement to the police of 3 June 1978, which will be quoted at length during Mr Challes's evidence later in the trial. This denied any homosexual relationship with Scott, denied that Thorpe had been party to any conspiracy to kill or injure or frighten Scott, denied any knowledge of Newton's dog shooting and "possible abortive attempt on Scott's life," or of payments made to Newton or Scott and claimed that he had lodged Hayward's £20,000 with accountants as an "iron reserve" for future elections. Mr Taylor maintained there were a number of "palpable untruths" in this statement, most particularly with regard to the £20,000 of Mr Hayward's money which, so far from being kept by accountants as an iron reserve, had immediately been syphoned off to Mr Holmes.

Mr Taylor ended his speech after seven and a half hours on his feet. It had been remarkable for the clarity of its exposition, but also for its lack of indignation when describing details of the alleged crime. His concern, it would appear, was simply to establish the truth as he saw it. He paid the jury the compliment of supposing they would be able to understand simple, clear English. An interview with one of the jurors which appeared in the New Statesman *a month after the trial, suggests that this confidence may have been misplaced. As Peter Chippindale and David Leigh wrote* (New Statesman, *27 July 1979*):

"The picture that appears is one of an intelligent, conscientious cross-section of citizens, confronted with a mass of scarcely comprehensible evidence, in circumstances where a sensible judgment about its value was nearly impossible to make."

The unnamed juror claimed to find evidence about the money transactions, in particular, "baffling." He said, "We didn't know exactly how the money went to Holmes."

Under the circumstances, one can conclude only that Mr Taylor had been wasting his time.

He concluded his opening statement:

"We submit that Mr Thorpe instigated and was party to a conspiracy to kill Mr Scott and that Mr Holmes was party to it and acted as its manager keeping Mr Thorpe in the background, and that Mr Deakin and Mr Le Mesurier were also party to the conspiracy working under Mr Holmes to hire and pay Newton for his services."

He ended by reminding them that nothing he had said was evidence. He was going to call his first witness, Mr Peter Bessell. Would they now lis..n to the evidence?

3

Mr Peter Bessell

At Minehead, Mr Peter Bessell's appearance was announced dramatically by Mr Taylor rather in the manner of a conjuror pulling a rabbit from his hat. The week before, there had been strenuous attempts by Thorpe's lawyers to have Bessell's evidence excluded. The Lord Chief Justice had heard how his immunity from the Director of Public Prosecution was so all embracing as to give him immunity from prosecution for perjury, should he choose to perjure himself at the trial. Mr Taylor pointed out that no such immunity was included, and the Lord Chief Justice accordingly found against the application. In the course of his pleading, Mr Carman had threatened that in cross-examination he was going to take Mr Bessell so thoroughly through all his business transactions as to discredit him utterly. Mr Taylor ended his opening speech at Minehead on the first day of the hearing with the story of how Thorpe had tried to persuade Mr Hayward to put pressure on Mr Bessell not to come to England.

"Despite this attempt to keep Mr Bessell away," proclaimed Mr Taylor, "and despite threats made in open court of what would face him, Mr Bessell is here and I propose to call him."

No such dramatic introduction awaited him in the Old Bailey on the fourth day of the trial. He had already put in an appearance on the second day of the trial – in the absence of the jury – to receive a severe wigging from the judge, accompanied by threats, for having mentioned to a journalist before the trial started that he still drank as many cups of tea as formerly.

On this, his second appearance, the thin, suntanned former MP once again walked through the well of the court to the witness-box in his dark blue pinstripe suit with a blue check shirt and dark tie, a pair of spectacles dangling from a cord round his neck. He had come from California, but somehow Mr Bessell gave the impression of having come from another planet. His manner was that of a creature from outer space going bravely to its execution – an impression that was somewhat reinforced by the judge's attitude to him.

No sooner had Mr Bessell taken the oath in his deep, science-fiction voice than Mr Justice Cantley indicated that he wished to speak to him. First, the judge said that he could sit down if he wished, as his evidence was expected to last for some time. Then the judge leant forward, no trace of cordiality on his face or in his manner, and addressed the witness with fierce, almost insulting clarity, about his evidence:

"You have been given an extensive immunity and I want to make it perfectly clear that the immunity does not extend to perjury in this trial," said the judge.

"I understand that, my lord," said Mr Bessell. *Perhaps I imagined it, but it seemed to me that in the face of the judge's hostility, Mr Bessell's voice already had a fatalistic, whipped-dog undertone to it. At Minehead, he had spoken confidently and even with a note of self-righteousness from time to time. One could see from the start that Mr Justice Cantley was not going to let him get away with any of that. Mr Bessell was not on trial and his business record may have attracted criticism – like Thorpe's over London and County Securities – but never criminal proceedings. Yet there was to be no suggestion that Peter Bessell, too, was a man of "unblemished reputation." Only the four defendants were to be described in those terms, whatever the evidence to the contrary.*

There could be no doubt that Mr Bessell was perfectly well aware that he had no immunity where perjury was concerned. This had been the main issue in the Divisional Court preliminary hearing. Mr Justice Cantley could not have supposed he was informing the witness of anything he did not already know. The only effect of such a warning, given to a witness before he has started giving evidence, was to cast doubt in advance on the truthfulness of what he was going to say.

There was no suggestion, at any stage, that Mr Bessell had ever committed perjury in the past. The kindest interpretation of the judge's behaviour at this point might be that he was simply being gratuitously offensive. But this was the moment if one has to put a finger on it when it became apparent that the judge's determination to be fair to Thorpe was going to extend to the denigration and belittling of Crown witnesses.

As soon as Mr Bessell had taken the oath and listened to the judge's warning, Mr Taylor stood up and asked for a brief adjournment while he had talks with Mr Carman, Thorpe's lawyer. Eventually the jury came back and the Crown's first witness was able to start his evidence. This is the story which Mr Peter Bessell told:

He had known Thorpe since 1955, when they were both Liberal candidates. When Mr Bessell became a Liberal MP in 1964 for the neighbouring constituency of Bodmin, they became still closer friends.

In the spring of 1965, Thorpe confessed to him that he was a homosexual. This perturbed Mr Bessell, who wanted Thorpe to be leader of the Liberal Party. Shortly afterwards Thorpe invited him to lunch at the Ritz Hotel and showed him the Dublin letter from Norman Scott to his mother, Mrs Ursula Thorpe, which had already been read to the jury. Thorpe told him, apropos the allegations made in the letter, that the contents were basically correct. Bessell volunteered to go to Dublin, see Scott and assess the situation.

He arrived there a few days later and first saw Father Sweetman, a Roman Catholic priest who was looking after Scott. Later he saw Scott and suggested to him that he was trying to blackmail Thorpe, which was an extradictable offence. Scott was alarmed by this, but told him he was concerned to recover his luggage from Switzerland and regain his national insurance cards, which Thorpe has taken.

When Mr Bessell reported to Thorpe the existence of a bundle of incriminating letters in this luggage, the two of them arranged to have the luggage collected. Thorpe was alarmed by the possibility of a police investigation into his homosexual liaison with Scott, particularly since Scott had given some documents, including letters, to the London police in December 1962. Accordingly, Mr Bessell arranged to speak to a Parliamentary Under Secretary at the Home Office – Mr George Thomas, later Speaker of the House of Commons – and to the then Home Secretary, Sir Frank Soskice. Afterwards, Mr Bessell told Thorpe he had no great cause for concern; he mentioned a file which had been on Sir Frank's desk and said the Home Secretary had referred to a number of letters.

Mr Bessell arranged for his secretary to collect Scott's suitcase from Victoria Station, where it had eventually turned up, and take it to Thorpe's flat in Marsham Court. There Thorpe opened it and removed two bundles of letters. The suitcase was then sent to Scott in Dublin.

In 1967 Thorpe duly became leader of the Liberal Party. Mr Bessell told Thorpe that if anything about his private life came out, he would have to resign. Thorpe agreed and said that if anything of this sort came out he would be forced to take his own life to avoid damaging the party.

Scott wrote to Mr Bessell on 20 April 1967 mentioning a

proposed trip to America. However, the journey never materialised, and Scott was taken to a psychiatric unit, where he told a doctor everything about his relationship with Thorpe. Mr Bessell suggested he should see Scott in London and Thorpe agreed. Mr Bessell started paying Scott a "retainer" of between £5 and £7 a week until such time as Scott should sort out his problems and find a job. Thorpe refunded most of this momey.

In 1968, Mr Bessell mentioned to Thorpe that Scott claimed that he still had some letters in his possession, in addition to those that had been recovered from the suitcase. They hatched a plot to recover the letters, with David Holmes – one of the accused – posing as a reporter, but this came to nothing when Scott said he had destroyed the letters.

In November or December of the same year he met Thorpe in Thorpe's room at the House of Commons. Thorpe was depressed about Scott whom he saw as a continuing threat to his career, and said that if Scott could not find a job in America they would have to get rid of him. Thorpe suggested various ways of getting rid of the body: burying it, tying weights to it and dropping it in a river; cementing it into a motorway under construction; finally dropping it down a disused tin mine in Cornwall. Mr Bessell raised detailed objections to all these proposals and also told Thorpe that it was an immoral suggestion, to which Thorpe replied, "It's no worse than killing a sick dog." Thorpe suggested David Holmes as the murderer, to which Mr Bessell replied, "Rubbish, David is too wet." He thought Holmes too incompetent for the job, but they both agreed that they could not do it. Thorpe said, "David is completely loyal and if he were instructed properly he would be able to carry it out."

Mr Bessell was not certain how serious Thorpe was at this stage, and had no intention of taking any part in the murder himself, but agreed to be present at a meeting between Holmes and Thorpe if only to prevent the plan going any further.

In February 1969 Mr Bessell met Thorpe and Holmes in Thorpe's room. Thorpe asked him to lock the door and sit down. The plan was that Holmes, posing as a reporter from *Der Spiegel*, should take Scott to Plymouth as for a meeting with his editor, who wished to be convinced of the truth of Scott's story, Holmes should get Scott drunk, take him to a lonely spot in Cornwall and shoot him. Thorpe put this forward as a practical plan, something that Holmes should do, but Holmes looked petrified. Eventually, Bessell managed to catch his eye and winked, after which Holmes relaxed.

Thorpe, however, was treating the matter in deadly seriousness. Both Bessell and Holmes tried to laugh him out of it, pointing to the practical difficulties, whether of shooting or poisoning, but Thorpe was not to be put off, and the matter was left that Holmes should do some research into slow-working poisons and report back on his findings to Thorpe.

At this point the court adjourned for the weekend. Mr Bessell's narrative was to be resumed on Monday 14 May.

Day five: 14 May 1979
Mr Bessell's narrative continued

A few weeks after this meeting, Holmes had done no research into slow-working poisons and Thorpe was agitating for further news when Mr Bessell heard that Scott had married on 13 May 1969. Thorpe was relieved to hear this but thought the "ultimate solution" might still be necessary. Holmes did not disguise his relief.

Soon afterwards Mr Bessell was telephoned by Scott who said that his wife was pregnant and she could not get maternity benefits owing to the absence of his national insurance cards. He was in genuine financial trouble and hysterically threatened to sell his story to a newspaper. Mr Bessell arranged for some welfare payments to be made to him, but avoided discussing the matter with Thorpe for fear he would revive the homicide plan.

Shortly afterwards, Scott and his wife started divorce proceedings. This alarmed both Thorpe and Bessell, since a divorce hearing would give Scott another opportunity to refer to his relationship with Thorpe. They put Scott in touch with a solicitor, Mr Leonard Ross, hoping to keep him quiet. Thorpe kept repeating that the position was such as to demand the ultimate solution, and suggested that Bessell and Holmes should kill him in Florida.

Bessell and Holmes pretended to take this seriously, meeting in Florida and even going so far as to buy a toy gun. The judge at this point commented, "It sounds crazy." Mr Bessell replied "I agree, sir." On his return to England, Holmes told Thorpe that the plan had failed because Scott did not come out to America, and there the matter rested for a time.

In May 1971 Scott's divorce was still pending and Mr Bessell was still in England when he received a telephone call from Mr Emlyn Hooson, the Liberal MP for Montgomeryshire: Mr Hooson had learned of Thorpe's relationship with Scott; he was informing the Liberal Chief Whip, Mr David Steel, and expected Thorpe to resign. This incident coincided with the Liberal Party investigation of May 1971, which decided to ignore Scott's allegations.

Mr Bessell then disappeared from the story until 19 January 1976 when Holmes visited him in Oceanside, California, where he had settled after the collapse of his businesses. Holmes told him that Scott has been causing trouble in Thorpe's constituency; more recently he had befriended an airline pilot whom he later black-mailed over a compromising photograph; in the course of an argu-ment, the pilot had shot Scott's dog; the pilot was going to be charged with this, and there was a danger that Scott would use his status as witness to repeat his story of a relationship with Thorpe.

Holmes told him that Thorpe had consulted with Lord Goodman, the well-known solicitor, who had produced a plan of action: Mr Bessell should write a letter to Scott's solicitor, saying that Scott had blackmailed him years before. If Scott did not men-tion Thorpe's name in the case against the airline pilot, Mr Bessell would take no action; but if he did, Mr Bessell would sign an affidavit accusing him. The effect of this letter would be to discour-age Scott from making an outburst against Thorpe in court.

Mr Bessell was uneasy about this, as the story was untrue and he was not prepared to testify on oath. Holmes assured him there was no question of this. Mr Bessell said that in any case the press would ignore the ravings of a layabout who had taken to blackmail. Holmes said that the letters which Mr Bessell had written to Scott, accompanying the "retainer" had been preserved by Scott and constituted a great danger to Thorpe. Under these circumstances, Mr Bessell agreed to write a mendacious letter accusing Scott of having blackmailed him.

Holmes gave him the name of Mr Michael Barnes as the man to whom the latter should be written, saying this was Newton's solicitor. He then produced a draft letter in Thorpe's handwriting which Mr Bessell, for various reasons, rejected. He wrote his own letter. It said that Scott threatened to expose the fact that Mr Bessell was having a relationship with his private secretary, which would have been damaging to his family and to his political career. It concluded by saying of Scott, "I have no doubt that he is vicious. He does not hesitate to turn upon those who have tried to help him."

All this was quite untrue. After the letter was written, Holmes telephoned Thorpe's house in England and left a message, presum-ably with Thorpe's second wife, Marion: "Mission accomplished."

This alarmed Mr Bessell and made him suspicious. On the way to take Holmes to the airport, Mr Bessell questioned him further and he admitted that he had hired Newton to kill Scott. He said he had been persuaded that this was the only solution.

This made Mr Bessell even more worried about the letter he had written. He asked for it back, but was not given it.

On 1 February 1976 Holmes telephoned Mr Bessell and told him that Scott had repeated his allegation about Thorpe before·a social security tribunal; the letter was therefore no longer needed and could be destroyed. Thorpe had issued a brief statement, on Lord Goodman's advice, denying it.

Next day Thorpe telephoned Mr Bessell, who told him he was going to deny he had ever been blackmailed by Scott – the contents of Mr Bessell's letter had already been leaked to the press. Thorpe became agitated and begged him not to do so. Mr Bessell told him he had already told the *Daily Mail* that there was no affidavit, no document deposited with solicitors. Thorpe replied that eventually he would have to sue somebody, and it might as well be the *Daily Mail*. Mr Bessell advised against this reminding him of the outcome of the Oscar Wilde libel action against Lord Queensberry, which ended with Wilde in prison for sodomy. Thorpe replied, "I know, I know," and sounded very depressed.

Later Thorpe urged him to make no comment on the grounds that he might be called upon to give evidence in a criminal matter. This astounded Mr Bessell, who had made it plain that on oath he would have to tell the truth. Thorpe agreed that Holmes had hired Newton, and in a later telephone conversation about a meeting of the Parliamentary Party to discuss his future, said, "It's hell. I wake up every morning with that terrible sick feeling."

On 19 February 1976 Thorpe wrote to him begging him not to withdraw the Barnes letter, as it would suggest that someone was lying. "The press are still being bloody and trying to destroy me," he wrote. "Harold on the other hand, is being quite superb" – a reference to the then Prime Minister, Mr Harold Wilson, who was on record as believing that the whole case against Thorpe was trumped up by South African interests to discredit the Liberal Party.

In May 1976 Mr Bessell met Douglas Thompson of the *Daily Mail* and told him that the Barnes letter – accusing Scott of black-mailing him – was a lie. His reason for this was that he had heard that Scott was suing the Commissioner of the Metropolitan Police for the return of letters handed to Chelsea police station in December 1962 which provided evidence of Scott's relationship with Thorpe. He decided it would be best for the party to make a clean breast of things. Holmes rang him twice asking him to deny the story, but he refused, saying the time had come to tell the truth. He had not spoken to Holmes or Thorpe again.

That ended Mr Bessell's narrative, as it was given in answer to Mr Taylor's examination-in-chief at the Old Bailey. The charge against Thorpe, of inciting Holmes to murder Scott relied entirely on Mr Bessell's uncorroborated evidence. A large part of the case against Thorpe on the charge of conspiracy to murder relied on Mr Bessell's evidence of earlier conversations with him on this matter and of later conversations with Holmes. Reference was also made to a cryptic reply by Thorpe in a telephone conversation with Bessell – referred to as the "Isaac Foot" answer – which might have been interpreted as an admission by Thorpe of involvement in the conspiracy to murder. Since it plainly was not so interpreted, was confusing in itself and was left more or less hanging in the air by Mr Taylor, I have not even included it in my summary of Mr Bessell's evidence. But on the point whether the conspiracy was to murder or to frighten, Mr Bessell's narrative plainly added weighty circumstantial corroboration to Newton's later claim that he was hired to murder Scott, if either could be believed.

One should perhaps emphasise again that the foregoing is Mr Bessell's version of events. There is reason to suppose that both Thorpe and Holmes would have disputed large parts of it if they had chosen to give evidence in their own defence.

4

The Agony of Mr Peter Bessell

Day six: 15 May 1979
On the previous day, in the course of discussing his disappearance in Mexico at a time when he was having some difficulty with creditors, Mr Bessell revealed that he had suffered a suspected coronary attack and continued to suffer from emphysema, a form of irreversible damage to the lung. Many of those in court, when Mr Bessell took the stand to face cross-examination, wondered whether he would survive the ordeal physically. Any aspect of his past commercial and political life was liable to be thrown in his face in a cross-examination which might last up to five days. With his strange, croaky voice, slight figure and unusual colouring, he did not inspire confidence as being a very robust man. In the relaxed atmosphere of Minehead, where everyone wore informal dress in a small courtroom presided over by benign or at any rate impartial magistrates, he had borne up very well – occasionally, perhaps, even overplaying his hand and allowing a slightly peevish note to creep into his evidence. In the Old Bailey, before a hostile judge, he never cut the same figure. It was as if we were listening to the ghost of a man giving a performance which had been carefully rehearsed when the body was animated. His memory remained impressive and he made few mistakes, but his manner was more that of a penitent seeking forgiveness than a prosecution witness. Perhaps he had decided that if he was going to destroy his old friend and collaborator Jeremy Thorpe he should also destroy himself in the process. It was not an attitude which married well with the posture of a man who stood to gain a considerable sum of money from his old friend's conviction. A more sympathetic judge might have been impressed by his breast-beating readiness to own up to past sins, but a jury composed in large part of lower-middle class Londoners was more likely to be impressed by the pecuniary aspect.

Mr Mathew's cross-examination
Mr Bessell was cross-examined first by Mr John Mathew QC, for

Holmes. As a cross-examiner, his manner was frankly old fashioned: sneering, hectoring, fixing his eyes at some point in the back of the court and repeating questions in a way which insinuated that the witness was either trying to evade them or was likely to contradict himself second time around. At Minehead, without his wig, he seemed a more formidable figure. Mr Bessell answered him coolly, for the most part, but his own history was not so straightforward as to enable him to meet all Mr Mathew's innuendoes with a simple denial.

In retrospect, Mr Mathew's approach was probably the most effective one with the jury. In the New Statesman *interview with an unnamed juror after the trial, it emerged that Mr Bessell's financial interest in a conviction was what most discredited him. Mr Mathew's constant rehearsal of past untruths and endless reiteration of money matters already discussed and agreed obviously impressed the jury. But his long, repetitive harangue was tedious for quicker minds in the court.*

He began by rehearsing a few of Mr Bessell's admissions in Minehead.

Mathew: "There are a number of compelling reasons, aren't there, why your evidence should not be believed?"

Bessell: "I do not accept that, sir."

Mathew: "You have told a considerable number of lies about this matter over a period of years?"

Bessell: "Yes, sir, but it was in defence of Mr Thorpe's position."

Mathew: "Do you accept that you have a credibility problem?"

Bessell: "For the same reasons, yes, sir."

Mr Mathew then suggested that Mr Bessell not only had a credibility problem but also every motive to exaggerate and sensationalise, since he was making a lot of money out of the case.

He then referred to the wide immunity given to Mr Bessell, that no criminal proceedings would be instituted against him by the police or anybody else in respect of anything arising out of the court proceedings. He asked Mr Bessell what, exactly, he expected to arise out of the court proceedings which might have resulted in a prosecution. There must have been a good reason for the immunity, he said, and proceeded to suggest a few. Would it not be true to say that in January 1974 Mr Bessell had fled from his creditors?

Bessell: "I disappeared for a time, it is true."

Mathew: "That does not answer my question. You fled from your creditors?"

Bessell: "Very well, that is a fair statement."

This was the first sign of the hare on the run, and Mr Mathew was on its trail like a very experienced old beagle.

Mathew: The lamentable last act of a discredited figure, do you agree with that relating to you at that time?

Bessell: Regretfully, I do admit that, sir.

Mathew: Do you also agree, speaking after you disappeared – a discredited politician?

Bessell: No, sir.

Mathew: A disastrous businessman?

Bessell: Yes. Yes, I think that is fair.

It emerged that Mr Bessell had asked Jack Hayward, the Bahamas-based philanthropist, for half a million dollars to bribe an American official over a property deal they were both involved in, intending to convert the money to his own use. Mr Bessell had been more robust about this episode at Minehead, pointing out that Thorpe had been involved with him in the attempted fraud. Perhaps it was a gentlemanly horror of repeating himself, perhaps he had forgotten this aspect, perhaps he did not wish to bring it up for some other reason.

Mathew: "I suggest that you will go to any dishonest lengths to get yourself out of your backwoods lifestyle in California, that you will go to any dishonest lengths to make money."

Bessell: "No, that is not true. What you describe as my backwoods life is most unfair with respect to my way of life there."

Next Mr Mathew cross-examined him about the book which he intended to write. Mr Bessell had entered into a contract with the *Sunday Telegraph* in September 1978 – the month after Thorpe and his co-defendants were arrested – by which he would receive £50,000 for the serialisation, but only £25,000 if, for legal reasons, the newspaper was unable to serialise it – in other words, if Thorpe and his three co-defendants were acquitted.

Mathew: "Mr Newton's writing a book. Mr Scott's writing a book – everybody's writing a book, aren't they? And all trying to make as much money as possible out of the drama that is going on in court. You're on that bandwagon, aren't you?"

Mr Mathew hammered on with the fact that Mr Bessell stood to make more money from a conviction than an acquittal, suggesting that his evidence had been concocted with a view to making money.

Mathew: "And the truth of the matter is that as soon as you realised what the press wanted, you embellished, exaggerated and lied?"

Bessell: "No, sir."

Next the suggestion was that Mr Bessell had worked with the two journalists, Penrose and Courtiour, to co-ordinate the evidence of the Crown witnesses.

Mathew: "And you knew, Mr Bessell, that these two journalists had been going from one witness to another . . . and getting their version?"

Bessell: "At that stage I was not aware of that. All I knew at that stage was that they were talking to Sir Harold Wilson."

Just as Mr Lewis Hawser had cut in at the Newton trial in March 1976, so Mr Mathew cut in now to put a stop to the mention of another public figure's name.

Mathew: "I didn't ask you about Harold Wilson."

Bessell: "I'm sorry."

In September 1976, said Mr Bessell, he had composed his *aide-mémoire* of 100 closely typed pages about the Thorpe case, but he disputed that he had written it for the purposes of drafting a book. At this point the judge chose to intervene. In case the jury had been in any doubt about his attitude to Mr Bessell's evidence, he thought they should be given a further clue.

"You must have written the *aide-mémoire* for some purpose," observed Mr Justice Cantley in what might be described as a voice of cheerful scepticism.

Mr Bessell replied that he wrote it to remind himself of events; in the event of his death, it would be available for others. It was not for the prime purpose of writing a book. Mr Mathew resumed his cross-examination.

The only lies Mr Bessell could remember telling to Penrose and Courtiour were about some connections he might have had in Washington.

These provide the most puzzling and least satisfactory section of The Pencourt File, *seeming to suggest that Mr Bessell had relations with the CIA or some other United States Security Agency. It is an aspect of the case which has never been explained satisfactorily, one way or the other.*

Mathew: "Would you agree that you were working fairly closely with them on their book?"

Bessell: "Yes, sir. But you have read that out of context. You were referring – because I know the phrase – to a letter I wrote to Lady Falkender."

Mathew: "It may well have come from a letter."

So great was his respect for public figures that Mr Mathew seemed unable to get the name of Sir Harold Wilson's personal secretary past his lips, but he proceeded to read from the letter which Mr Bessell had written her.

At one point Mr Bessell had used the word "exaggeration" to describe a statement which could, he later admitted, be more accurately described as a "lie." Mr Mathew made merry for a time of this use of "exaggeration."

Mathew: "Was it not typical of your 'exaggeration,' Mr Bessell, when you recounted how Mr Holmes pretended to be a reporter from a German newspaper in order to trick Scott out of two letters?"

Mr Bessell denied this. Mr Mathew went on to suggest that there might have been some light-hearted banter about getting rid of Scott, but nothing of a serious nature was ever said.

Bessell: "I cannot accept that. It was a serious proposition."

Mathew: "Why didn't you take it seriously, Mr Bessell?"

Bessell: "I accept that I should have taken it a great deal more seriously."

Mathew: "Why didn't you take it seriously, Mr Bessell?"

Eventually Mr Bessell replied that it was his knowledge of Thorpe's character which prevented him from taking it seriously.

Mathew: "Why didn't you do something about it?"

Bessell: "I recognise it was irresponsible of me not to have taken some action at the outset. But I hoped and believed that Holmes and I would succeed in persuading Thorpe that this was a nonsensical plan . . . I accept that I perhaps should have taken some other action, but I did not."

Perhaps this passage conveys in some manner how the Mathew method of repeating a question worked on Mr Bessell to induce the -confessional spirit.

Mr Mathew then pointed out a few inconsistencies between what Mr Bessell had originally told Penrose and Courtiour and what he later said in court. To the observer, they did not seem important to the main story, but Mr Bessell accepted that he had made mistakes when talking to the journalists before compiling his recollections. Pushed further by Mr Mathew, he accepted that it was "absolutely contrary to what he had sworn as true facts to the jury."

Mathew: "There was much more at stake later – serialisation rights, the book, money – all sorts of things had entered into it."

Mr Mathew thought he had discovered a most important inconsistency in Mr Bessell's original account (to Penrose and Courtiour) of his first discussion with Thorpe about Scott. In the earlier version, this had taken place at Thorpe's flat, in the later versions – sworn on oath – in Thorpe's room at the House of Commons. From this Mr Mathew moved on and questioned various details of his account of meeting Holmes in America over the Barnes letter. The careless listener might have supposed that these details, too, were disputed by an independent witness.

Next, Mr Bessell was asked about his attitude to Thorpe and Holmes after the alleged murder attempt. Why had he continued helping them after he had decided they were guilty of attempted murder? Mr Mathew quoted a statement of Mr Bessell on American television in August 1978:

"It comes down to . . . a very simple issue. What he [Thorpe] did was to arrange for a friend of his, David Holmes, to hire a gunman to do that which Jeremy Thorpe could not do himself – kill Norman Scott. Against this background, the issue of personal loyalty does not arise. Whether it is the assassination of Thomas à Becket, Julius Caesar, John F. Kennedy or even Norman Scott, it is still one person depriving another of his life and that is a crime which in a civilised society is intolerable."

Mr Bessell explained that these had become his sentiments after May 1976, but it took him a long time to come to terms with the question of whether personal loyalty took precedence over the nature of his crime. Of an earlier occasion, when he had twice told Thorpe that he was anxious to do anything he could to help, Mr Bessell said:

"It is hard, I know, to explain it, but my regard and affection for Thorpe were, at that stage, unaltered. I was appalled by what happened. I wanted to put it out of my mind. I wanted to concentrate on the fact that Scott was alive and unharmed and I did not want to destroy a friendship which I valued. It was very wrong and irresponsible of me, but that is what I did."

One began to wonder whether Mr Bessell's irreversible deterioration of the lungs would be much improved by all this breast-beating.

Mr Mathew drew attention to the tapes of telephone conversations between him and Holmes of April 1976, in which Bessell urged Holmes to "take good care" of himself and described him as "a good and faithful servant of our friend." Mr Mathew suggested these were "total hypocrisy." Mr Bessell agreed.

Tapes were now produced, so judge and barristers laboriously prepared to put on earphones to listen to them. They cannot have liked what they heard. Once again important names were being bandied around. Holmes, in Manchester, was talking to Bessell, in

California, complaining that newspapers had got hold of the fact that he was refusing to make a statement to the police.

Holmes: "Bear in mind that I only talked to the Deputy Director of Public Prosecutions, and then at his request, not a statement but just a talk."

Holmes maintained that the newspapermen could have heard from only two people, and added: "Nothing would make me believe that the Deputy Director of Public Prosecutions had done it."

Bessell: "Are you doing anything about that? I mean, is anybody?"

Holmes: "Well I am not, but Harold is."

Bessell: "Yes, that will do. That will do very nicely."

Holmes: "Because he is furious."

Bessell: "Yes."

Holmes: "What is more, my statement was vetted by him twice . . . he was, er, could not have been more helpful, not with me, but I used David Freeman who is his solicitor as well as . . ."

Bessell: "Of course he is."

Holmes: "I could not use the other obvious candidate because a mutual friend is using him."

Bessell: "You mean Goodman?"

Holmes: "Yes."

Needless to say, no questions were asked about this passage. What it seems to mean, if it means anything, is that Holmes was claiming his statement had been read and altered by Sir Harold Wilson, the newly resigned Prime Minister, to whom it had been shown by their common solicitor. Mr David Freeman. Lord Goodman, of course, stopped representing Thorpe shortly afterwards.

Later, Bessell asked: "Goodman is still holding his hand?"

Holmes: "Absolutely."

Holmes went on: "I have deliberately emerged in the last two days as being a total fool."

Bessell: "Yes, which is very wise. I think you are right."

Holmes: "Yes, absolutely. I mean, we decided that this is how I would play it. To look at my interviews, anyone would think I was ga-ga."

Bessell: "No, I do not think that. I am sure they would not think that."

Holmes: "You need not be polite. It was quite deliberate on my part."

In a second, twenty-minute tape, Mr Bessell mentioned that Jack

Hayward had got his address, and Holmes told him: "We are actively defusing him."

Towards the end of the conversation, Mr Bessell delivered a moving encomium to Holmes: "David, you have been through a tough time and we have been very sorry for you. It is indeed difficult when you have to take what you have had to take. You have been, to use a sentimental term, a good and faithful servant to our friend. I do not mean that in a belittling way, but I mean in the sense that you have been a most honourable friend and you do not deserve to suffer."

One part of this exchange of 20 April 1976 was seized upon with a certain glee by *Private Eye* magazine and printed in its issue of 25 May 1979.

Bessell: "I have been really anxious on your behalf."

Holmes: "Well, that's extremely nice of you. There is one marvellous piece of news about that. Jimmy Goldsmith has actually got criminal libel proceedings against *Private Eye*."

Bessell: "Oh really?"

Holmes: "It would have been a major criminal offence."

Bessell: "Yes of course it would. Oh my God, that would finish them, which would cause me no grief."

Holmes: "Not only against the editor, but against every member of staff, every member of the Board, and every distributor."

Bessell: "Yes, good. Well, that may close them down. You say it has reduced them by seventy per cent?"

Holmes: "That has cheered me immensely . . ."

Holmes: "My solicitor, Freeman, says there is no point in suing unless you are going to do exactly what whatsisname is doing – there is no point in starting."

Bessell: "Right."

Holmes: "He has to be a very rich man to sue that number of people."

Bessell: "Right, exactly."

Holmes: "Goldsmith, mercifully, is a multi-millionaire, so he is going to do it."

Bessell: "Good, well that's splendid. That's splendid. More power to his elbow."

Holmes: "I know. That cheered me up no end."

Bessell: "Yes, I should think so."

When Mr Mathew handed the witness over to Mr Carman, he had re-established the familiar fact of Mr Bessell's pecuniary interest in a conviction and he had established a few fairly unimportant inconsis-

tencies between Mr Bessell's earlier account of events to journalists and his later account to the court on oath. He had succeeded in throwing a certain amount of dirt at Mr Bessell, to prompt the suspicion that the witness might be a double-dyed villain, prepared to send an old colleague to prison on a trumped up charge in order to sell the false story to newspapers afterwards, and he had left hanging in the air, incompletely explained, the question of how Mr Bessell's attitude to Thorpe had changed from the "dear and wonderful friend" of 4 February 1976 – after the alleged murder attempt – to someone about whom he was determined to tell the bitter truth in May of the same year. But so far as his client Holmes was concerned, he had failed to shake Mr Bessell from his central assertion, that "the question of frightening Mr Scott never arose at any time during the conversation I had with your client." Since the essence of Holmes's defence was that the admitted conspiracy was to frighten, not to kill, Mr Mathew's cross-examination might be judged inconclusive in any ideal state where the jury was intelligent and the judge had an open mind as to facts and was concerned only to establish the truth. But in an imperfect world, where the scales of justice must be unevenly balanced, as Mr Carman put it in his opening submissions, in favour of the accused, Mr Mathew had probably managed to sow a little doubt in the mind of the jury. Mr Bessell had no advocate present to argue the improbability of the defence's explanation, that three key witnesses concocted a false charge in order to sell the details of it in books and newspaper articles. The central question left in the mind of the jury was whether or not they trusted Mr Bessell, which is not quite the same thing as whether or not he was telling the truth.

But the most important effect of Mr Mathew's bullying tactics, his sneers, innuendoes and imputations of improper motive at every point, was to soften up the witness for his next ordeal, when Mr Bessell faced two and a half days' cross-examination by George Carman QC, representing Jeremy Thorpe.

Mr Carman's cross-examination

Mr Carman started by probing Mr Bessell's relationship with Thorpe. The witness agreed that Thorpe was a dedicated MP, a distinguished and successful leader of the Liberal Party. In the past, they had been loyal friends. Thorpe had done many kindnesses to Mr Bessell, including helping him when he was in business difficulties and, with his wife Marion, giving Mr Bessell's wife a home when he was in America. Thorpe was a popular MP in the House of

Commons who was "totally stricken with grief" when his first wife was tragically killed.

There were four possible reasons for Mr Bessell's voluntary return to England to give evidence, said Mr Carman. The first was a sense of justice; the second, loyalty to the Liberal Party; the third, revenge; the fourth, money. Mr Bessell accepted the first two, denied the last two.

Mr Carman then began to discuss Mr Bessell's character. Mr Bessell said he had tried to be honourable and now regarded himself as an honourable man. He did not think "hypocrite" a fair description, although he had occasionally told lies. He accepted that his attempt to defraud a benefactor of the Liberal Party was not a loyal action. He agreed that he was a lay preacher at the same time as knowing of the Liberal leader's serious proposal to murder another human being.

Carman: "Did that trouble your conscience?"

Bessell: "No, sir, it did not."

Carman: "Did you not feel it was your duty to tell the party that its leader was a man intent on murder?"

Bessell: "My first loyalty was to Thorpe. I thought it could be prevented. I saw no purpose in seeking to damage his career in that way."

Carman: "Didn't you think Mr Thorpe must have needed to see a psychiatrist?"

Bessell: "Yes, I suppose that is true."

Mr Bessell had not done anything about it, however, he said. Mr Carman enlarged on the witness's "incredible attitude" before producing what was to prove the surprise of the afternoon.

Carman: "A lot of things you have done are incredible and disgraceful are they not? Let us pass on to something even more totally incredible. Before Mr Thorpe, on your account of the matter, had in mind sending Mr Scott to his death in 1971, in the United States, you have asserted he proposed the murder of another person to you in 1970?"

Bessell: "Yes, sir."

Carman: "A man called Hetherington?"

Bessell: "Yes, sir."

Mr Carman wittily added that this man Hetherington was not to be confused with the present Director of Public Prosecutions, Sir Thomas "Tony" Hetherington. *This provoked a burst of sycophantic laughter from every quarter, but Mr Carman never told the court who Hetherington was or why Thorpe wanted him murdered. Readers of* The Pencourt File *might have remembered that he was a black-mailer who had knowledge of the Scott affair just before the 1970 election and whom Mr Bessell, by his account, had paid and fright-ened away by a ruse.* But so far as the jury was concerned, his name *was left hanging in the air, as an example of Mr Bessell's preposterous allegations about his former friend. Psychologically, this was prob-ably a shrewd move by Mr Carman: if the jury were prepared to believe Thorpe capable of arranging the murder of Scott, they might equally well believe him capable of arranging to murder Hethering-ton. By approaching it from the other side – the prosecution offered no evidence on the Hetherington allegation and did not include it in their charges against Thorpe – Mr Carman hoped to cast doubt on the conspiracy to murder Scott.*

Mr Bessell seemed surprised that Hetherington's name had been mentioned. *This made one wonder whether he had not been wrongly told of some agreement between prosecution and defence to exclude the name of Hetherington, as being of no advantage to either side.*

Carman: "If your evidence has a vestige of truth, the leader of the Liberal Party had proposed the death not only of Norman Scott but of another person ... this time it was not the unfortunate Mr Holmes but you who were to be the assassin?"

Bessell: "That is correct."

Carman: "What steps did you take to acquaint the Liberal Party, police, doctors, Mrs Thorpe, with the fact that the leader of the Liberal Party was insane?"

Bessell: "None, sir."

Carman: "Yet when he got his vote of confidence in 1976 you were delighted?"

Bessell: "Yes, sir."

Carman: "Does this make you a thoroughly amoral person?"

Bessell: "I think it does."

Carman: "If you were publicly preaching Christianity, add hypocrite?"

Bessell: "Yes."

Carman: "Amoral, hypocrite, liar – is that not a scoundrel?"

Mr Bessell did not think so. There were limits to his self-abasement. Earlier, he had even managed to produce one fairly spirited reply. When questioned on whether the morality of the Ten Commandments – "Thou Shalt not Kill" – troubled him, he replied: "If the morality of it had not, sir, I would not be in this place at this time."

But the truth was apparent, that Mr Carman had a cowed Mr

Bessell eating out of his hand. Time and again he coaxed these admissions which, offered in a penitential spirit, became extremely damaging to the prosecution case when repeated by Mr Carman later. For a time, it seemed touch and go whether Mr Bessell would own up to being a scoundrel.

Mr Carman next took the witness through an episode when he had apparently been involved with a claim on the Romanov millions with someone who might have been a descendant of Tsar Nicholas II. Had Mr Bessell claimed to be a friend of Henry Kissinger? No, an acquaintance. Dr Kissinger later denied this. Next, Mr Carman took us, step by step, through Bessell's earlier career.

Now fifty-nine, he went to school in Bath and was eighteen when war broke out.

Carman: "Did you fight during the war?"

No, Mr Bessell had first registered as a conscientious objector. Later he asked for his name to be removed from the register, lectured on music to the armed forces, then went into the tailoring business, which was a reserved occupation. After a period in dry-cleaning he went into property development with an office in New York and driving a Cadillac. His commercial world shattered in the early 1970s. Mr Carman continued to question him about the lies he had told; he said he may have told some on minor matters but not in relation to this case.

Carman: "Have you told any whoppers since 1976?"

Bessell: "Not to my knowledge."

Carman: "You have told quite a few in this case, haven't you?"

Bessell: "No."

Mr Carman then asked Mr Justice Cantley if that would be a convenient time to adjourn. The time was 4.15 pm – exactly the same time as the judge had himself adjourned the trial, on his own initiative, at the end of the third day. Mr Bessell had been giving evidence all day, as well as on the previous two days, but on this occasion the judge decided otherwise.

"Oh, I think we have got time for one whopper if you like."

Mr Justice Cantley, it would appear, needed no convincing by this stage. His use of the word "whopper" when Mr Carman had just used it to describe evidence the witness had already given, shows a robust independence of mind, of course. It also left the jury in no doubt what he thought of the witness's evidence. Perhaps it did not occur to the judge that in his duty to give Thorpe the benefit of every possible doubt he also had a duty to be fair to Mr Bessell. Or perhaps it was simply the case that he had made up his mind and felt confident that he knew best.

At the end of the sixth day, the first rumours went round journalists attending the trial that neither Thorpe nor Holmes was going to give evidence. I scribbled the rumour in my notebook, adding: "Surely false."

Day seven: 16 May 1979

"We have dealt with your character as a liar outside the court. I now want to very firmly put to you a lie you have told on oath in this court, reminding you of course, that you are not immune from perjury," began Mr Carman on the second day of his cross-examination of Mr Bessell.

People in court sat forward on their seats, but nothing very dramatic emerged from this opening. The day was to be devoted to a process of attrition, constantly denouncing Mr Bessell as a liar, weaving together lies he had told on minor or irrelevant matters with statements he had made about Thorpe to suggest that the two should be given the same value. A further theme of the day's cross-examination was that Mr Bessell was betraying a friend for money.

The first alleged lie on oath concerned a very minor matter – whether he had insisted on the journalists Penrose and Courtiour being present through his first series of interviews with Chief Superintendent Challes. Mr Bessell explained that the reason he wanted them present was that he had been unhappy about the earlier police investigation. He failed to see how the question of perjury arose.

"You may in a moment," said Mr Carman threateningly. It turned out that there may have been a difference of recollection between the police officer and the witness about the degree of insistence involved.

Mr Carman then moved to another subject: the suggestion by Penrose and Courtiour that Bessell should co-author a book with them.

Carman: "You were giving house-room to the journalists who proposed to you to write a book, to share the spoils of the book, which was to follow on the trial and imprisonment of a former dear and loyal friend."

He then returned to the *Sunday Telegraph* contract, pointing out yet again how it was worth £25,000 on an acquittal, £50,000 on a conviction.

Carman: "It's what you might call in popular language a 'double your money' contract. Half on acquittal and double on conviction."

Bessell: "I accept that."

It may have been tedious for those of us in court to listen to this repetition, but Mr Carman was almost certainly right to repeat it. A juror who was interviewed in the New Statesman *after the case revealed that this point impressed him conclusively in his assessment of Mr Bessell's evidence. According to the two writers of this article, "Peter Bessell – just as many observers calculated he must be – was by this means almost wholly destroyed as a credible witness." The juror spoke to them of "the difference of twenty-five grand on a conviction. This was very important. I wrote it in big letters on one page – 'Half Price Acquittal' . . . It impressed me a great deal. I think it must have impressed the others."*

To anybody outside Britain, and to most people inside it, the Sunday Telegraph's *contract will be incomprehensible unless they have studied the scope and application of Britain's libel laws. These would forbid the publication of Mr Bessell's testimony outside the privileged circumstance of court proceedings unless it had been found proven in the court.*

Earlier, Mr Carman had made much of the value of the contract, despite Mr Bessell's evidence that he would see very little of the £50,000. It worked out at £1.66 per word, said Mr Carman, or about the industrial weekly wage per paragraph: "Do you still say that money doesn't play any part in your coming to England?"

Once again Mr Bessell was asked if it did not prick his conscience to make a contract to write about someone he had earlier described as a true and faithful friend.

Bessell: "No, sir, it did not. I would not have been here if I had not believed it was my responsibility to give evidence which must inevitably, if it is believed, contribute towards a conviction."

Carman: "Does it not prick your conscience to have entered into a contract by which you and your family achieve double the money on the conviction of a former true and loyal friend?"

Bessell: "Yes, it does."

Carman: "You are prepared to betray a friend for money, aren't you?"

Bessell: "I think that is an overstatement."

After persisting in the suggestion that Mr Bessell, like another witness (Newton) to be heard later, was "in the case to milk it for all it is worth," Mr Carman turned to the details of the witness's financial record. His creditors had been persuaded to settle for seventeen and a half per cent at the time he had disappeared in Mexico. So the *Sunday Telegraph* money must assume some prominence in his financial affairs, suggested Mr Carman.

Bessell: "Yes, sir."

Mr Carman suggested that Mr Bessell's status as a potential witness had made the book potentially more profitable.

Bessell: "I think that is undeniable. I accept that."

Carman: "Your role as witness enhances your chance of selling the book?"

Bessell: "That is fair comment."

He maintained that money played no part in his decision to give evidence but agreed that giving evidence provided additional opportunity to publish a profitable book.

Mr Carman read a long letter which Mr Bessell had written to Lady Falkender on 22 July 1978 – a fortnight before Thorpe was arrested – about the book he was proposing to write. First, he discussed his relationship with Penrose and Courtiour, then the effect of the case on Sir Harold Wilson.

> The Jeremy Thorpe affair is likely to be long drawn out and may assume almost vast proportions before we are all through with it.
>
> Therefore it follows that Sir Harold's role will be mulled over – perhaps mauled over is a better term – for decades.
>
> I am convinced, based on my long and intimate knowledge of Jeremy, that in his fear and despair, and sad though it is, he ruthlessly misused and misled Sir Harold. I intend to make this point as strongly as I am able and to do it in a way that does not imply I am merely a star-struck admirer of Sir Harold's. In addition I want to quote some of Sir Harold's conversations with Pencourt as no more than samples of his sense of humour and willingness to take people on trust. In my view it would be tragic if Sir Harold's role should become a matter of needless and mischievous speculation. All the same, I am quite determined that my book shall be factual and able to resist any challenge.
>
> I have, of course, a credibility problem largely of my own making, partly of Jeremy's, and I must therefore be abnormally careful in my writing.

The letter suggested that he might send parts of his manuscript that referred to Sir Harold Wilson and that Lady Falkender might supply "appropriate suggestions and corrections."

Mr Carman revealed that Lady Falkender had passed the letter straight to Thorpe's solicitors. He suggested that the letter showed an intention to sensationalise the book for greater profit. Mr Bessell agreed that one of the book's themes was that there had been a widespread cover-up of Thorpe's activities, and Mr Carman asked who it was, in addition to Sir Harold Wilson, who might be implicated in such an alleged cover-up.

Carman: "He is in very good company indeed, in some of the names you purport to implicate or involve in that cover-up. I am going to give, I hope responsibly, a comprehensive list. The list, I make it clear in open court, is an indication of your wicked irresponsibility in order to make money. I am going to give you a list of people you have potentially in your book."

The tone of Mr Carman's remarks might seem to give support to earlier suspicions that all the counsel involved had received the firmest possible instructions – not to say warnings – from the judge not to bandy around names of men in public life – the great and the good – in such a way as to smear them. As Mr Carman went through his list, Mr Bessell indicated whether they might find themselves named in his book:

"The Director of Public Prosecutions?" – "No."

"Lord Rawlinson, the former Attorney-General?" – "No."

"Scotland Yard?" – "Yes."

"Mrs Thatcher, the Prime Minister?" – "Just mentioned."

Carman: "Is the *Sunday Times* mentioned, and does it attract special venom?"

Bessell: "No, I accept that the *Sunday Times* may well have been misled and misquoted. I have made the point abundantly clear."

"Sir Frank Soskice, the former Home Secretary?" – "Yes, but exonerated from any cover-up."

"Mr Reginald Maudling, another former Home Secretary?" – "I reported what I was told."

Carman: "I am merely trying to demonstrate to what lengths you are prepared to go to make your book sensational."

Bessell: "I am trying to show how mistaken you are."

"Lord Goodman?" – "Just in Holmes's report of him."

Bessell: "Lord Goodman will have no cause for complaint."

Carman: "No doubt Lord Goodman will be relieved to hear that."

This produced laughter in the court, because Lord Goodman had issued a blanket denial and given an indignant interview to the *Daily Telegraph* in which he talked of Mr Bessell's "demented allegations" during the Minehead committal proceedings. Mr Bessell was purporting to describe only what Holmes had told him about Lord Goodman's role.

Other, less important names were suggested, including Mr David Ennals, the former Secretary of State for Social Services, but Mr Bessell said they either were not named or were exonerated of any impropriety.

Mr Carman now turned to a study of Mr Bessell's political record, suggesting he was "a good Janus, capable of facing both ways."

Carman: "You can be all things to all men at the same time."

Bessell: "Yes, to some extent that is true."

The examples which Mr Carman provided of Mr Bessell facing both ways were fascinating. In 1967, during the Liberal Party leadership contest between Liberal MPs, he had assured both Thorpe and Emlyn Hooson of his support. He explained this by his hesitations about Thorpe's homosexual record, and said he later withdrew his support for Hooson and reverted to Thorpe. Then in 1968, said Mr Carman, Bessell did "a most extraordinary thing."

Carman: "As a Liberal MP you made informal approaches to the Labour and Conservative chief whips at about the same time with a view to joining one of the other parties."

When Mr Bessell admitted that he had, indeed, held these informal talks, the court collapsed in laughter. Only those who live reasonably close to the British Parliament, with its rigid two-party system, will be able to appreciate how extraordinarily funny this admission was. Mr Bessell put quite a brave face on it, saying that both these chief whips were interested in converting him. He pointed out that others had crossed the floor of the house, naming Mr Reg Prentice, a former Cabinet minister in the Labour Government, then serving as a junior minister under Mrs Thatcher.

Yes, yes, said the judge, leaning forward. He quite understood that and also that Mr Bessell might be seeking conversion to one side or the other. "It is the oscillation which interests me," he said, and the court collapsed again.

This was the first moment of pure merriment since the start of the proceedings, and although few newspapers bothered to report it next day, it added nothing to the figure – whether dignified or penitential – which Mr Bessell was trying to cut in court.

Mr Carman next took the Crown witness through a long series of lies which he had told – and agreed he had told – to protect Thorpe from the consequences of his homosexual activities. Among them were lies to Scott – pretending to disbelieve his story – to Father Sweetman, Scott's mentor in Dublin – pretending Scott had admitted there was no truth in his allegations about Thorpe – and to numerous parliamentary colleagues.

Mr Justice Cantley, exhilarated, perhaps, by the success of his little joke about the oscillating politician, seemed to take over the cross-examination at one point, suggesting that Mr Bessell had never before mentioned these attempts to discourage Scott. Mr Bessell would not have needed to be very sensitive, one felt, to guess that the judge did not believe them now, which was odd, as there were letters to prove the point.

Mr Bessell said he had told Sir Frank Soskice, then the Home Secretary, that he thought Scott's allegations about Thorpe were probably true. He said the same to various MPs but denied it to others.

Reverting to the Hetherington story of the day before, Mr Carman commented on the ruses which Mr Bessell claimed to have used against the blackmailer: "You seem almost unable to talk to any human being on any matter of consequence without introducing a lie." He described Mr Bessell's account of the Hetherington episode as an *Alice in Wonderland* version, and the judge interrupted at one point to ask Mr Bessell, poker-faced, whether he had in fact murdered Hetherington.

Carman: "If the jury are to believe at all that the leader of the Liberal Party had seriously proposed to you not one but two murders – I suggest it is a figment of your imagination – you must have thought you had a ghastly maniac leading the Liberal Party."

Bessell: "Yes, at one stage I thought Mr Thorpe had a crazy, sick obsession about murder."

Carman: "I thought you said he was a man of the highest political integrity . . . you cannot lead a political party in the House of Commons and spend your time plotting murders as well and do both jobs properly."

Mr Bessell again regretted that he had put his loyalty to Thorpe before what was clearly his duty. Mr Carman suggested that the only conversations between the two about murdering people had been light-hearted fantasies, and Mr Bessell denied this again.

Carman: "You haven't left out any other murder proposals have you? You are not going to tell us of a third or fourth murder proposal tomorrow are you?"

Bessell: "No, sir."

On that light-hearted note, the court adjourned for the day. *This powerful line of defence does not explain how a conspiracy of some sort definitely arose – whether or not Thorpe was party to it – or how a*

*dog was shot and a man frightened out of his wits on Porlock Moor
by someone who claimed to have been hired to murder him. Indeed
no attempt was ever made to reconcile the extreme unlikelihood of a
leading politician being involved in a criminal conspiracy to protect
himself with the fact that a criminal conspiracy of some sort or
another had definitely been formed for the purpose – with or without
Thorpe's knowledge. But at this stage we did not know that Holmes,
at least, would have pleaded guilty to a charge of conspiracy to
frighten. This was not finally revealed until after the verdict, when Mr
Mathew was pleading for his client's costs.*

*But this more light-hearted approach may have impressed the
judge, whose summing up at the end of the day was accompanied with
many smiles, nods and mysterious little chuckles.*

Day eight: 17 May 1979

The third day of Mr Bessell's cross-examination opened dramatically with Mr Carman producing a copy of the *Western Morning
News* dated 16 June 1970 which proved Mr Bessell had got his dates
wrong over his claimed payment of £170 to the blackmailer
Hetherington. It showed a photograph of Mr Bessell standing with
Thorpe and another Liberal MP on a political platform with the
headline "Thorpe Calls Powell 'Stark, Staring Bonkers'." Earlier,
Mr Bessell had said he could not remember standing with Thorpe
on a political platform at that time.

Carman: "It takes a long time to nail down some of your lies. Do
you now agree that your story about meeting Hetherington is a lie?"

Mr Carman then reminded the witness – at some length – about
a further lapse of his memory, when he originally told Penrose
and Courtiour that it had been in Thorpe's flat that the murder
of Norman Scott was first discussed.

Mr Bessell then discussed his addiction to the sleeping drug,
Mandrax. This had muddled his moral values at the time of his
attempted fraud on Jack Hayward, he said. Mr Hayward had once
contributed £150,000 to the Liberal Party, and Mr Bessell involved
himself in a scheme to sell Mr Hayward's interests in the Bahamas
to the Mobil Oil Corporation for something between $70 and $90
million. Mr Bessell had asked for $700,000 to pay an American
commission, intending to keep the money for his own use. He had
untruthfully said the money was needed to pay a broker called
George Lawrence, on the staff of Senator Buckley, a Conservative
from New York who was close to Nixon. Thorpe was aware of this

fraud, said Mr Bessell, and had indeed proposed it, but did not stand to gain anything by it.

Carman: "That, I suggest, is another very wicked invention by you. Mr Thorpe was totally deceived by you at that time, as well as Mr Hayward, I suggest."

Mr Bessell repeated that there was no selfish motive so far as Thorpe was concerned. Mr Carman took him through a couple of letters he had written to Thorpe at this time – one of them, said Mr Bessell, was written for Thorpe to show to Mr Hayward – asking him, sentence by sentence, whether the sentence was true, false, or partly true. *By my count, the letter contained one true statement, four which were either untrue or partly untrue.*

After this exercise, Mr Bessell was back in his penitential mood. Not for the first time, one found oneself admiring the skill with which Mr Carman was handling him.

Carman: "So you deserved to be put behind bars, did you, in January 1974?"

Bessell: "Yes. What I had done in respect of Mr Hayward was in my view totally unforgivable, inexcusable, and therefore deserving punishment."

Carman: "Did you use Mr Thorpe as the innocent dupe to your fraud?"

Bessell: "No I did not. It had been agreed between us."

Carman: "That puts you not only in the role of a liar but you are back again as a hypocrite?"

Bessell: "No, I should have rejected the idea. I should not have allowed Mr Thorpe or myself to have any part in this disgraceful, inexcusable, totally damnable episode."

Carman: "Mr Bessell, I do not wish you to use this box as a confessional box, I just want to find out the truth of what you say and the extent that your evidence can be relied upon."

Bessell: "I am sorry, sir. I was merely expressing the emotion of the moment."

After the lunch break, Mr Carman returned to the Hayward fraud.

Carman: "Would it be a fair assessment to say that you had demonstrated you are a man capable of consummate deviousness in his business and personal activities?"

Bessell: "I have to reply that you have shown undoubtedly that I have been guilty of deviousness, that I have been guilty of quite disgraceful behaviour."

Mr Carman asked the witness what he thought of Norman Scott, who was to be the next witness. Had Mr Bessell discovered him to be a liar?

Mr Bessell said Scott was a pathetic creature who nearly always had a hard luck story; he tended to exaggerate his misfortunes, and was always putting the blame for his own weaknesses or misfortunes on someone else, Mr Bessell felt. He had also found him to be financially dishonest.

This was a strange, inconsequential passage towards the end of the cross-examination. In other moods and at other times Mr Bessell had seemed to speak of Scott with greater affection than this. It was almost as if, after nearly ten hours of giving evidence, he was saying exactly what Mr Carman wanted him to say.

Mr Carman then turned to various newspaper articles about him, most particularly the extraordinary pieces which appeared in the *Sunday Times* on 14 March 1976, where, on the front page, Jeremy Thorpe had attacked Norman Scott as an "incorrigible liar" under the leading headline "The Lies of Norman Scott," and inside a full-page article had described Mr Bessell as a scoundrel who was probably being blackmailed by Scott over some commercial malpractice. This article appeared two days before Scott was due to give evidence at the trial of Newton, in Exeter. Mr Bessell agreed that he was "appalled by this article": "It was the last straw, if you like, that broke this particular camel's back."

Carman: "I suggest it was not the last straw, but the thing which turned your tongue to venom and your mind to malice was that Mr Thorpe had provided the *Sunday Times* with information about you."

Mr Bessell denied this.

At the very end of his cross-examination, after a little knockabout turn (in which the judge gleefully joined) about the mercenary attitude of journalists, who were thought only to be interested in the profit and circulation of their newspapers, Mr Carman turned to the question of suicide. Mr Bessell, who now looked thoroughly exhausted after his ten hours in the witness-box, agreed that he had contemplated suicide in 1971 and 1973. After a few routine insinuations – that by his method of suicide he was planning to defraud his insurance – Mr Carman asked his last question.

Carman: "May I suggest to you that you have reached the stage of being incapable of belief by anyone else?"

Mr Bessell paused a long time before answering. For a terrible moment, it seemed as if he was going to agree, thereby destroying the whole ten hours of agony with one syllable. He was exhausted, confused and full of the self-loathing which sometimes seems to be the Methodist equivalent of Catholic penance. For the space of fifteen seconds, as I say, it was touch and go. Then a very strange thing happened. Whether Mr Justice Cantley took pity on him, or whether he did not want to see Mr Carman get away with it so easily we shall probably never know, but it was the judge who saved him – the same judge whose previous interruptions might have been calculated to answer this very question.

"You can't expect him to agree to that," said Mr Justice Cantley. "You're wasting our time. That is a question for you to put to the jury, not to him."

This interruption brought Mr Bessell to his senses. "If I believed I were no longer capable of being believed," he said, "I would not be here at the Old Bailey. I would be at Oceanside, California."

That ended Mr Bessell's cross-examination. Mr Taylor rose to his feet and pointed out that his witness was plainly too tired to face re-examination that day. The court adjourned.

Day nine: 18 May 1979
Before Mr Bessell could be re-examined on the fourth day of his stand in the witness-box, Mr Carman staged one of his dramatic pre-trial interruptions. It appeared that Mr Bessell had been conferring with his solicitor, in defiance of the judge's order that he was to confer with nobody.

Mr Bessell said that he did not know the ban extended to conferences with his solicitor, and apologised. Once again, Mr Carman took the opportunity of accusing him of lying on oath.

It appeared that he had remembered something about the dates of the Hetherington incident and dictated some notes for his solicitor, Mr Lionel Phillips, to give to Mr Taylor, the prosecution counsel. Mr Taylor, appalled by the impropriety of this, had handed the notes to the defence, who raised the matter now in the presence of the jury. Other counsel in court were mildly surprised by the furore which developed from this. Nobody disputed the impropriety of a witness trying to contact his solicitor; but gravity would depend on the circumstances. In this case, the circumstances did not seem to be grave. The judge, however, perhaps regretting his leniency of the day before, was disposed to take the matter very seriously indeed, especially after reassuring himself and the court that Mr Bessell's solicitor was the husband of his literary agent. Once again the spectre of other people making money had arisen.

Whatever the reason, Mr Justice Cantley decided to humiliate the witness publicly, and in the presence of the jury, before he had finished giving evidence. Addressing him savagely, and in terms which were more appropriate to a convicted criminal than a witness who had voluntarily and in all innocence handed the court the evidence of his *faux pas*, the judge reminded Mr Bessell of his order that he was to talk to no one. Mr Bessell apologised, and accepted that he had disobeyed it. The judge commented, "You may have to accept more than that."

At the end of the day's evidence, again in open court, the judge was to send for Mr Phillips, who was represented, and emphasised once again how he thought it a "bad feature" that his wife should be Mr Bessell's literary agent.

Mr Justice Cantley: "Your disobedience is all the more remarkable because you are a solicitor who should have known better. There are several courses open to me, including immediate imprisonment or a fine. Indeed, I had thought of something quite drastic by way of an example to other solicitors. But I shall accept that, however astonishingly, you did this innocently because we would not have caught you otherwise. You handed this to the prosecution and thereby informed the court of what you had done.

"Although your conduct has been extremely stupid, it has not been ill-founded. For this reason I will rebuke you for your action but take no further action."

The court was to adjourn at the end of the day on that note – a further nail in the coffin of Mr Bessell's credibility. Once again, it had been delivered by the judge; this time, in the opinion of many people present, quite gratuitously.

Meanwhile, even the normally urbane Mr Taylor seemed ruffled by this display of judicial spleen when he rose for his brief re-examination of the witness. Before starting his re-examination, he addressed two questions to Mr Bessell about the matter which had gone before.

Taylor: "To whom do you look for legal advice?"

Bessell: "To my solicitor, sir."

Taylor: "When you spoke to him this morning . . . did he seem to deter you in any way?"

Bessell: "No, sir."

That closed the matter. Nobody suggested that it was an elementary injustice that a witness who had submitted to having his character torn to shreds and who was not legally represented in court, should be debarred from consulting his solicitor to put the record straight on a few minor points. So far as Mr Bessell was represented in court, as a Crown witness, it was by the Crown counsel, yet he was forbidden to communicate with Mr Taylor. It was an episode which left a nasty taste in the mouth of many who witnessed it, not least for the savagery with which the judge rebuked him in front of the jury.

Re-examination necessarily covered only a very few points raised in cross-examination. Mr Taylor produced a letter from Mr Bessell to Thorpe which had accompanied his "Mandrax" letter. It was highly facetious in tone, starting "My Lord" – Mr Bessell explained it was normal for him to address the former Liberal leader as Lord Thorpe of Barnstaple, and Thorpe called him Baron Besili [sic] of Bodmin. It left no doubt that the earlier letter had been written for the purpose of convincing Mr Hayward that Thorpe was not involved in the fraud.

If Norman Scott had been following Mr Bessell's evidence and the court's treatment of its chief prosecution witness, this might explain why, when he took his stand in the witness-box, he had the air of a little rabbit who was very frightened indeed.

5

Tale of a Flopsy Bunny

Mr Norman Scott

At Minehead, his tidy appearance and soft, almost prissy manner had come as a surprise. This was the man whose accusations against the former Liberal leader, relentlessly but also courageously pressed in the face of an extraordinarily powerful campaign of discouragement, had led to what looked like a murder attempt against him, the subsequent arrest and trial of a powerful public figure. By one account, he was a poisonous and successful blackmailer, by another a hysterical, probably paranoid fantasist; by either account he was wilfully destroying the reputation, and possibly life, of an honourable and popular figure, one of the few trustworthy men in public life, and one who had already endured more than his share of suffering in the tragic death of his first wife – possibly as a result of Scott's harassment. Nobody, in any saloon bar throughout the land, had a good word to say for Norman Scott. Mr Taylor, in his gentlemanly way, seemed as much concerned to correct the general opprobrium attaching to his witness as he was to establish the truth of Scott's narrative. The purpose of his evidence was to establish a motive for the alleged crime, and this motive was as valid if Scott was an unprincipled blackmailer or liar as it was if Scott was sincere, misunderstood and deeply wronged. By generously supporting the more favourable interpretation of Scott's motives, Mr Taylor may have encouraged the misapprehension of which Scott himself frequently complained – that he was on trial as much as Thorpe, and the jury were being invited to choose between the two.

At Minehead, his story at least had the dramatic impact of its novelty. By the time he appeared at the Old Bailey, everybody knew what he was going to say. Those who expressed an anxiety about the effect of reporting the Minehead proceedings on public attitudes to Thorpe seldom paused to consider its effect on public attitudes to Scott.

Unlike Mr Bessell, he had not learned his story by heart, although he had probably told it even more often. He was vague about dates, frequently forgetful, and easily flustered. Where, at Minehead, he had possessed a fine indignation which managed to carry him through these lapses, in the Old Bailey even his petulant outbursts seemed rehearsed. His manner, at the outset, was nervous and distracted. This is the story which Norman Scott told.

Scott first met the defendant Thorpe in 1960 when he was working as a stable lad for a man who called himself the Honourable Brecht Van de Vater. His real name was Norman Vater. He was a friend of Thorpe, already an MP. After staying the night with Vater, Thorpe met the young Scott and asked him if he was happy. When Scott said he was, Thorpe replied that if ever he had cause to be worried – Vater was rather a strange person in many ways – he should get in touch with the MP.

Soon after, Scott suffered a nervous breakdown and left Vater's employment for a psychiatric clinic where he was heavily sedated. On leaving the clinic he went to see Thorpe in the House of Commons. Thorpe said he would take care of him and told him to collect his Jack Russell terrier, Mrs Tish. First, Thorpe took him to the house of a friend (*at Minehead he said the friend was called Tony, but this information was denied the Old Bailey at this stage*) in Dulwich. Two men were there, and Thorpe asked them to look after Scott if ever he was in trouble. Then Thorpe took him to the house of his mother, Mrs Ursula Thorpe, in Surrey, saying he would be introduced as Peter, from Colchester, member of a camera crew accompanying Thorpe to Malta next day. He signed the visitors' book with this name, adding "Johnstone," "Harrison," "Thomson" or something like that.

That night he went to his room and Thorpe gave him a glass of water for some pills he had to take. Thorpe also gave him a book, *Giovanni's Room* by James Baldwin, the story of a homosexual relationship. After he had been reading the book for about forty-five minutes. Thorpe came into his room in dressing-gown and pyjamas and sat on his bed.

They discussed Scott's problems with his employer. Vater was an undischarged bankrupt, and Scott maintained that he had run up bills in Scott's name. Thorpe remarked that he looked like a frightened rabbit and Scott, overwhelmed by Thorpe's kindness, broke down and cried. Thorpe put his arm around Scott and said, "Poor bunny." Later Thorpe got into bed with him, produced a towel which he put underneath Scott and some substance from a tube in

his pocket which he put on his penis, turned Scott over and buggered him or, as Scott put it, "made love to me." Scott, while this
was happening, bit the pillow and tried not to scream for fear of
upsetting Mrs Thorpe.

Scott had had relationships with both men and women before, but
had never previously been buggered. After this act, Thorpe wiped
himself and went out, patting Scott's thigh. Scott lay in bed crying
with his dog Mrs Tish for company. He did not see Thorpe again
that night – at Minehead, he said that Thorpe came back two hours
later and buggered him again – but next morning, at about seven-
thirty, Thorpe came in and asked him how he liked his eggs boiled.
Then he had breakfast with Thorpe and his mother, Mrs Ursula
Thorpe.

Later, they were driven to London by Thorpe's secretary,
Jennifer King, who lived in a village called Limpsfield. Thorpe gave
him some money to find a flat near the House of Commons where
Thorpe would come and visit him. Scott told him that Vater held his
national insurance cards which had not been paid.

Scott found a room at 21 Draycott Place, Chelsea. On his return
from Malta a fortnight later, Thorpe visited him there and sexual
intercourse occurred. Thorpe visited him most evenings when he
was in London, and sometimes they went out together – to the
House of Commons, the Reform Club, or a Chelsea restaurant.

Over Christmas 1961, Thorpe sent him to stay with some friends,
the Colliers, in North Devon. Thorpe and his mother were staying
nearby at the Broomhills Hotel. After lunch there, Thorpe suggested his mother and the Colliers should go for a walk in the
garden; he took Scott to his bathroom and further sexual activity
occurred.

Scott was not happy about the sexual side of their relationship,
which saddened and sickened him. On one occasion, after he had
been staying with the Colliers for six weeks, with Thorpe visiting
him at the weekends, he was driving with Thorpe in a motorcar
when Thorpe tried to kiss him and he threatened to expose Thorpe
in public. Thorpe laughed at his distress and said Scott could not
hurt him because he, Thorpe, was a friend of the Director of Public
Prosecutions, who, he said, was Sir Norman Skelhorn.

At this time, on Thorpe's suggestion, he put an advertisement in
Country Life describing himself as an ex-public schoolboy of
twenty-one willing to work on a farm with horses. He received many
replies from homosexuals. While staying with the Colliers he
received a letter from Thorpe which he produced:

My dear Norman,

Since letters normally go to the House, yours arrived all by
itself at my breakfast table at the Reform and gave me tremendous pleasure. I cannot tell you just how happy I am to feel you
are really settling down and feeling life has something to offer.
This is really wonderful and you can always feel that whatever
happens Jimmy and Mary [Collier] and I are right behind you.

The next thing is to solve your financial problem and this James
Walters [a solicitor] and I are on to.

The really important thing is that you are now a member of a
family doing a useful job of work – with Tish – which you enjoy.
Hooray. Faced with all that, no more bloody clinics.

I think you can take the Ann Gray incident as over and done
with. Enclosed another ltr. I suggest you keep them all – just in
case – but will you send back the photo? Thank the guy but say
you are fixed up. In haste.

Bunnies *can* (and *will*) go to France.

Yours affectionately,
Jeremy
I miss you.

Ann Gray was a girl-friend of Scott who lived in Draycott Place and
who claimed he had stolen her sheepskin coat. The police came to
interview him about this in Thorpe's new office in Bridge Street,
Westminster. When the police arrived. Scott's fly-buttons were
undone and Thorpe was fondling him. They stopped. Thorpe put his
hand to his mouth and motioned him to sit down. He later made a
statement to the police about the sheepskin coat which did not
mention his relationship with Thorpe.

Scott was describing once again the reference to bunnies when
the court adjourned for the weekend.

Day ten: 21 May 1979
Scott's narrative continued

By the end of 1962, Scott was unhappy about the relationship and
wished to kill himself and Thorpe. During the year he had been to
stay in Minehead with a Dr Lister who was treating him for his
nerves. While he was there, his dog Mrs Tish killed all Dr Lister's
ducks and had to be put down. He thought they would send him
away if she killed more poultry, and was very unhappy. After
leaving the Listers, Scott returned to his mother, but she did not

have much money. Then he started going to stay with Jeremy Thorpe at Marsham Court, Victoria. The flat had a single bed in it; after sexual activity, Thorpe would tell him to get the camp bed out, and Scott slept on that.

On 19 December 1962 he mentioned to a friend of his who was also a friend of Thorpe, Caroline Barrington-Ward, that he wished to kill himself and Thorpe. Two hours later he went to the Easton Hotel, in Victoria. By chance the receptionist there was Mary Collier at whose house he had spent the previous Christmas in North Devon. After she had spoken to him, she summoned two policemen who took him to a police station where he made a long statement about his relationship with Thorpe. He also handed the police two letters and a postcard; the letters were returned to him fourteen years later, in 1976, after he had taken out a writ against the Commissioner of Metropolitan Police, Sir Robert Mark.

In 1963 Scott went to live in Northern Ireland, occasionally returning to England to see Thorpe, who had said he was going to stamp Scott's national insurance card. His relations with Thorpe continued as before.

At this point the judge interrupted to ask a question about the cards, saying he did not want to hear about the relations. It provoked an outburst from Scott: "Believe me, sir, I don't want to talk about the relationship ever again . . . Every time I came over it was solely for one reason. It was not to pick up the insurance cards. It was so he could screw me, sir."

On returning from Ireland, Scott held a few jobs but lost them again because of telling lies; he went back to Thorpe at Marsham Court. Shortly afterwards he went to take up a job with horses in Switzerland, his fare being paid by Thorpe. He packed all Thorpe's letters in his suitcase, but the suitcase was mislaid. He left after a night, went back to Thorpe, and then to Southern Ireland. He did not get his suitcase back until 1965.

In Ireland he met a priest called Father Sweetman who was kind to him, but Scott treated him badly. Eventually, he decided to write to Thorpe's mother, Mrs Ursula Thorpe, asking her to intercede for him in the matter of the luggage – Thorpe had been very angry when Scott mentioned some letters contained in the suitcase. He later regretted writing to Mrs Thorpe, but he thought she already knew about their relationship.

After he sent the letter, he met Mr Bessell in Dublin who told him he had an extradition order from Sir Frank Soskice, the Home Secretary, to take him back to England on a charge of blackmail. He welcomed this, as he had never blackmailed anybody, and was scarcely in a position to do so having already made a statement to the police. Mr Bessell promised to sort out the luggage and gave him £5 to buy food. Some time later his luggage arrived without the letters.

At about this time he changed his name from Josiffe to Scott, because the name Josiffe caused trouble in the modelling world where people thought he was called Joe Sieff. He realised he had been duped by Thorpe and Bessell in the matter of the letters and feared that without the evidence of his relationship in the letters he might be committed to a mental hospital.

After receiving a letter from Scott, Mr Bessell started making payments to him of about £5 a week, which Scott regarded as being in lieu of unemployment benefit. These payments stopped when Scott went to live with a man called Conway, but when he and Conway split up he needed his insurance cards again, and received £75 from Mr Bessell to set up as a model. In August or September 1968 he had about 500 copies printed of a folio of photographs which were his brochure as a male model.

On 13 May 1969 Scott married Susan Myers. Soon after, his wife was pregnant and they were starving. He threatened to write to Thorpe's wife Caroline, but did not speak to her on the telephone. His son was born in November 1969. Shortly afterwards his marriage broke up.

Mr Bessell wrote to him suggesting the name of a solicitor to handle his divorce, Mr Leonard Ross. Later, Scott realised that this was only to protect Thorpe. Mr Bessell said he should keep out of London during the divorce, and said he would pay the rent for him to live in Tal-y-bont, North Wales.

While there, Scott befriended Mrs Gwen Parry-Jones, a widow, and Mr Keith Rose, a local garage proprietor. Mr Rose wrote to Thorpe about the state Scott was in, and received a snubbing reply from Thorpe's personal assistant: "Mr Thorpe asks me to say he has no obligation to this gentleman."

Scott and Mrs Parry-Jones became lovers. She wrote to Mr Emlyn Hooson, Liberal MP for Montgomeryshire. Together she and Scott went to London to face a Liberal Party enquiry into Scott's allegations. Scott spoke to David Steel, the Liberal Chief Whip, Mr Hooson and Lord Byers, Chairman of the Liberal Party. On 10 June and 14 June 1971, Scott made further statements to the police, and tried to get back letters he had given the police in 1962.

In March 1972 Mrs Parry-Jones died. Scott was of the opinion she killed herself. At the inquest, Scott described his relationship with Thorpe. An open verdict was recorded.

After a time he went to live at the Old Rectory, South Molton, in Thorpe's constituency. Earlier, Scott had met a South African journalist called Gordon Winter to whom he told his story. Winter tape-recorded an interview with him and took copies of documents; Scott complained to him of the Liberal Party cover-up, claiming that three respected Liberal MPs had brushed his complaints under the carpet.

He was suffering from anxiety neurosis. A Dr Gleadle in South Molton prescribed drugs. He was drinking a lot in pubs and talking about his relationship with Jeremy Thorpe. Dr Gleadle paid him £2,500 for his file of documents and said he was to talk to nobody. Luckily, Gordon Winter had taken copies of the documents.

In February 1975 Scott was telephoned by a man who said he was called Steiner, working for either *Der Spiegel* or *Stern*, the German magazine. They arranged to meet at the Imperial Hotel, Barnstaple, Scott bringing copies of documents supplied by Winter. When Scott went there, his documents were stolen, probably by two men who came into the hotel.

On another occasion, he was telephoned by a man who said he was called Ian Wright, working for an Italian fashion house called Pensiero fashions. The man offered him £400 a week to model some clothes and suggested he go to the Royal Garden Hotel, Kensington. Scott refused.

Later Scott went to live at the Market Inn, Barnstaple, managed by Mrs Edna Friendship, from mid-September to mid-October 1975. He was telephoned by a man called Masterson who spoke with a public school accent. He was writing an article about the affair and asked Scott to go to the Holiday Inn at Bristol, where a room would be booked for him. Scott agreed but did not turn up. Masterson telephoned angrily, and Scott suggested he should come to Barnstaple, but he heard no more from Masterson.

In October 1975 he was approached by a stranger in the Pannier Market, Barnstaple, who told him he was in great danger. There was someone coming from Canada who had been paid to kill him. The man said a woman wanted to see him at a place called Knowstone nearby. Scott asked if the woman was Marion Thorpe, and the man agreed it was. Scott said she would have to come to his hotel. The man said he was being paid to protect Scott, and wanted to know why. Scott was frightened and asked Mrs Friendship to take down the number of the man's car, which she did. The man, who said he was called Peter Keene, took notes on pink slips of paper as Scott told him his story.

Keene, whom Scott later identified as Andrew Newton, told him that his son might be harmed before he was, and this suggestion made Scott so unhappy that he cried.

Later Keene left but on 23 October – the day before the alleged murder attempt – Scott received a called from a telephone box. The caller appeared to be in a hurry. "Hello, this is Andy," he began. Scott said he did not know anyone called Andy and the caller said, "It's Peter." Keene then said that the man from Canada was in the country and was coming to kill him. He had to see Mr Scott.

They met by arrangement at 6 pm on 24 October 1975 outside the Delve's Hotel in Combe Martin. Scott took his Great Dane bitch, called Rinka, with him. Keene (Newton) said, "I will not have that bloody dog." Scott insisted on taking the dog with them in the car to Porlock, where Newton said he had to recruit a young woman for his business of private investigator.

The day's hearing ended there, with a warning from the judge that Scott should not talk about his evidence to anyone.

Day eleven: 22 May 1979
When they reached Porlock, Newton told Scott to wait for him in the Castle Hotel while he interviewed the young woman. At 8.20 pm Scott saw Newton's car outside and asked him why he had not come into the pub. Newton replied, "Oh no, I can't be seen with you."

Scott and his dog Rinka climbed into the car and they set off towards Combe Martin. As they climbed out of Porlock towards the moors, the car began swinging from side to side. Scott suggested that Newton must be tired and offered to drive.

Newton replied, "Yes, I'm knackered."

They stopped in a lay-by. Both men and the dog got out.

Newton said, "Oh no, this is it," and shot the dog.

It took some time for Scott to realise what he had done – it was a wild and windy, wet night. When Scott realised that Rinka had been killed, he said, "You can't involve Rinka. You can't involve Rinka," Scott shook the dog, shouting at her, "Are you all right?"

Scott saw Newton standing in front of the headlights, shaking the pistol, and screamed at him, "Why did you do it?"

Newton pointed the pistol at him, and Scott ran away. Then he decided he might as well die with his dog and returned. Newton levelled the gun at him again and started swearing. Then he jumped into the car, slammed the door, and shouting, "I will get you," turned the car round and drove back towards Porlock.

Scott, meanwhile, tried to resuscitate the dog for about ten minutes, all alone on the moors, giving it the kiss of life. Then he saw headlights and was picked up by a passing car.

In March of the next year he gave evidence at the trial of Newton. Newton was charged with being in possession of a gun with intent to endanger life. He was convicted and sentenced to two years' imprisonment.

6

Rabbit Redux

Norman Scott cross-examined

Throughout his examination-in-chief, Scott spoke very quietly. Sometimes his voice sank to a whisper, and he had to be asked to speak up. Although he had plainly told the story many times before, he still wept at the appropriate moments – when Rinka was shot, when Mrs Parry-Jones died – with every sign of spontaneity. Having seen the performance once before, I judged his first appearance, at Minehead, the better of the two and this was the opinion of most journalists who attended both. But on that occasion, as I say, his evidence had the advantage of novelty, and a very startling tale it was to hear for the first time.

Under cross-examination, he became noisier and more emotional. Unlike Mr Bessell, he had been allowed to give his evidence-in-chief without a barrage of questions or sceptical interruptions from the judge, but the atmosphere of the court was very different from Minehead, where the magistrates interrupted not at all. Where, at Minehead, his rages had been impressive, here they seemed either petulant or rehearsed and seldom very effective.

Short cross-examinations by Mr Mathew, for Holmes, by Mr Williams, for Deakin, and by Mr Cowley, for Le Mesurier, produced nothing which at the time seemed of much importance, nor does it in retrospect. Scott's role was to establish a motive for the conspiracy and to establish the likelihood of Thorpe's involvement in it. His evidence had no bearing on Le Mesurier and little enough on Deakin and Holmes unless they were the people who stole his papers from the Imperial Hotel, Barnstaple. But Mr Taylor had made no attempts to establish this, and even if it was true, it only indicated their involvement in a conspiracy of some sort – which neither had denied – and not in a conspiracy to murder.

Scott agreed with Mr Mathew on this occasion that Newton, on approaching him for the first time in the Pannier Market, Barnstaple, had said he wanted to talk about "this blackmail" –

something Scott had doubted, or even seemed to deny, on previous occasions. He agreed that Newton had said that if he handed his documents to Thorpe's solicitor in Barnstaple, Michael Barnes, he would receive a large sum of money.

Mr Williams, for Deakin, made a great business of writing names on paper for the judge's eyes only, and discussing how it would be improper to discuss whom Scott might have met in Dulwich. It was at this point that Scott said he never learned "Tony's" full name. We never learned the relevance of this passage to Mr Williams's defence of Deakin.

In answer to another question, Scott said he was not sure whether it was he or his wife Susan who had spoken to Caroline Thorpe on the telephone, but whichever it was had referred to Scott's allegations about Thorpe.

He agreed that he had named prominent people as being involved in his affairs. Mr Williams seemed to be daring him to name a particular name, but Scott declined to do so and the judge intervened anxiously: "A lot of scandal may be very interesting, but it is not relevant."

After further cryptic conversation between them – Scott agreed he had told Newton that people of influence were engaged in a cover-up – Mr Williams sat down and Mr Denis Cowley QC, for Le Mesurier, broke his long silence to ask a single, equally mysterious question of the witness.

Cowley: "Did you speak to Caroline Thorpe but the once?"
Scott: "Yes."

Then – the moment we had all been waiting for, Mr Carman stood up. At Minehead, Scott was cross-examined by Thorpe's solicitor, Sir David Napley, a former president of the Law Society, whose knighthood hung over the court like a plumed helmet over the Castle of Otranto. Napley's cross-examination may have been ponderous, and without much subtlety – on at least one occasion it degenerated into farce – but it was extremely thorough, and provided most of the answers which Carman required for his cross-examination. A problem for Carman was that Scott was extremely vague about dates and minor details of that sort. If ever Mr Carman tried to attach significance to these inconsistencies, he was made to look a fool. But where Napley had been hectoring in manner, Mr Carman tried a gentler approach, as if he were dealing with an invalid who, however tiresome, required sympathetic treatment.

His first question set the tone beautifully. Was Scott undergoing any medical treatment at the present time, he asked tenderly?

No. Scott agreed he had undergone medical treatment – and like many persistent invalids seemed disposed to talk about it – but not for two and a half years. He had a history of nervous problems and was once compulsorily detained in hospital.

Scott seemed a little nervous when Mr Carman took him back to the time when, after leaving Norman Vater's employment, he had been a patient of Dr Willems at the Ashurst Clinic. After discharging himself, Scott went to live with a couple in Oxfordshire, and was readmitted in October 1961. This was a month before he presented himself to Thorpe at the House of Commons and was taken to spend the night in Mrs Ursula Thorpe's house in Surrey. At this stage, he had met Thorpe only briefly at Vater's house. This passage proved one of the most extraordinary moments of the trial:

Scott: "I was very drugged at the time, and some details of the incident might have gone out of my mind."

Carman: "You don't remember telling them that you knew Jeremy Thorpe?"

Scott: "I still had a bundle of love letters of Jeremy Thorpe that he had written to Van de Vater."

Carman: "Never mind what you say are love letters between Mr Thorpe and Van de Vater, answer the question."

The judge: "You are not giving a proper answer. That was just a bit of dirt thrown in. Listen to the question and answer, and behave yourself."

In their anxiety to prevent any irrelevant accusations being made against Thorpe, both the judge and Mr Carman seem to have missed the significance of these letters – that through the accident of Vater's having the same Christian name as himself, Scott had been using them to support claims of a homosexual relationship with Thorpe even before any such relationship had occurred, by Scott's later account. In other words, by Scott's own admission, he had been lying about a relationship with Thorpe even before the alleged relationship started. This could have been a most damaging admission, lending powerful support to Thorpe's claim that no homosexual acts had taken place between them. But because the admission slipped out under these circumstances, Mr Carman made little of it at the time.

Carman: "You met Mr Thorpe and talked to him for five minutes or less. He hadn't written you a single letter before you went to the House of Commons, neither had you written a single letter to Mr Thorpe before that. Why did you say Mr Thorpe was a friend of yours when all you had done was to speak to him for less than five minutes?"

Scott: "Because when I had had the therapy at the hospital I was going through a delusion and I had these letters. I was using these letters to say that I had had a relationship with him already . . ."

Carman: "You were saying you had a sexual relationship with Mr Thorpe before you went to the House of Commons?"

Scott: "Yes."

Carman: "Quite obviously, that was not true?"

Scott: "No, it wasn't."

Carman: "In fairness to you, were you saying it because you were suffering from a delusion?"

Scott: "Yes."

Mr Carman went on to discuss various other delusions from which Scott had suffered – that his parents had been killed in a plane crash, that he was the son of an earl.

Carman: "Was that another delusion?"

Scott: "No, it was a lie."

Scott explained he told this lie because he was trying to get a job, and he thought it would be difficult to get a job with horses unless he was a certain type of person. He changed his name to Scott while he was in Dublin in 1966–67, because Scott was the family name of the Earl of Eldon.

Scott: "I pretended I was the son of the Earl of Eldon."

Carman: "Do you think that was a wicked thing?"

Scott: "Yes I do. But I have done so many wicked things in the past."

This was a foolish sort of general admission to make in court if one is a witness, and Scott may have realised it when he added:

"I have not lied since that wretched man tried to kill me because I suddenly realised there was no point in all this lying."

That, indeed, was the essence of both Crown witnesses' stand – that whereas Mr Bessell and Scott had both lied frequently in the past, they had now decided to tell the truth. The trouble with this as a witness-box posture was that unless they were prepared to repeat it with every question, as Mr Carman took them through their previous lies, it appeared to the careless or inattentive listener as if Mr Carman had caught them out again, thereby seeming to discredit their protestations.

Scott agreed that he used to pretend he knew great or famous people and that he was well connected. Mr Carman did not name these people, nor did he ask Scott whether he had ever claimed sexual connection with them. *This may have been in deference to the judge's known sensitivity on this point, or possibly the result of*

agreement between defence and prosecuting counsel – part of the
quid pro quo *whereby no evidence of Thorpe's previous homosexual
activity was produced. If so, I can only suggest that Mr Carman drove
the harder bargain. But of course any such theory must rest on
speculation.*

Next, Mr Carman referred Scott to his statement made at Chelsea
police station on the night of 19 December 1962. At that time, it will
be remembered, Scott had told a young woman called Caroline
Barrington-Ward that he proposed to kill Thorpe. She told the
police who took a long detailed statement from him accusing
Thorpe of homosexual relations, which were still a criminal offence.
Police investigations were not pursued, and indeed nobody learned
about this first police statement until 1976, after the first police
investigation into the dog-shooting was finished.

Mr Carman read from the statement which began:

"I have come to the police to tell you of my homosexual relations
with Jeremy Thorpe, who is a Liberal MP, because these relations
have caused me so much purgatory."

In this account, Mr Carman pointed out, Scott seemed to deny
that actual penetration had occurred on the first occasion, in Mrs
Ursula Thorpe's home. One passage read: "I am almost certain his
penis did not go into my anus. I am not sure whether he ejaculated,
but he seemed satisfied."

This was very different, of course, from Scott's later account of
biting the pillow to prevent himself crying out with pain, or (at
Minehead) of feeling that Thorpe might be sawing him in half with
his penis. Scott explained the discrepancy by saying that he was
nervous of police prosecution for buggery in December 1962.

Scott: "At the beginning of my statement I was trying to make
myself out a cleaner person than I was."

But later in the 1962 statement, as his confidence grew, he
admitted to buggery having occurred on many occasions, in
Draycott Place and elsewhere, and even claimed, on one occasion,
to have buggered Thorpe.

"But I did not ejaculate. I felt sick."

This statement described the Bridge Street episode, when detec-
tives called at a time when "Jeremy was trying to kiss me" but
placed the incident in the Liberal whip's room in the House of
Commons, rather than in Thorpe's Bridge Street office.

It also included the famous remark by Thorpe: "He said that
he couldn't be hurt, and that I could not harm him or his character
if I told the police or anyone, because, he said, MPs have some

sort of privilege, and he was a friend of the Director of Public Prosecutions."

This was a curious statement for Thorpe to have made in 1961 or 1962 because the Director of Public Prosecutions then was old Sir Theobald Mathew, father of John Mathew QC, who by coincidence was representing Thorpe's co-defendant, David Holmes. Nobody doubts that Thorpe was a friend of the man who replaced him on Sir Theobald's death in February 1964 – Norman Skelhorn, a fellow barrister on the Western circuit. Skelhorn's tenure of the post was a short one when compared to Sir Theobald's twenty years – he resigned in 1977, the year that the second police investigation into the Thorpe affair was eventually launched. Perhaps Thorpe was also a friend of Mr Mathew's father, despite the difference in their ages. Stranger things have happened. There was a friend and Oxford contemporary of Thorpe's in the DPP's office at the time – Christopher Bonan – but his name was never mentioned. Since Thorpe declined to give evidence, we may never know the true explanation. Nobody has suggested any connection between Thorpe and the DPP responsible for the form of the prosecution against him, Sir Thomas "Tony" Hetherington, although there were many jokes, inevitably, about the "man called Hetherington" of Mr Bessell's evidence. It was widely felt, at the end of the day, that alternative or lesser charges would have resulted in conviction where at any rate some of the defendants were concerned.

Towards the end of the morning's cross-examination, Scott reaffirmed that he had been driven to London Airport after the pillow-biting incident by Thorpe's secretary, Miss Jennifer King. Mr Carman said Miss King – now a married woman – would be produced, and strongly hinted that she would deny the incident. For the purposes of identification, he would show Scott the lady concerned.

The door opened and a plump, dark, middle-aged woman walked around the well of the court, rather like Banquo's ghost. It was a fine, melodramatic moment, like the one at Minehead when Scott said that he could prove he had had a homosexual relationship with Thorpe if Thorpe was prepared to submit to a medical examination. When asked what secret matters would be revealed, Scott wrote, "He has nodules under his arm," on a piece of paper which he handed to Sir David Napley.

On this occasion there was a similar anti-climax. Scott stared blankly at the woman and said he wasn't sure whether she was Miss Jennifer King or not.

It seemed odd at the time that Mr Carman should go to such lengths to establish what could only have been a minor and unimportant inaccuracy in Scott's narrative. If anyone remembered at the end of the day it would have seemed even odder, because Miss King was never called as a witness and so never revealed whether she had or had not made the car journey. Perhaps Mr Carman felt he had already made the point. Or perhaps, as I believe, he still intended to call defence witnesses at this stage.

If by the end of the morning's evidence Scott had been subdued, the afternoon found him in a louder, more emphatic mood, sometimes even aggressive. His outbursts were less effective in the large courtroom than they had been in the Magistrates' Court at Minehead, but the afternoon was to bring what, in the context of the defence, was an important admission by Mr Carman – that Thorpe, indeed had been a man of homosexual tendencies at the time in question. Up to this moment, it had been assumed that he would deny it. It was the first wavering from his front of unassailable rectitude.

The first outburst came within minutes after the luncheon recess, and it occurred to me that Scott had perhaps eaten something disagreeable during the lunch hour. Mr Carman was asking about the Bridge Street episode, when Scott suddenly started shouting.

Carman: "Mr Thorpe had arranged for the police to come by appointment?"

Scott: "Yes," then (shouting), "Jeremy Thorpe lives on a knife-edge of danger."

Carmen (quietly): "What about you?"

Scott (even louder): "I don't at all. I have certainly lived in danger of my life for many years because of your client."

A little later, Mr Carman asked Scott if he felt vindictive towards Thorpe.

Scott: "I feel nothing, neither vindictiveness nor anything at all, just great pity. The man has destroyed me totally. Thorpe has destroyed me, or endeavoured to destroy me, but I don't want to be destroyed, and I do not wish to destroy him."

It occurred to me at the time that Scott would have been more convincing and therefore his whole evidence more credible, if he had agreed that vindictiveness was part of his motive. But Scott plainly did not see himself in that light. The next outburst came soon afterwards.

Carman: "You do appreciate that Mr Thorpe has consistently denied any homosexual relationship with you?"

Scott: "Yes, sir."

Carman: "Are you claiming the sexual activity on the first night at the home of Mrs [Ursula] Thorpe was without your consent?"

At this point Scott became extremely emotional and started shouting.

Scott: "There was nothing I could do because I was in their house, tired and very woozy. I was broken and crying. I did not know what was happening until it was too late. I assure you it happened."

Carman: "Do not get excited."

Scott (shouting): "I am not getting excited but it is stupid. Do you think I enjoy saying these terrible things or talking about it? It is most horrendous."

The judge: "If you only spoke like that when you began your evidence, we could have heard everything you said. It shows you can speak up."

The situation was fraught, and I could scacely believe my ears at this point. Unless I was very much mistaken the judge, having seen that Scott was in a highly emotional state, was deliberately baiting him, rather as one might approach a lunatic waving a knife in the street and give him a prod with one's umbrella – uncertain of what will happen next, but sure that it will be interesting.

If so, he was not slow in getting his results. Scott was trying to enlarge on an answer he had given when the judge rebuked him for interrupting counsel. Scott's anger burst out.

Scott: "Sir, I am in contempt of this court. I will not answer any more questions."

The judge: "You may find that an uncomfortable place to be."

Scott: "I have gone on enough over the years with this story. I will not say any more."

The judge: "Do you want to go home now?"

Scott: "I don't mind where I go. I won't have myself destroyed in this way when he knows very well his client is lying. I have had enough."

Carman: "I am sorry Mr Scott, but it is my professional duty to ask a considerable number of further questions. Are you going to answer them?"

Scott: "I have nothing to say."

There was an awkward pause. Mr Carman, I thought, looked as if he was enjoying himself. I found myself wondering whether he had really thought this matter through, and what would be the effect on the jury's mind if an important prosecution witness was sent down to cool his heels in the cells. At one point the judge had seemed prepared to send Scott home, which would have been an unusual development.

But the judge was obviously debating several possible courses of action. His next question was asked with an air of detached curiosity.

The judge: "Are you going to answer further questions?"

Scott: "No, sir."

There was another awkward pause, then –

Scott: "Not if I am going to be treated as a most dreadful criminal. I am not a liar."

I thought I detected a weakening of Scott's resolve in this after-thought, but the judge, if he had decided to press the matter, could easily have had the witness striking new attitudes of defiance. Instead Mr Justice Cantley addressed him in a quiet, reasonable voice, without a hint of scorn, rather as one might speak to a recalcitrant child. It worked, and Scott reverted to the role of the child called to order.

The judge: "Now listen here. There are two sides to this case. You have made allegations against Mr Thorpe, and it is his counsel's duty to put Thorpe's version. It necessarily involves this sort of questioning. That is why you are being questioned, and the jury in the end will decide what is the right answer. The jury are entitled to hear both sides. Every witness has to endure counsel's questions."

If Scott had known that Thorpe would not have to endure any counsel's questions, or that the jury would be treated to Mr Justice Cantley's "last word" before deciding what was the right answer, he might have reacted differently. As it was, he calmed down and looked penitent.

Scott: "Yes, sir. I am sorry, I am sorry."

Next Carman went through all the money Scott stood to receive for his story for the *Daily Mirror* – not much, as it turned out, when compared with Peter Bessell's contract with the *Sunday Telegraph*. This was a boring passage for the press, who had heard it all before, but we later learned how much importance judge and jury attached to it. He asked what was the "going rate" for a Norman Scott photograph.

Scott: "I have no idea, it seems very cheap at the moment."

The last time he had had a physical relationship with Thorpe was on the night before he went to Switzerland in December 1964, said Scott.

Carman: "What obligation does Mr Thorpe owe you now?"

Scott: "He owes me to tell the truth about the whole story. He has a moral obligation."

A little later, Scott agreed that he had been paid £2,500 by David Holmes for a bundle of letters from Mr Bessell. He had no idea why the letters were worth so much. Later, Scott wanted to get copies of these letters from a South African journalist, Gordon Winter, to whom he had given them earlier. He was asked why.

Scott: "I was afraid I would be committed because of the whole story, because of my lies in the past . . . I felt that people would regard my story as too fanciful for words and I would be committed to a lunatic asylum."

The purpose of this cross-examination was presumably to establish Scott either as a blackmailer or as someone obsessed with revenge. It is hard to see, logically, what the defence had to gain by establishing either of these two points, since they pointed to a motive for murder, and Scott's evidence was only of relevance in establishing this motive. But Mr Carman may have reckoned that Scott, in seeking to deny that he was either a blackmailer or inspired by revenge, would arouse scepticism in the jury which might then reflect on the main body of his evidence.

Carman: "Are you not being vindictive?"

Scott: "No, sir, merely answering questions."

Carman: "You were trying to destroy Mr Thorpe?"

Scott: "No I was not. I went with Mrs Parry-Jones [to the Liberal Party enquiry] to sort out the problems of my national insurance. National insurance is my lifeblood. It has been throughout all this sordid time."

This remark – "National insurance is my lifeblood" – which surely deserves a place in the dictionary of quotations – may have contributed to the judge's celebrated conclusion (in his summing up) that Scott was a sponger. The judge also seemed to have decided at the end of the day that Scott was both a blackmailer and a man obsessed with revenge. Despite this, he seemed to invite the jury to disbelieve Scott's evidence – which, as I say, was designed only to establish a motive for the murder conspiracy. Plainly, the judge did not like Scott very much, and one can perhaps understand why.

Carman: "Did you boast of sexual affairs with well-known actors – I don't want any names."

Scott: "I have boasted of friendships with actors."

Carman: "Why did you do that?"

Scott: "Because I did – I just did."

One quiet remark by Scott at this stage struck a poignant note for at least one of the journalists present.

Scott: "I did not think this court would ever sit, I can assure you. I thought the establishment would cover it up."

Carman: "Have you an obsession about this?"

Scott: "Of course I had. So would you if people were trying to kill you."

After playing around a little on the theme that Scott's relations with the two journalists Penrose and Courtiour were too close – this line of defence was never really developed – Mr Carman produced what was to be the main defence posture in face of Scott's evidence.

Carman: "You knew Thorpe to be a man of homosexual tendencies in 1961?"

Scott: "Yes, sir."

Carman: "He was the most famous and distinguished person you had met at that time?"

Scott: "Yes, sir. I think so."

Carman: "You were flattered that for a short time he introduced you into a different social world. I suggest you were upset and annoyed because he did not want to have sexual relationships with you."

Scott: "Of course that is ridiculous because he did."

Scott had just repeated his denial that he tried to make money out of the relationship by talking about it when Mr Taylor rose to re-examine.

Mr Taylor's re-examination

The doughty chief prosecutor was not going to leave the jury in any doubt of his belief that Thorpe had had a homosexual relationship with Scott. Strangely enough, he seemed to see this point as central to the existence of a murder conspiracy. Equally plainly, it was a matter on which the judge was unhappy to dwell. Mr Taylor's main reason for believing in the homosexual relationship, which had been sworn by Scott and corroborated by Mr Bessell, was the bunnies letter. This puzzled some observers, who did not find the letter conclusive.

Mr Taylor's first question was a not very subtle reintroduction of the letter.

Taylor: "You remember that you told Mr Carman earlier in the cross-examination that you knew of Mr Thorpe's sexual tendencies before you went to see him at the House of Commons. It has been suggested that you were upset and annoyed because Mr Thorpe did not have sexual relations with you. What was your state of mind when Mr Thorpe wrote you a letter which ended: 'Bunnies *can* and *will* go to France. Yours affectionately, Jeremy?' "

Scott: "I was pleased and proud."

Mr Taylor then turned to some letters written by Thorpe to the character called Norman Vater or Van de Vater. Scott agreed he had stolen them from Van de Vater on leaving his employment.

Taylor: "What was the nature of these letters?"

Scott: "They were love letters."

Carman: "I object. What is the relevance of these letters?"

The judge: "What is the relevance? It will be too late, when we get the answer, to know whether we ought to have had it."

Despite spirited objections from Mr Taylor, the judge forebade further questions about these letters. The jury must have been puzzled by the judge's behaviour – if indeed, they had any intellectual curiosity in the matter. We journalists who had been following the case knew the reason – that one of them, in a facetious aside, mentioned the famous Person whose name the judge was determined to keep out of the case at all costs.

By forbidding any questions about Thorpe's correspondence with Vater the judge prevented Mr Taylor explaining the circumstances in which Scott came to boast of a sexual relationship with Thorpe at a time when Scott scarcely knew him. But the ban on discussing this correspondence did not extend to the judge's summing up, where he referred to the theft of the letters as an important indication that Scott was a blackmailer ergo *odious, unreliable, not to be believed.*

In re-examination Mr Taylor also produced a few details of Scott's tribulations before coming to court which he had, for some reason, omitted at the beginning. Scott described how he had been beaten up by two men in Barnstaple in February 1975 who had come out of the shadows and said, "Hello, Mr Josiffe." On that occasion he was left unconscious with his teeth broken and taken to hospital. On another occasion he was frightened by people who landed a helicopter near his cottage on Exmoor. Finally, he received Scott's assurance that money received from television and newspaper concerns had not affected his evidence.

If Mr Taylor hoped to win the judge's sympathy for his witness by this account of Scott's tribulations, or to impress the judge with Scott's disinterestedness by this assurance, he was plainly going to be disappointed. The judge indicated that he had some questions to ask the witness.

The judge: "How are you supporting yourself now?"

Scott: "I am self-employed. I give dressage lessons."

Taylor: "You tell me you hunt."

Scott: "Yes, sir."

The judge: "Sounds very comfortably off."

Taylor: "How many horses have you got?"

Scott: "Three, including a pony which is for my daughter."

The judge: "How did you manage to get money to start the business?"

Scott: "I used money from the television people."

The judge ordered Scott to return next day with his contract from Mirror Newspapers so that he could be questioned on it. *Like nearly all the judge's contributions throughout the trial the effect of this interruption was to inform the jury in no uncertain terms that he, Sir Joseph Cantley OBE, had grave doubts about the witness. But he agreed that both Scott and Mr Bessell could be released after the matter had been dealt with.*

At the end of the eleventh day of the trial Mr Taylor revealed that the prosecution case was running one day ahead of its programme. *It would appear that he had been expecting Mr Carman to cross-examine Scott at greater length. Scott himself seemed to be suffering from anti-climax. This was, after all, the moment he had been expecting, in one form or another, for nearly seventeen years – and Thorpe's counsel had dealt with him in a single day.*

The court adjourned.

7

The Hit Man

The morning was taken up with minor witnesses and written statements. First, a handwriting expert and forensic scientist, Dr
R. J. Toddy, told the court that the entry for Scott's first visit to Mrs
Ursula Thorpe's home on 8 November 1961 had, indeed, been
tampered with. Scott claimed he had signed it with a false name, but
the original writing had been erased and the words Norman and
Lianche superimposed.

Mrs Mary Collier, wife of the former Liberal candidate for
Tiverton, Mr James Collier, agreed that Scott had come with his dog
Mrs Tish to stay with them, at Thorpe's request, around Christmas
1961. She had been present at the luncheon at Broomhills Hotel.
She had also been receptionist at the Easton Court Hotel when
Scott was seen by police officers from Chelsea police station. She
denied that Scott had discussed his sex life with her, or that she and
Thorpe had discussed Scott's sexual orientation.

Her husband, James Collier, had nothing to add to this, except
that Scott and Thorpe had been absent for about twenty minutes
after the Broomhills lunch. Thorpe had stated quite openly that he
had some shirts which might fit Scott.

Other evidence was heard from Mr Arthur Rose, a neighbour of
Scott and Mrs Parry-Jones in North Wales; Mr Thomas Daley, a
personal assistant to Thorpe; Major Hambro, a Somerset farmer
who briefly employed Scott at Thorpe's request; Mrs Diana
Attabey, a former secretary of Mr Bessell who arranged for Scott's
suitcase to be taken from Victoria Station to Mr Bessell's office in
Clarges Street – she was telephoned unusually by Thorpe, who
wished to know whether the suitcase was safe, with the greeting
"Diana darling, are you in a gorgeous negligee?" and assured him
all was well: Mrs Sheila James, née Skelton, another Bessell secretary, who confirmed payments to Scott; Mrs Zena King, yet another;
Mr Leonard Ross, who was Mr Bessell's solicitor and acted for Scott

over his divorce, until he was dismissed by Scott for deleting Thorpe's name from the proceedings. His fees and expenses of £77.55 were paid by Thorpe in April 1973. None of these witnesses added anything substantive to the case against the four defendants; all were concerned with Thorpe's possible motive for the crime.

After the luncheon recess, Scott was recalled to the witness-box and questioned by Mr Carman about his contract with the *Daily Mirror*, which had been signed during the period Scott was giving evidence under oath at the Minehead hearing.

It seemed an extraordinarily modest proposal. The advance of £3,000 – half on signature, half on delivery – would be shared between Scott and a Mr Dan Wooding, who had the job of converting Scott's 86,000 word synopsis into a coherent narrative, with Scott receiving 60%, Wooding 40%.

Throughout this episode the judge appeared to be in a curiously elated mood, interrupting constantly with frivolous or mildly sarcastic observations. He remarked how modest it was of Mr Wooding not to want his name on the cover, and chuckled to himself for some time over this sally. He observed that the comic strip rights were also covered by the contract. The general tone of these procedings succeeded in annoying Scott again. He became very angry over suggestions that Penrose and Courtiour had orchestrated the story against Thorpe, and announced that he no longer wished the book to be published. That was the last we saw of him.

Mr Bull, junior counsel for the prosecution, then read a statement by Mrs Edna Friendship, licensee of the Market Inn, Barnstaple, who reported seeing Newton on his first approaches to Scott in October 1975.

Mr Andrew Newton

Finally, Newton arrived in the witness-box and affirmed, rather than take the oath. At Minehead Andrew Gino Newton, the airline pilot who claimed to have accepted the contract to kill Scott – first from Deakin, then more positively from Holmes – was at pains to create a debonair impression, arriving in a balaclava helmet in an Opel with blackened windows, narrowly missing photographers as he roared up to the courtroom. He seemed vague to the point almost of half-wittedness about the evidence he was giving, off-hand and at times distinctly cocky. Obviously addicted to thrillers, he reverted sometimes to bizarre criminal slang and plainly enjoyed the idea of himself as a character in some American pulp crime novel.

At Number One Court of the Old Bailey he was more subdued, at any rate to begin with. This may have been the result of a bizarre circumstance, witnessed with great amusement by the press representatives and lawyers who wandered in and out of court during the earlier proceedings. Scott and Newton were both waiting in the hall outside the court. They had last seen each other at Newton's trial in Exeter, when Newton was untruthfully claiming to have been blackmailed by Scott, and Scott's evidence sent him to prison. Before that, of course, they had last seen each other on Porlock Moor over the corpse of Rinka, when Newton appeared to be having difficulty with his pistol. Outside Number One Court, both were waiting to be called as Crown witnesses. They studiously ignored each other, would-be murderer and would-be victim, both pacing nervously around at opposite ends of the handsome marble hall.

Before Newton started on the main part of his evidence, there was an application from defence counsel that Stuart Kuttner, a journalist employed by the *Evening News*, should leave the courtroom. Kuttner had been involved in negotiations with Newton which, by Newton's account (which the *Evening News* and Kuttner himself were later to deny) were of a very dubious nature. Newton's suggestion was that Kuttner had offered him large, specified sums of money contingent on the conviction of various named people, starting with Sir Harold Wilson, the former Prime Minister, on a charge of conspiracy to murder Norman Scott. Thorpe and Holmes were also named and priced, according to Newton.

The judge agreed with alacrity that Mr Kuttner should leave the court during Newton's evidence. *It is hard to see exactly what was achieved by this since there was no question of calling him as a witness. The only effect must have been to reinforce Mr Carman's half-argued suggestion of a press conspiracy against Thorpe, dictated by commercial considerations and the desire for sensationalism. Certainly, it made not one tittle of difference to the conduct of the trial whether Kuttner was present or not, and he could have read all the evidence immediately afterwards. But the application for his removal had come, on Newton's suggestion, from Mr Mathew, counsel for Holmes.*

Newton's manner, at the beginning of his evidence, was subdued, as I have said. He seemed nervous of the judge, who interrupted from time to time to correct Newton's extraordinarily prolix manner of speaking. He also seemed to suspect, possibly not without reason, that the judge was mocking him.

This is the story which Newton told:

During 1974 and 1975 Newton was a pilot with British Island Airways, mainly on domestic flights out of Blackpool, Gatwick and Manchester. Early in 1975 he was living in Blackpool. A friend from his days at Chiswick Polytechnic, David Miller, who ran a silk-screen printing business in Cardiff, took him to a trade dinner party on 26 February 1975 at the Savoy Hotel, Blackpool, where he met the defendant George Deakin, a man he knew slightly. As the result of an earlier conversation with Miller, Newton approached Deakin and said: "I understand you want someone bumped off. If you have got nobody, I am your man" – or words to that effect.

Taylor: "What was it that you were volunteering to do?"

Newton: "Initially to take out a contract on a person unknown . . ."

Taylor: "What do you mean – take out a contract?"

Newton: "By contract I mean that somebody was to be eliminated."

Taylor: "Would a shorter term be to kill someone?"

The judge: "Murder."

Deakin at this stage was "interested" in his proposal, but Newton became so drunk at the dinner party that he could remember no more. Three weeks later he met Deakin at Miller's business premises in Cardiff, and the sum of £15,000 was mentioned. Later he arranged to meet Deakin at the Aust Service Station on the M4 motorway. Deakin gave him some photographs of Scott, said "that's him," and revealed that the fee was £10,000, not £15,000. He mentioned the town of Dunstable.

Taylor: "Did you ask any questions?"

Newton: "Yes, only the sort of questions you would expect a hit man to ask." There was laughter in court. "I say this only from what I had seen in films."

Newton said he asked Deakin whether there was a burglar alarm and if the man had any dogs. He was told there was no dog.

This produced a certain amount of laughter in court.

Newton: "It bothered me. If I had to approach Mr Scott, I would not want a dog to attack me."

Loud laughter, called to order.

The judge: "This is certainly not funny."

Newton asked, but was not told, who wished to have the man killed and why. He went to Dunstable but could find no trace of anyone called Norman Scott. Deakin then gave him the number of

David Holmes in Manchester. Holmes told him that Scott did not live in Dunstable but Barnstaple, Devon.

He arranged to meet Holmes over coffee in the Royal Court Hotel, Sloane Square, London. Holmes confirmed the offer of £10,000 and said he would be happier to have Scott vanish off the face of the earth without leaving a body. The method of disposal was left to Newton.

Newton telephoned Scott at the Market Inn, Barnstaple, claiming to represent the Pensiero Group of Italy and saying he wanted to hire Scott for some modelling work. It was agreed that Scott should go to Royal Garden Hotel, Kensington, where Newton booked a room for him. That day Newton bought a coal chisel and a bunch of flowers, intending to hide the chisel within the bunch of flowers when he called at the hotel, and then to use the chisel to hit Scott over the head and kill him. However, Scott did not turn up for the appointment. Newton was greatly relieved by this. Holmes did not sound too surprised by this development when Newton told him on the telephone. "Leave it to me," said Holmes. "I will set something up."

Newton was being shown the chisel − an ugly object, looking more like a crowbar, and identifying it as the one he had purchased with the flowers, when the court adjourned until next day.

Day thirteen: 24 May 1979
Mr Newton's story continued

After the episode of the coal chisel and the missed appointment in the Royal Garden Hotel, Newton realised he had not the stomach to murder.

Newton: "It was something I did not want to do. It was something I knew from that day on I could not carry out. It was something I had found out about myself as a person."

On another occasion, Newton looked at the judge with what might have been puppyish appeal.

Newton: "I am asking you to believe that after the Royal Garden Hotel the scene changed. Hopefully, I thought it would fizzle out."

Holmes now told Newton that he had spoken to Scott using the name Masterson as an alias. Posing as a press association reporter, he had arranged to interview Scott at the Holiday Inn, Bristol. Newton was expected to turn up and kill Scott, but once again, Scott was not there. This was a "traumatic experience" for Newton who resolved not to go on with the killing. He feared for his own safety at this stage. He decided on delaying tactics, and telephoned Holmes from Bristol.

Newton: "I told Holmes to leave everything to me because I wanted the reins back in my hands so that I could manipulate the situation and hopefully defuse it."

He had an idea he might be able to frighten Scott and borrowed a gun for the purpose from a friend in London. On 11 October 1975 he drove down to Barnstaple from Blackpool and spotted his quarry in the Three Tuns public house. He approached him next morning in the Pannier Market and said to him, "I want to talk about this blackmail." Scott burst into a sweat and started stuttering. They went to the Imperial Hotel where Scott said he was living in fear of his life. As they talked, Newton took the notes on pink paper which were produced in court, although never read out.

Scott said he thought Newton might have been hired to kill him – Newton replied that on the contrary, he had been hired to protect him. Scott suggested that Marion Thorpe might have hired him for this purpose, and Newton agreed to this, although the whole story was then untrue. Newton asked why he was being hired to protect Scott, and Scott poured out the story of his life. Newton suggested that if the threats on Scott's life were to do with the letters, he should come to some arrangement with Thorpe's solicitors. Scott was against the idea. Newton received the impression that although the prospect of £5,000 was attractive to Scott, being able to ruin Thorpe was even more attractive.

Newton told him that a man from Canada was coming to kill him. This was a lie but it brought them closer together.

Scott showed him some letters from Thorpe and Bessell. When Newton mentioned this to Holmes later, Holmes asked if the letters were originals. Newton said they were, and Holmes said: "Oh, Jesus Christ!"

The arrangement to murder Scott still stood.

Newton: "After much thought, the thing that came to my mind was to try and frighten Scott with a bungled murder attempt. The plan was to have a firearm, to lure Scott into an open place and to try and shoot him, and have the gun jam."

Newton got in touch with Scott, using the false name of Peter Keene, and they arranged to meet in a hotel at Combe Martin, in Devon, on 24 October. He drove there with his gun and ammunition in a car borrowed from his girl-friend.

Scott turned up with a huge dog, and refused to leave it behind on the drive to Porlock, so the dog came along too. On the return

journey, Newton pretended to be tired. Scott offered to drive.
Newton stopped in a lay-by. All three got out of the car and Newton
shot the dog.

Newton: "Well, once the dog was out of the way I could carry on
with the plan of frightening Scott. If I had tried levelling the gun at
Scott I could not have been sure that the dog would not have had a
go at me. The dog was a monstrous size . . . so I shot it."

Then he levelled the gun at Scott and said, "It's your turn now."
Next he said, "Oh it's jammed," and walked to the front of the car,
pretending to unjam it. Once again he pointed the gun at Scott, but
Scott just stood staring at his dead dog.

Newton: "Scott still stood there. He made no move to go so I got
back in the car and said, 'I will see you another time.' It's as stupid
and as simple as that."

When Scott asked him what he had done to the dog, he replied
that he had tranquillised it. Afterwards, he reversed his car and
drove back to Porlock.

*Newton's insistence that he had no intention of killing Scott after
the Royal Garden Hotel incident did not, of course, destroy the
Crown case for conspiracy to murder, but it certainly confused it
from the point of view of the jurors, who were later to be bombarded
by defence representations that there had been no conspiracy to
murder in the first place.*

Newton now asked the judge if he could make some explanation
about the shooting, and when the judge demurred, he launched into
a confused speech which he had obviously been preparing.

Newton: "The trouble of being in this witness-box . . . I felt that
when I was on trial at Exeter that it wasn't me on trial but Jeremy
Thorpe and others. As I stand in this witness-box I have a big
stigma. Obviously I have done a lot of things of which I am not
proud and a lot of things which have made it difficult for me. There
is still one stigma which sticks with me. It is what actually happened
on the moor that night which has not been fully explained and I
would like a chance to explain it."

The judge: "You can tell the court something which happened on
the moor that night, but you are not to express your thoughts or
theories."

Newton: "Well, the thing I'm trying to say . . . all right, I
have admitted trying to kill Norman Scott at the Royal Garden
Hotel . . ."

The judge: "You are not on trial here, you know."

Newton: "I am sorry, my lord, I am."

The judge: "Well you're not. Take that from me and don't talk nonsense. You can tell us if there is anything which happened on the moor, but you are not going to make a speech to the jury."

Newton: "That's all right. What I wanted to say probably would not interest you."

With a withering, hurt glance at the judge, Newton continued his story.

After the dog-shooting incident on the moor, said Newton, he drove to his friend David Miller's business premises in Cardiff and made a great pretence of unjamming the pistol. The same night he washed the inside of the car, where the seats were covered with dog's blood. He then went away on holiday with his girl-friend and Miller to the Far East, having first telephoned Deakin from Heathrow Airport and told him what had happened.

On 18 November 1975 he and Miller were met by police on their return to England. After being interviewed he was arrested and subsequently tried for being in possession of a firearm with intent to endanger life. While on bail he had six or seven meetings with Holmes, in the course of which Holmes gave him £400 and learned of news about the forthcoming trial. Newton invented a defence that Scott was blackmailing him over a nude photograph which would be shown to his employers; he intended to frighten Scott into returning the photograph and stopping the blackmail. There had been no intention to endanger life. This defence, Newton said, was his own invention and a lie. Holmes told him he would be paid £5,000, but he might go to prison for six months. Holmes assured him that Thorpe and other important people were anxious to help his defence, and steps were being taken. The £5,000 would be paid after the trial, or when he came out of prison. There was a tacit agreement that no names would be mentioned at the trial.

The trial started at Exeter Crown Court on 16 March 1976. He was convicted and given a two-year prison sentence, being released on parole on 16 April 1977. Soon afterwards he met David Miller in Cardiff, who took him to a suspicious rendezvous with Le Mesurier at a remote spot in North Wales. Le Mesurier was sitting in a mini-car. He pointed over Newton's shoulder and said, "Telephoto lenses, what is going on?"

Newton was suspicious, fearing a set-up. He thought he would be murdered and encased in concrete. Both men were alarmed when a car passed them with a woman dangling out of it with a camera. A man was at the wheel.

These, it later emerged, were private enquiry agents hired by Miller for the purpose of collecting souvenirs of the occasion.

They drove off to a cement or brick factory compound, and Le Mesurier said he had something for him but "the people in London" wanted to be sure he would keep quiet. Newton was now very scared, but he took the money and let himself be driven by Miller to Cardiff station where he took a train to London and counted the money in a toilet. He hid the £5,000 in his mother's Chiswick home; later he told the police where they could find it. They recovered £3,190, the rest having been spent.

Newton devoted the next few weeks to recording conversations with Holmes and other conspirators, although he could not get through to Thorpe. He thought the conspirators should find him a job, and wanted the tapes as security. Holmes suggested he should go to South Africa for a job. Newton made various tape recordings of conversations with Holmes in an attempt to implicate him in the conspiracy to murder, as a protection for himself in the event of anything happening to him. He felt the South African suggestion was bogus, being an attempt to implicate the South African government in some anti-Thorpe plot.

He was told to contact General Peter Walls in Salisbury, Rhodesia, but was unable to do so. The police later took possession of his tape-recordings, and he was given immunity from further prosecution by the Director of Public Prosecutions.

That ended Newton's evidence-in-chief. Before the court adjourned, Mr Taylor announced he would be playing some of Newton's tape-recordings. Judge, jury, legal advisers and police put on special headphones. Journalists and members of the public followed as best they could from the public address system. The first tape was nearly inaudible, but agreed typescripts were made available to judge, jury and lawyers.

The first conversation was between Newton and Holmes, the second between Newton and Le Mesurier. So was the third, lasting eighteen minutes. Newton is anxious to secure a job, but is told that Holmes, too, is in job difficulties because of his connection with the Thorpe case. They gossip about press interest in the police enquiry. Le Mesurier claims that Penrose and Courtiour are having trouble getting their book published.

Le Mesurier: "Seven publishers have turned it down so we don't think that's going to be a great danger . . . The danger for you and I and for anyone else for that matter . . . is that the whole lot is raked up again. But they've got to prove it."

Newton: "Holmes told me that people higher up than him are involved – the press, for example, suspect Goodman's part in this."

Le Mesurier: "Yeh, well, he's chairman of the Press Council."

Newton: "Is he really?"

Le Mesurier: "Yeh, so what editor is going to have a go at him if it happened?"

Newton: "I know how it was done, how the whole thing was set up and so do you, right?"

Le Mesurier: "We know from where it came ... it's just five people know ... I am assured that they are the only people that absolutely know all about it."

Newton: "They feel a Thomas à Becket was done – you know, with Thorpe sort of raving that would nobody rid me of this man."

Le Mesurier: "Yes."

Newton: "And somebody obliged."

Le Mesurier: "Yes."

Newton: "And who was closer perhaps than Holmes, you know."

Le Mesurier: "Yes."

The last tape was between Newton and Holmes. It lasted nearly half an hour. Newton tells of an incident which he thought had been an attempt on his life when a lorry jack-knifes on him.

Newton: "It took three blinking attempts to run me over, you know, and I take great exception to this."

Holmes: "I assure you the incident had nothing to do with me."

Later, when Newton mentions "John the carpet" (Le Mesurier), he is rebuked again by Holmes.

Holmes: "Stop producing names in every conversation because, I mean, the whole thing terrifies me. I know who you are talking about – get on."

The tape ended with the sentence which was held by the prosecution to implicate Holmes in a conspiracy to murder, rather than frighten. *Listening to it, and knowing Newton's motive for holding the conversation, one could scarcely see it as conclusive. At most, it offered a doubtful corroboration to Newton's claim that he was hired to murder Scott. But on a charge of conspiracy to frighten, or even of criminal assault, it is hard to see that Holmes's goose would not have been cooked.*

Newton: "... there is a charge, you know, a conspiracy to bloody ..."

Holmes: "I'm remembering that very carefully."

Newton: "... to murder, right, so now ... let's keep it quiet, OK?"

Holmes: "Just fine, and you may rely on that."
The trial was adjourned until next day.

Day fourteen: 15 May 1979
Mr Mathew's cross-examination
From the outset, Mr Mathew made it plain that he was not going to
deny that there had been a plot to frighten Norman Scott, or that
Holmes had hired Newton for that purpose. Newton agreed that it
had been his intention to frighten Scott, and claimed that he had
successfully done so, but resolutely maintained that he had been
hired to kill him. Mr Mathew was concerned to suggest that Newton
was lying on this point, being inspired by greed and the prospect of
reward. His cross-examination was directed towards establishing
that offers of money had been made, money had been received,
further money was expected, and Newton was an untrustworthy
witness on his previous record. None of these propositions was
difficult to establish. Mr Mathew's three and a half hours of examination proved the most entertaining passage of the trial, at any rate
for most people attending it. The judge appeared to find his own
summing up at the end even funnier.

Newton cheerfully agreed that he had told many lies about the
case, and that it created a problem, when telling lies, to remember
what he had said on previous occasions. Mathew's sneering manner
did not seem to rattle him in the least.

Mathew: "You find it difficult to remember what is fact and what
is fiction?"

Newton: "I think you are falling into the realms of sorcery with
words."

Mathew: "I was quoting what you said on a previous occasion."

Newton: "I am being taken out of context."

Mathew: "I will put it into context. Did you answer, in reply to the
very first question which was put to you in cross-examination at
Minehead: 'I do sometimes find it difficult to distinguish between
fact and fantasy regarding this case?'"

Newton: "Oh yes, I do remember saying that."

Mathew: "It accurately described your state of mind at
Minehead?"

Newton: "Yes."

Mathew: "But not now?"

Newton: "Not now."

First point to Mr Mathew. But Newton's was the voice of the New

Age: flippant, cynical, self-righteous, stupid and television-fed into a
sort of mindless conceit. Newton was not going to be browbeaten.

Mathew: "You present the facts in a way beneficial to yourself,
and that is the only criteria you apply?"

Newton: "I wish you would stop prostituting yourself. You say
that your client was not guilty of murder . . ."

Mr Mathew interrupted what might have been a most entertaining harangue.

Mathew: "You lied on oath during your trial at Exeter Crown
Court over the dog-shooting incident?"

Newton: "Yes, I was trying to save my own skin in the same way
that the defendants are."

Mr Mathew took him in detail through all the lies he had told at
Exeter, and the wealth of false evidence he had produced to corroborate the untrue story that Scott had been blackmailing him.

Mathew: "It comes to this – in order to protect yourself you
were prepared falsely to accuse someone of a very serious crime,
blackmail?"

Newton: "Yes, with the help of your client."

Perhaps Newton's cheerfulness derived from the fact that he had
been given immunity from prosecution for his perjury at Exeter. A
letter from the Director of Public Prosecutions gave him this immun-
ity on the conspiracy charge – and also immunity from prosecution
for attempted murder. Yet for some reason which the judge never
allowed him to explain, Newton was gloomily insistent that he did not
attempt to murder Scott, that he only pretended the gun had jammed.
He could still be prosecuted for perjury in the Old Bailey, he pointed
out. Mr Mathew chose to ignore this point.

Mathew: "This has opened the door to you because you have now
arrived at what can only be described as a money-making situation,
would you agree?"

Newton: "Yes, money has been made."

Mathew: "And is still to be made?"

Newton: "That is debatable."

The witness revealed that he had great difficulty finding employment since the story of the dog-shooting episode became common
knowledge, although he had made many attempts. Mr Mathew
reminded him that at Minehead he had said he was devoting himself
substantially to negotiating the sale of his book of memoirs.

Newton: "You are splitting hairs and trying to put up a big
smoke-screen. I personally have never approached a company to
try to sell my story. In fact, they have been coming to me. Unlike

one of the defendants – they themselves tried to sell the story – so you cannot accuse me of being more enterprising. Your client in fact tried to sell stories. When you take away a person's livelihood how else is he supposed to live?"

Mathew: "You were resolved to milk this case as hard as you could. Is that a correct statement?"

Newton: "No. You are way off mark . . ."

Mathew: "Did you say at Minehead, 'This case is the sole source of income I have. It is right to say I am resolved to milk it as hard as I can'?"

Newton: "Yes. That was a statement of fact at Minehead, but not before Minehead."

Mathew: "Is it correct that your state of mind at that time was that you were resolved to milk it as hard as you can?"

Newton: "At that time."

Mathew: "Does that remain your state of mind and intention?"

Newton: "Most certainly it is."

The judge: "You are still resolved to milk the case as hard as you can?"

Newton: "Yes, sir."

The judge: "I see."

Newton did not appear to see any inconsistency between this answer and his earlier one to Mr Mathew – "No, you are way off mark." No doubt it was all a question of mood. His answer to the next question, given in even more emphatic terms, was possibly even more damaging to his credibility.

Mathew: "It is going to be a very much easier case to milk and you are going to obtain a great deal more milk if these defendants are convicted on this charge – correct?"

Newton: "That is absolutely correct."

Mr Mathew next took Newton through the various sums he had already received for his story from newspapers and television companies. These amounted to £10,950 made up as follows:

Evening News	£3,000
Der Spiegel	£4,000
Daily Express	£600
American Broadcasting Corporation	£2,000
Columbia Broadcasting Corporation	£500
Canadian Television	£850

Later, Newton was questioned about his dealings with Penrose and Courtiour. He denied entering into any arrangements with them, but claimed his then solicitor had done so behind his back.

The judge: "Not on his own behalf, surely?"

Newton: "There's other crooks around, you know."

The judge: "Was he trying to sell things?"

Newton: "You've hit it right on the head, my lord. He undertook to sell – or as he put it, give – some tapes to Barrie Penrose and Roger Courtiour. I am getting the Law Society to look into it."

The judge: "You can get the money back from the solicitors, you know?"

Newton: "Good. I'm glad to hear it. And I hope they come up before you."

There was much good-natured laughter at that point.

Two journalists who visited him in prison were Keith Dovkants and Stuart Kuttner, then both working for the *Evening Standard*. Later, when Mr Kuttner was working for the *Evening News*, Newton demanded £100,000 for his story or possibly £80,000 but Kuttner would not offer more than £40,000 and no agreement was reached. Or that seemed to be what Newton and Mr Mathew agreed between them. The *Evening News* later denied it all, as it denied the extraordinary suggestions which followed (these alleged negotiations took place in the early autumn of 1977, before Newton had been given immunity from prosecution).

Mathew: "That figure was offered on the basis – and only on the basis – that you were prepared to say that this was a conspiracy to murder, rather than an agreement to do anything else, correct?"

Newton: "Yes, I was expected to say exactly what happened."

Mathew: "Is it right that Mr Kuttner made it clear to you that he was out to get Mr Holmes for a conspiracy to murder?"

Newton: "Absolutely."

Mathew: "It was made absolutely clear to you, was it not, that there was really only any money in this story if it was a conspiracy to murder – they weren't interested in anything else, were they?"

Newton: "No, they were interested anyway. But obviously the story had a higher premium with the conspiracy to murder."

Mathew: "Did you say to Mr Kuttner at any time these words: 'Supposing I was only sent money to put the frighteners on him, how would that sound?' "

Newton: "Yes, I did."

Mr Mathew put it to him that he had denied this three times at Minehead (*although my notes of the Minehead cross-examination only give Newton as saying that he can't remember*). Newton's explanation for this odd question scarcely made it any clearer.

Newton: "I said that because we were with solicitors, I wanted to find out the prices on the various people's heads, what the price was for conspiracy to murder and conspiracy to frighten."

The suggestion was that these were probing questions. At that time Newton had no immunity and was still pretending that the story he told at his trial was true. However, Newton agreed with Mr Mathew that Kuttner made it clear he was only interested in a conspiracy to murder. This, according to Newton, was the tariff proposed by Kuttner for convictions on a charge of conspiracy to murder:

> For Harold Wilson's head   £150,000
> For Jeremy Thorpe's head $200,000
> For David Holmes's head $130,000

Newton said the offer was open to anyone but agreed that it had, in fact, been made to him. He spoke with scorn about "these Paradisal promises which people make – they don't materialise." At Minehead, he had referred to Kuttner as a "dreamboat journalist," and it plainly rankled that no contract had ever materialised. He was never offered more than £35,000 and did not sign the contract, although one was drawn up. No, he did not have a copy of the contract.

The judge (to Mr Mathew): "Perhaps you could serve a witness summons on the *Evening News* and make them produce it."

Mr Mathew: "Thank you very much, my lord."

But he did not take advantage of the judge's thoughtful suggestion, perhaps suspecting that the unsigned contract would prove less exciting than Newton's description of the original proposals.

Newton could not recall being introduced on American television as "Andrew Newton, trying to make a buck and apparently doing a pretty good job of it." But he agreed it was a true description.

Mathew: "You have the clearest possible motive to perjure yourself in this case?"

Newton: "Yes, I have."

Mr Mathew referred Newton to a conflict of testimony between himself and Miller about Miller's degree of involvement in the murder conspiracy. At Minehead, Miller had referred to Newton as a habitual liar.

Newton: "That is quite possible."

Mathew: "He called you 'chicken-brain.' "

Newton: "I would go along with that."

Mathew: "He said, 'I am sure Newton can tell fact from fantasy, but he tells lies anyway.' "

No further attempt was made to exploit the spectacle of thieves falling out – possibly because Newton refused to be drawn into attacking Miller.

Mathew: "I will be suggesting to you that so far as Mr Holmes is concerned you were never asked to do anything than put the fear of God into Scott."

Newton denied this.

Mathew: "He told you that the first action he wanted taken was for an offer to be made to get this man Scott to return all the documents he had and to sign a document saying everything he was saying was a pack of lies."

Newton: "Absolutely not."

Newton said it was a good story, but untrue. He had thought it up himself when he first met Scott in the Imperial Hotel, Barnstaple.

Mathew: "You were being asked by Mr Holmes that if that failed, in some way which was left to you, you were to frighten Mr Scott to such an extent that he would finally keep quiet about his allegations."

Newton: "I daresay that if you repeat it often enough someone will believe you, but that is a pack of lies."

Mr Mathew went on to suggest that Newton had suggested killing Scott – "it would be much cleaner" – and Holmes had forbidden him to do anything of the sort. Newton interrupted from time to time with various disavowals. "Absolutely incorrect;" "no chance;" "nice one, but you're absolutely wrong."

But this, it appeared, was to be Holmes's defence: that he had hired Newton to frighten Scott at most, that Newton had suggested killing him but Holmes had explicitly repudiated the idea. If Mr Holmes had decided to give evidence, this is what he would have said, and we would have been given a chance to judge who was lying. However, for some reason at which we are not even allowed to guess, Holmes decided not to give evidence, and the jury decided to disbelieve Newton anyway.

Next, Mr Mathew started pouring scorn on Newton's story of the appointment in the Royal Garden Hotel. Scott had no memory of any such arrangement, said Mr Mathew.

Mathew: "The truth is there was no firm arrangement for Scott to go to the Royal Garden Hotel. You say you were going to beat him to death in a hotel bedroom – that's nonsense, isn't it?"

Newton: "I wish it was."

Mathew: "And the flowers were a little embellishment?"

Newton: "No."

The judge: "But you were going to meet a man. Why was it necessary to have a bunch of flowers?"

Newton explained that he intended to disguise the chisel in the flowers. In case he was stopped by a security guard, he would say he was delivering the flowers.

Newton: "I mean you know that was what 'appened."

Newton was at last beginning to look rattled by this combined onslaught from judge and counsel. He referred to an earlier statement to the police.

Newton: "What I am saying is I lied, of course I lied, as your clients are going to lie."

In this matter, of course, he was wrong. Mr Mathew's client, Holmes, was not going to open his mouth at all, but none of us knew it at this stage.

Mathew: "You know perfectly well that you had bricks to break up, and that one of the reasons you bought the chisel was for the bricks, isn't it?"

The judge (fiercely): "Isn't it? Remember, Mr Newton, there are three answers to any question – 'yes,' 'no,' and 'don't know' – but answer it you must and don't fool about."

Newton: "Yes."

Mathew: "Why didn't you tell us that ten minutes ago?"

Newton: "It is difficult to remember incidents of four years earlier."

Mathew: "It was very convenient, wasn't it? It was an implement you could tell the police, and anyone else who came to pay you money, that was to be used to kill Norman Scott. That is true, isn't it?"

Newton: "No."

The morning's cross-examination ended with a discussion of the plan to kill Scott in the Holiday Inn, Bristol. Newton said that although he had no intention of killing Scott by then, he went to Bristol because this was what Holmes required him to do, and he feared for his safety. This was because of the two attempts to run him over which he had described the day before.

The afternoon started with a fine flurry of drama. Mr Mathew had been given an American police report of the traffic incident when Newton claimed that three attempts were made to run him over by a lorry which jack-knifed. The American police reports were supplied to Mr Mathew by the Director of Public Prosecutions.

Mr Mathew suggested that they showed Newton's account of the incident to be a pack of lies. Newton denied he had even made a statement to the police about the incident and said the police report was invented.

Mathew: "If it was invented, it was apparently invented by the Department of Justice of the FBI."

Newton agreed that he was the man knocked over.

Mathew: "But you're not the pedestrian who made the complaint to the police?"

At this point the judge moved in and accused Newton of laughing.

Newton: "I am not laughing. I'm just frustrated."

Mathew: "Oh no you're not. You're not frustrated, you are a liar, aren't you? You can't laugh this one off."

Most people in court, apart from the main participants were laughing by now, but Mr Mathew seemed determined that he had caught Newton out in a major lie. Newton was suitably indignant. The spectacle of three highly indignant people – witness, counsel and judge – all talking at cross-purposes struck me, at any rate, as very droll. Mr Mathew quoted from the alleged police report, saying that "complainant (ie the pedestrian on-looker) also stated he did not think the driver was aware of striking him (ie Newton) for he was hit with the rear end of the trailer."

Newton stoutly reaffirmed that the driver made three attempts to run him over. His indignation, as Mathew put the American police report to him, was a beautiful sight.

Newton: "I don't know who invented this. Perhaps you had better ask the politicians or something . . . How dandy that is. How nice! . . . The FBI – oh how convenient! You see what they're doing in Cuba and Chile. We have a piece of paper by the FBI. How ridiculous. Oh, take it away."

The judge: "No, we won't take it away. We want to give it an exhibit number."

Mathew: "Are you aware these documents came into the possession of defence counsel after enquiries made by the Director of Public Prosecutions?"

Newton: "Yes."

Mathew: "Are you suggesting the DPP has deliberately invented this in order to demonstrate that you are a perjurer?"

Newton: "I'm just in ignorance of who has concocted it – but I certainly know why. This is an absolute farce."

Mathew: "Talk as long as you like, but there's no way you can get around the fact that you have been proved before this jury to be an unmitigated liar, on oath, in that witness-box. Is that a fact?"

Newton: ". . . One day someone will write his memoirs about this and you'll look back and think 'Oh, perhaps Newton was telling the truth.' I suppose we've got to wait twenty-five years for that."

The most hilarious aspect of this episode was that everyone else – apart from judge, counsel and witness – could see that it was almost entirely irrelevant. Mr Mathew invested it with histrionic solemnity, and the judge always seemed delighted that any Crown witness should be shown a liar; accordingly, Newton over-reacted in his own implausible way. But the worst light this exchange threw on him was to suggest he had exaggerated in the account of his adventures with a lorry in America – at a time when he was plainly both frightened and concussed. Either way, the story had absolutely nothing to do with his evidence against Holmes and the other alleged conspirators – it was as if Mr Mathew had trapped Newton into repeating some childhood lie about seeing dragons. But both Mr Mathew and the judge seemed to see it as a major breakthrough.

Next Mr Mathew asked about the incident on Porlock Moor when, as Newton now claimed, he pretended his gun had jammed. At Exeter he had said he intended to shoot and miss Scott, but the gun had jammed anyway after he had shot the dog. Mr Mathew asked which of the two versions was to be believed, and Newton said the second – he was pretending the gun had jammed.

Both Mr Mathew and the judge seemed in some difficulty here. They were determined that Newton was a villain and was lying when he said he had only pretended the gun had jammed, and convinced that the gun had indeed jammed; but this did not help the defence case much, except to show Newton's general unreliability. If the gun had genuinely jammed, it might have been a genuine murder attempt. This was unhelpful to Mr Mathew, who was briefed that it was a plot to frighten Scott, and unhelpful to the judge, who seemed anxious that men of the defendants' "unblemished reputation" should not be convicted on such disreputable evidence.

The judge: "What were the reasons behind these differing versions?"

Newton: "I invented the story in the cells while I was in Bridgwater. . . I was telling lies left, right and centre to save my own skin."

The judge: "Your second version would have done quite well at Exeter."

Mr Mathew pursued the matter, insisting that Newton was lying and the gun had genuinely jammed. Why had Newton told the man who supplied the gun – Mr Meighan – that it had jammed?"

Newton: "I did not tell Mr Meighan that the gun had jammed."'

Mathew: "An agreed statement will be read later (from Mr Meaghen) saying that you told him the gun had jammed."

Newton: "It was easier to pretend the gun had jammed than explain you were a coward and couldn't go through with it. Here I am a hit man, and not a hair on him was touched."

Mr Mathew said it was not disputed that meetings between Newton and Holmes took place, and it was not disputed that money had passed between them. All that was disputed was the nature of Newton's brief.

Newton: "I am telling you what the brief was, and that was to murder."

There was a mysterious difference of opinion between Newton and Mr Mathew about how much money Holmes had paid Newton between the dog-shooting and the Exeter trial. Newton said it was £300 and £100, denying that it was £300 and £500, as Mr Mathew had apparently been instructed.

Newton also agreed that a letter purporting to be from him in prison to Holmes had, in fact, been forged by Barrie Penrose; that when he visited Holmes in Manchester, it was to collect supporting evidence for his *Evening News* story; that he telephoned Holmes in order to get incriminating evidence by deceit and trickery.

Mathew: "Trickery and deceit have been your trademark throughout this matter haven't they?"

Newton: "Yes."

On that note, Mr Mathew sat down after three and a half hours of cross-examination. *He had succeeded beyond reasonable doubt in demonstrating that Newton was an unreliable witness. All that was required was his client as witness to demonstrate that Newton was not telling the truth. The questions left in my mind were how many hit men, called to give evidence against the people who hired them, would be any more reliable; and, in the absence of more reliable evidence than that, how the hirers of a hit man could ever be convicted?*

Mr Williams's cross-examination
Mr Williams next stood up to start his cross-examination on behalf of Deakin. He revealed a mean, Welsh, insinuating manner from the start, but Newton seemed relieved to be rid of Mr Mathew, and agreed in answer to Mr Williams's question that Deakin was only on

the periphery of the matter and that he had no knowledge of Le Mesurier's involvement.

Newton also agreed that nobody else could confirm his claim that Deakin was asking for a murder, or that he even met Deakin at Aust Fenny – someting Deakin had always denied.

He had not read the book called *The Thorpe Committal*; he had tried *The Pencourt File* but could only manage about a third of it. Mr Williams did not really get into his stride on his first day of cross-examination, and the court adjourned at rather an unfortunate moment for him. He brought up the matter of Newton's balaclava helmet at Minehead.

Williams: "Do you know what a buffoon is, Mr Newton?"

Newton: "Yes, I think so."

Williams: "A buffoon would be someone who lacked moral sense?"

Newton seemed uncertain on this point. I should have thought Mr Williams had got it wrong. This is no part of the definition of a buffoon.

Williams: "Why did you wear that absurd hat at Minehead?"

Newton: "I didn't want to make the press's job any easier."

Williams: "Do you agree that it was the action of a buffoon?"

Newton: "No. One is entitled to wear what one wants. After all, I mean to say, you wear what is on your head."

This reference to his expensive horse-hair wig did not seem to please Mr Williams. The court adjourned for four days, until the following Tuesday.

Day fifteen: 29 May 1979

Newton's cross-examination resumed

Mr Williams opened his second day of cross-examination with questions about a book which Newton was writing and for which he hoped to receive £50,000. Somewhere, Mr Williams had found a copy of its synopsis. It was apparently called *The Autobiography of Andrew Gino Newton*. He read extracts from the synopsis with considerable comic effect.

"It begins with his own graphic account of the shooting . . . switches back to Andrew Newton's life as a well-paid airline pilot living a glamorous bachelor existence . . . The proposal to be a hired killer, fascinating acquaintances, meetings with amazing characters, and plots . . . all leading to the first meeting with Scott.

"His own reactions begin to play an important part as the moment to put the gun to Scott's head draws near . . . weeks in which he was a hunted quarry by the police . . . After the shooting the conspirators tried to murder him . . . his arrest, his trial and the beginning of the cover-up. His efforts to protect names of leading politicians . . . highly placed people in another attempt on his life . . . There will be evidence for the first time of a police conspiracy or a Mafia-type 'code of silence.' "

Williams: "Are you saying there is a police conspiracy, a cover-up like the Mafia, or were you saying it then?"

Newton: "I am not saying it now. I had my suspicions at the time. We are all marionettes, you know. At that time I was certainly suspicious."

Newton explained the hyperbole of this synopsis by the fact that he had not seen it before, but insisted that at least one attempt on his life had been made. He seemed to have forgotten the American episode over the Bank Holiday weekend, but repeated that two men in a red Mini had nearly run him over in Bath Road, Chiswick, while he was awaiting trial. These were presumably the "highly placed people."

Williams: "The opportunity of making cash from your story will be limited if all or some of the accused on trial are acquitted."

Newton: "I realise that is a possibility."

The judge: "It would be a different book, wouldn't it, unless you lost all your money in damages for libel?"

Newton: "I think my lord is correct."

Watching Mr Justice Cantley chuckling and nodding to himself after this interruption, one began to receive the impression that if his lordship had any say in the matter there would be considerable difficulty over the publication of The Autobiography of Andrew Gino Newton.

Newton denied that his need for cash was pressing, but agreed that he was living on the dole. He said he would consider offers from newspapers. If anyone came along and wanted to make an offer, he would listen.

Newton: "I cannot say that someone with money could not influence me, but what other alternative have I?"

Next Mr Williams took him through the Showman's Dinner at Blackpool on the night of 26 February 1975 when, by his account, the murder proposal was first mentioned. A puritanical hiss began to appear in Mr Williams's musical Welsh lilt when the excesses of the evening were mentioned. Sodom and Gomorrah had had nothing on Blackpool that night.

Newton agreed that there had been topless women present.

Williams: "You were placing meringues on strategic places of these half-naked women?"

Newton: "I do not recall that."

Newton could remember nothing of a fight with the boy-friend of one of these half-naked women, nor of being taken home dead drunk by Deakin.

Newton: "I think you would probably agree it is a different world after sixteen pints."

But he vividly remembered his earlier conversation with Deakin, when Miller had been present. There was a table of Welshmen nearby.

Williams: "Did they enter into the conversation?"

Newton: "I put it to you, if you proposition someone to murder you don't actually announce it on the tannoy."

He stuck to his story that he had approached Deakin with the words, "I understand you want someone bumped off, I am your man." Mr Williams suggested a different exchange – that Miller had walked up and said, "Andrew's the boy for that trouble of yours," and Deakin had replied, "It's not my bloody problem." Newton denied this version. He said he was interested in whether it was a man, a woman or a child to be killed, but agreed he did not ask the identity of the person involved from Deakin.

Williams: "I suggest the conversation about killing someone never happened."

Newton: "I expect you to say that, but it did."

Newton said the first time cash was discussed between himself and Deakin was during the meeting at Aust Service Station. Asked whether it had been discussed at the earlier meeting at Miller's premises in Cardiff, he said he could not remember.

Williams: "You could remember, or purport to remember, last Friday."

Newton: "'ell, I'm sorry, but I'm wrong then."

It was plain by this stage that Newton's memory was not of the best.

Williams: "You are just making it up as you go along, aren't you?"

Newton: "No, I'm not."

The judge moved in to point out a discrepancy in Newton's account of Deakin's answer to his question about whether there had been a consortium involved.

The judge: "Was the correct answer 'Yes' or 'No'?"

Newton: "I have decided to say 'Yes.' "

Williams: "Why did you ask if it was a consortium involved?"

Newton: "Because it sounded the sort of question a professional 'it man would ask."

Mr Williams was anxious to emphasise that his client's only role had been to pass Newton to Holmes as a man prepared to frighten Scott out of blackmailing Holmes's unnamed friend.

Williams: "Where was the money to be paid?"

Newton: "Presumably at some location on completion."

Williams: "I challenge that you even met Mr Deakin in Aust Service Station on any occasion."

Newton: "Well I did."

Next Mr Williams took him through the famous names and prominent people said to be involved.

Williams: "I want you to look at this piece of paper. Without mentioning any names."

It was the dreaded pink piece of paper. Within moments Mr Carman was on his feet asking for the jury to withdraw while he discussed the terrible risk that a certain name would accidentally be mentioned. The jury obediently filed out.

Most people in court were growing rather tired of these endless manoeuvres to prevent the name – possibly of Lord Snowdon – being mentioned in any context whatever, particularly as most of us knew perfectly well that nothing remotely incriminating or disreputable was alleged about him. But Mr Carman seemed to accept it as a badge of his client's honour that this name should not be mentioned – as if Thorpe, in some heroic posture or other, would sooner go to the firing squad than let the name of a (former) member of the Royal Family be impugned – and the judge seemed to respond to this. He made a few more hurtful remarks about the press to the effect that if the King of Siam were mentioned, in no matter how innocent a context, his name would be splashed all over the newspapers next day. I played with the idea of running a spoof headline in Private Eye, *"Thorpe Trial Judge Names King of Siam Shock Horror Sensation", but dismissed the plan. It was from this moment that I began to watch Mr Justice Cantley rather more closely. What had seemed a healthy scepticism, at the beginning of the trial, now began to seem alarmingly one-sided.*

Mr Williams promised to introduce no names, and Mr Taylor reassured the court yet again that he did not have the slightest intention of introducing the name. *Harold Wilson, Lady Falkender, Reginald Maudling, Lord Goodman could be dragged through the mud, one understood, but not this mysterious person.* The judge piously remarked that he could not rule out evidence just because he did not like the smell of the story. But it was plain that he intended to keep the cross-examination on a very tight rein.

Mr Williams denied Newton's story of a telephone call to Deakin from Heathrow Airport, when Newton was on his way to the Far East after shooting Rinka.

Williams: "I am suggesting that Deakin's only involvement was to put you in touch with Holmes on an agreement to frighten, and that other than that Deakin had no part in this matter at all. That is right, is it not?"

Newton: "No, it is not."

From the line taken by Mr Williams, it was reasonable to conclude that Deakin, as well as Holmes, would have pleaded guilty if the charge had merely been conspiracy to frighten.

Something of the nature of Newton's present relations with Miller could similarly be deduced from Newton's answer to a later question.

Newton: "Well, it surprises me that there are not five defendants in that box."

Mr Cowley's cross-examination

Cowley: "Mr Newton, in evidence last week you said these words, if I may remind you, you said, 'I am not saying that Le Mesurier was privy to a conspiracy against Scott.' "

Newton: "Yes I did."

Cowley: "I am going to spend the next quarter of an hour showing that that was a truthful and accurate observation."

Newton: "Thank you very much, sir."

Newton agreed he had never met nor heard of Le Mesurier until he met him fourteen months after the dog-shooting, when he received £5,000. Thereafter, the dialogue between Mr Cowley and Newton was largely made up of denials. Newton denied he had discussed the cover-up, and important people involved in it, with Le Mesurier. He denied he had mentioned Harold Wilson, Jeremy Thorpe, David Holmes, Peter Bessell, Lord Goodman, MI5. He denied that he had told Le Mesurier at any stage that the prosecution was not allowing him to tell the whole story.

The morning's proceedings ended on this note of denial. Newton was in a denying mood.

Newton: "I was not saying anything of the kind, let's put the record straight."

In the afternoon, Newton agreed that on taped conversations between them, Le Mesurier had described himself as an innocent bystander in the case. Mr Cowley also seemed to favour the idea that there had been a conspiracy to frighten.

Mr Taylor's re-examination

Re-examining, Mr Taylor returned to the question which Newton now admitted having asked the *Evening News*: "Supposing I was only sent money to put the frighteners on him, how would that sound?" Why, Mr Taylor asked, had Newton put that question?

Those of us who had been attending closely already knew the answer – because Newton did not, at that stage, have immunity from prosecution and was nervous of letting himself in for a life sentence. But Newton was tired and confused and had forgotten the reason. Mr Taylor had to put the question three times, while Newton mumbled about how he was hoping to confuse the *Evening News*. The judge eventually put a stop to this repetition and put the same question himself.

The reason he had introduced the suggestion of a conspiracy to frighten when the conspiracy had, in fact, been to murder, said Newton, was to confuse the *Evening News* for this reason:

Newton: "I didn't want to admit a conspiracy to murder because you wind up going in prison for life, that's why. If I was to admit a lesser charge of just frightening, then I wouldn't go to prison for life."

But his poor chicken-brain could not recall the vital word "immunity." Without further ado, Newton was dismissed.

After Newton's retirement, we heard the deposition of Dennis Meighan, who lent Newton the pistol. When Meighan asked what he wanted it for, Newton replied that it was to frighten a blackmailer. Later Newton telephoned to complain that the gun had jammed.

Mr Peter Prescott, a firearms expert from the Home Office forensic science laboratory, said he had tested the pistol, and it was prone to jam. It had jammed four times when he tested it.

Photographs of the pay-out, taken at the instance of Miller, were now exhibited. Presumably these were taken by the lady hanging out of the car and who had alarmed them so much. The court adjourned until the next day.

8

Miller's Tale

Day sixteen: 30 May 1979

David Miller, the Cardiff screen printer, was not such a flamboyant witness as his former friend, Newton. He had great difficulty in speaking up. The judge advised him that he was entitled to refuse to answer any questions which he felt might incriminate him. Unlike Newton and Mr Bessell, Miller had no formal immunity from prosecution although, on Newton's evidence, he was plainly a conspirator. This was his story:

Miller was a business associate of Deakin and old friend of Newton, having been at the Chiswick Polytechnic with him. Some time in 1974, Deakin asked Miller if he knew anybody who would frighten somebody for money. He replied that he knew somebody "who would do anything for a laugh and a giggle."

At the Showman's Dinner, in Blackpool, he introduced Newton to Deakin accordingly, and left them together. There was a great deal of drink at the dinner, with everyone being given a bottle of spirits – brandy or whisky. Newton became so drunk that Miller took him back to his flat, where Newton vomited. No more was said about the meeting with Deakin. This was 26 February 1975. *Earlier we had heard that Deakin performed this act of charity, but nobody chose to make anything of the discrepancy.*

Miller returned to his business premises after midnight on the night of 24 October 1975 – the night of the dog-shooting – and found Newton there. He had a pistol which was jammed. Miller helped him clear it, and Newton fired a bullet into the wall. Next morning, Miller lent him some rags to clean up the back seat and floor of his car, which were covered in blood.

Afterwards, Miller went on holiday with Newton and Newton's girl-friend, Eleanor Rooney. At the airport, Miller heard Newton telephone Deakin, saying everything had gone wrong and he had ended up shooting the dog. He came back from abroad with Newton on 18 November 1975 and the police were waiting for them.

Towards the end of Newton's prison sentence, he was telephoned by Deakin who said a gentleman wanted to see him to authenticate Newton's handwriting on a letter addressed to Holmes. This was Barrie Penrose's forgery, and it was Le Mesurier who brought it round.

He taped the conversations he had with Le Mesurier, which were played to the court. Le Mesurier said that arrangements made with Newton still stood. They did not want any trouble with the press. This is what Le Mesurier said to him:

"We want Andrew to know that 'cause if the press get hold of him and he starts blabbering . . . the geezer involved in this is Lord Goodman, defending solicitor.

"These writers already have had letters from Lord Goodman threatening them if they mention Holmes's name, they'll be sued for libel, criminal libel, fucking slander, not from some little solicitor tucked away in . . . this'll be Lord Goodman's office, so they ain't playing with the boys.

"You know they've got the money, the real money to go up, so if these two geezers who reckon they're going to write this book start any nonsense with Holmes in it, he'll hit on to three things, like Goldsmith just did, you know *Private Eye*, fucking closed *Private Eye* as you probably know. Well, the same thing applies here . . ."

Miller told Le Mesurier that he would get a message to Newton in prison that the deal would be honoured, and Newton would receive his money. He assured Le Mesurier that Newton would keep quiet about it – "he loves money, Andrew, that's his problem" – since he would not want to go back to prison for attempted murder. Le Mesurier said he had already been convicted of that, and Miller replied, "No he hasn't. He's been done for endangering life. He can be charged again. That's why they done him for endangering life."

After Newton was released from prison in April 1977, Miller was not happy about taking him to the pay-off meeting as he was concerned for his own safety, but he was to be paid £100 for doing so – the money to be paid by overcharging £100 on a printing order. To protect himself, he arranged for Dabs detective agency, of Cardiff, to record the meeting.

He collected Newton from the meeting and drove him to Cardiff Central station. On the way, Newton counted the money in his van. He met Le Mesurier again, who said that he was alarmed about the photographs taken at the pay-off meeting, in case *Private Eye* or a newspaper was involved.

Miller spoke to Deakin in October 1977 and said he had some

bad news. Articles had appeared in the London evening newspapers after a statement by Newton. Although Deakin's name was not mentioned yet, Miller said that Newton was going to name everyone. His motive was money. Deakin said he was going to deny everything except that as far as he was concerned they just wanted somebody to frighten somebody.

Miller told Deakin the newspapers were saying that the police intended to reopen enquiries, but suggested a lot of it was rubbish. Newton's account of the night on the moors was untrue, he said, because Newton hadn't admitted that he pointed the gun at Scott's head and it stuck. Deakin said: "I say, look, I knew very little about it, you know. They just wanted somebody to frighten somebody and I said it quite jokingly in a place in Blackpool . . . What went on afterwards I don't know because that's all I ever did and that was the end of it."

At the end of this conversation, Miller said that if it all came out the police would really go into it.

Deakin replied: "There's such a lot of high powers at the moment trying to hush it up still."

Miller answered: "Well, hopefully, yeah."

Cross-examined by Mr Mathew, for Holmes, Miller said he had never had any contact with Holmes in the matter.

It was not a difficult task for Mr Williams, in cross-examination, to cast doubt on the evidence of both Newton and Miller. Although Miller never took advantage of the judge's invitation to refuse to answer any question whose answer might tend to incriminate him, awareness that he had no immunity from prosecution seemed to have an unfortunate effect on his memory. When in doubt, he said he could not remember. Moreover, the fact that Newton's evidence might have tended to incriminate him rather jaundiced his attitude to the former pilot. Mr Taylor's task cannot have been made easier by having two of his witnesses at each other's throats, and Mr Williams moved in to take advantage.

Once again, Miller agreed that he had described Newton as an "habitual liar" and "chicken-brain." Asked to amplify this, he agreed that Newton would sometimes tell a story which had a grain of truth inflated to make it more exciting. It was a lie when Newton said he had been promised £15,000 for the job.

Mr Williams then took him through a police statement which Miller made before Newton's trial in March 1976. From what Mr Williams read of the statement, it seemed to support Newton's story – concocted for the benefit of the Exeter court – that he was being blackmailed by Scott. Miller agreed that his statement was untrue, and that it was a serious business to make a false police statement.

The statement said that Newton and Miller were both in the habit of answering advertisements in "contact" magazines promising sexual entertainment. As a result, they visited addresses throughout the country, sometimes together, sometimes separately. Miller had desisted from this practice several years earlier, but he knew Newton persisted in it. It was at this point that Miller's evidence started to wobble.

Williams: "Did you know at the time you made this statement that Mr Newton's defence was to be that of blackmail by Mr Scott arising from these advertisements?"

Miller: "No I did not . . . I only went to one party with Newton after an advertisement in one of those magazines."

The judge: "So there was therefore some truth in that part of the statement."

This admission may have been particularly interesting for journalists and lawyers following the case when, a few minutes later, Miller was listing the sums of money he received. He included the sum of £350 which he had received from the Daily Mirror *after successfully suing them for libel in a story about his attendance at wife-swapping parties – "which was not true," said Miller.*

Williams: "Had you been to a wife-swapping party?"

Miller: "I went to one party with Newton."

Williams: "Was it a party of that sort?"

Miller: "Yes."

Foreign journalists in court were puzzled by this. They were not familiar with the ancient British practice whereby the libel laws are slanted in such a way as to offer a secondary, tax-free income in most cases to any crook, coward, incompetent or voluptuary who manages to have his activities described in print outside the limited protection given to court reporting.

The judge: "Is *Contact* magazine a respectable publication? I don't know. I get the impression that there is something wrong with it."

Williams: "The reference to 'contact' magazines means a number of magazines. They are for people who wish to contact other people about sexual deviation."

Miller: "I would not put it like that. I would put it as a friendship club . . . a lonely hearts club."

Williams: "I suggest they are nothing like lonely hearts clubs. Why did you make such false statements?"

Miller: "I did not want to say anything about the shot dog incident. I did not want to put myself in trouble or any danger."

The judge: "Did you think that if the police were wondering if you were involved in the dog incident, they might be put off the scent by being told you were visiting 'lonely hearts' in various parts of the country?"

Miller: "Yes, my lord."

The judge had a pretty wit, but Miller was too easy game. He was as stupid as Newton, without any of Newton's panache, and unlike Newton, he was plainly frightened. He would probably have agreed to anything the judge put to him in a kindly or reasonable tone of voice, and was too stupid to realise the judge was laughing at him.

Miller agreed with Mr Williams that Newton had told him he was being blackmailed over some modelling photographs for male magazines. This may have corrected an earlier wobble in his evidence about his reasons for making the false police statement, but it did not seem important. He said his expenses in Exeter for Newton's trial had been paid by the *Daily Mirror*.

He had taped telephone calls with Newton and later learned that Newton was taping telephone calls with him. He had received £8,000 for his story from the *Sunday People* and smaller sums from other newspapers and television companies.

Williams: "At Minehead committal proceedings, did you say you had instructed solicitors to offer the money to a blind school?"

Miller: "Yes, but I have since kept the money."

Miller said he regarded the money, which was about double his business profit for 1975, as compensation for time off work, loss of business and being pestered by the press. The trial adjourned after Miller had promised to produce his *Sunday People* contract next day.

Day seventeen: 31 May 1979
Miller's cross-examination continued
The last stage of Mr Williams's cross-examination concentrated on Miller's reasons for making tapes, taking photographs and trying to get other people to incriminate themselves. Mr Williams maintained the reason was money, Miller that it was self-protection; as soon as his story had been published in the *Sunday People*, he felt safer.

Mr Cowley, for Le Mesurier, covered the same ground.

Cowley: "In the whole of these tapes you were putting false

matters in order to try to persuade Mr Le Mesurier either to incriminate himself or incriminate some other person?"

Miller: "That is correct."

Miller rejected Mr Cowley's suggestion that Le Mesurier had been no more than a contact man.

Minor witnesses and depositions

Mr Terence Gibbs won a large sum from Vernons Football Pools in May 1975. Vernons introduced him to Holmes as a financial adviser. On Holmes's advice, he invested £10,000 in Le Mesurier's carpet shop, later becoming a partner. He said it was quite evident to him that Holmes and Le Mesurier knew each other well. In November 1977 Le Mesurier told him he was worried about his involvement in the Newton affair and thought he would have to go to prison, although he said the stories were not true.

Mr Colin Lambert, a carpet salesman, was a former employee of Le Mesurier. Holmes was business consultant and adviser to the company. In 1977, after press publicity, he asked Le Mesurier whether he had paid Newton the £5,000. Le Mesurier replied, "Yes, I did," and added that Holmes thought they were going to prison.

On another occasion, Le Mesurier had said something to the effect that, "we should have hired someone like you, because the chap who went to do the shooting was an idiot." He did not elaborate whom he meant by "we." Mr Lambert explained the "someone like you" by pointing out that he had been a regular soldier in the infantry for nearly seventeen years – something which Le Mesurier knew well.

In cross-examination, Mr Cowley suggested that he had been sacked by Le Mesurier for claiming more commission on carpet sales than he was entitled to. Mr Lambert denied this hotly, and turned to the judge for protection.

Lambert: "I am being accused of being a crook here."

The judge: "It is the defence counsel's job to put questions of that sort. It is not very nice."

After conferring with the judge, Mr Cowley put no further questions.

9

First Tale of Mr Jeremy Thorpe

The next witness was Chief Superintendent Proven Sharpe, of the Devon and Cornwall Constabulary, the man who had conducted the first enquiry into Scott's allegations after the dog-shooting incident. He had been requested to hold an enquiry by the Director of Public Prosecutions early in 1976, and interviewed Thorpe at his Devon home on 8 February 1976. Among other Crown witnesses, Mr Bessell had already expressed the opinion that Mr Sharpe's enquiry was not pursued with much vigour.

Mr Sharpe's brief at that time had been to pursue three lines of enquiry: to find out whether there was any evidence to connect Newton with Thorpe or his associates; to investigate the circumstances under which the sum of £2,500 had been paid to Norman Scott; and to see if there was any evidence to support Newton's allegations of blackmail against Scott.

Thorpe agreed to make a statement which Mr Macreery wrote down. On hearing it read back to him, Thorpe had many corrections and alterations to make. This was the final draft of the statement which Thorpe signed next day:

I am the Member of Parliament for the North Devon constituency. I am in the process of drafting a comprehensive statement relating to my knowledge of Mr Norman Josiffe, otherwise known as Norman Scott, which, subject to the advice of my legal advisers, I would have no objection to supplying to those investigating this case. At this stage I have been interviewed on three specific points.

First, Mr Michael Barnes, solicitor, of The Square, Barnstaple. Mr Barnes has acted for me on a variety of business matters connected with my affairs in North Devon, in particular the purchase of my present house, the negotiation of a mortgage, the purchase of land belonging to my neighbours, and a number of other matters.

With regard to the Scott affair, to the best of my knowledge and belief, the only instruction which I gave to Mr Barnes was to warn my then Conservative opponent, Mr Keigwin, in either the 1970 or 1974 elections, that were the Scott matter to be raised, I would unquestionably issue a writ for defamation.

Apart from this, I have no recollection of giving Mr Barnes any further instructions on any matter relating to this. I have been asked whether I would object to Mr Barnes disclosing information which came to him in the course of his professional activities which could in any way be construed to affect or involve myself and Scott.

While this is obviously a matter for him to determine, speaking for myself I would have no conceivable objection.

Secondly, I have been asked for information I can produce relating to the alleged payment of £2,500 in respect of certain letters and/or documents.

Of this particular transaction I have no knowledge whatsoever. However, I do believe that Dr Gleadle made contact with Mr (now Lord) Banks around December 1973, or January 1974, indicating he, Dr Gleadle, was in possession of documents, which could be embarrassing for the Liberal Party and which the Liberal Party might wish to possess.

Lord Banks consulted Lord Wade. Lord Wade, at my suggestion, consulted the Liberal leader in the Lords, Lord Byers, who closely questioned Lord Banks as to whether Gleadle's suggestion was that either the documents be handed over, or bought.

On this point Lord Banks was uncertain. At a later date, which can be confirmed by consulting my office engagements diary, I was visited by the Rector of North Molton, who asked me whether I knew of a Norman Scott who was making serious allegations against me.

He alluded to the fact that there existed correspondence which could prove embarrassing either to me, Mr Peter Bessell, the Liberal Party, or all three. He also suggested that the Liberal Party might like to "set up" this young man financially and indicated that he felt that Scott's over-riding purpose was to destroy me.

He mentioned that he and Dr Gleadle, both of whom had been treating Scott over a period of time, were anxious to form a trust to set him up in some form of business, such as a riding establishment.

I concede that this conversation could be construed as a

veiled attempt at blackmail but knowing that Pennington's (the rector's) motive was to try to help Scott, to whom he administered both as a priest and as a member of the Samaritans, I did not so interpret it, although I robustly rejected the suggestion that I or any of my colleagues should be involved in these "good works."

I replied that I was certain that neither the Liberal Party nor myself nor Mr Bessell would have any interest in so assisting. I also indicated that I should be surprised if the documents to which he alluded differed materially from those which my colleagues had examined in 1971, to which I had immediate access to photostat and further photostats of which I believed were already in the possession of certain newspapers, none of which occasioned me concern.

I have not spoken to the vicar since. I should add that I have never seen Dr Gleadle, never corresponded with him, never spoken to him on the telephone nor had any communication with him, direct or indirect.

The third and final point relates to the reported incident of the dog on Exmoor on 24 October 1975. I have never met the accused, Mr Newton, I have never seen him, direct or indirect. In respect of this incident I again know no more than I have read in the press.

Mr Sharpe explained that he had never received the comprehensive statement promised. When he telephoned Thorpe to ask about it, Thorpe said that his legal adviser, Lord Goodman, was ill.

In reply to Mr Carman's cross-examination, Mr Sharpe agreed that Thorpe had volunteered this statement without his solicitor being present.

Mr Carman now moved into a very dangerous area. His instructions were that Thorpe had expressly asked the then Metropolitan Police Commissioner, Sir John Waldron, and the Home Secretary, Mr Reginald Maudling, to investigate Scott's allegations. Mr Sharpe replied that he knew nothing about that.

Carman (sarcastically): "Is it within police capacity to find out if what Mr Thorpe was saying is accurate?"

Sharpe: "I am sure it can be done. If you wish, I will see that it is done."

Finally, Mr Sharpe agreed that Thorpe had been polite, helpful and willing to provide a statement. *But it was Mr Carman's insistence that Thorpe had asked the Police Commissioner and Home Secretary to investigate Scott's charges which was to prove Mr*

Carman's greatest humiliation. Later, he was to have to withdraw the suggestion. Thorpe had made no such request. Yet Thorpe's solicitors had plainly briefed him in the strongest terms that the request had been made. It was a curious episode. Perhaps Thorpe had succeeded in convincing himself that this was the case. Perhaps it was simply a gamble that did not pay off. As Thorpe declined to give evidence, we shall probably never know.

This was not revealed until Chief Superintendent Challes gave evidence, five days later. While it might seem to upset the continuity of the trial narrative to anticipate his evidence, I suspect that it had already been upset by the speed of the trial. It seems probable that Mr Taylor intended to call the police witnesses all together, as he did at Minehead, but the pace of events meant that Mr Jack Hayward, the Bahamas-based millionaire, was not available. Mr Sharpe may have been speaking out of turn, but the five-day interlude gave Chief Superintendent Challes all the time he needed to make the fullest possible investigation into Thorpe's claims – something that happens all too rarely when the defence springs something on the Crown.

Finally, Chief Inspector Brian MacCreery, also of the Devon and Cornwall Constabulary, gave evidence of having been present at an interview between Holmes and Mr Sharpe at the Reform Club. *Most of the press had left the court by this stage, regarding MacCreery as a very minor witness – he was examined by Mr Bull, rather than by Mr Taylor. But this was the first I had ever heard of an interview between Holmes and the police at which Holmes had said anything much besides "No comment." The date of this interview was not given, but presumably it was in early 1976. It would be interesting to know whether it came before or after Holmes's admission to the press on 5 March 1976 that he had paid £2,500 to Scott for the Bessell letters.*

At this interview, Holmes agreed he was a personal friend of Thorpe but said he had never met Norman Scott. He said he had no connection, directly or indirectly with Newton. He described the circumstances of his arranging for Dr Gleadle to buy the letters from Scott for £2,500, suggested that the money was a personal payment and said that he had not discussed it with Thorpe. On this occasion, Holmes averred that he was concerned for the safety of Thorpe's son, Rupert, to whom he was godfather. He said he took the letters to Barnes, Thorpe's solicitor, and they burned them – "a most expensive bonfire."

Since the witnesses were running ahead of time, the trial was adjourned until the following Monday, 4 June.

10

Two Nice Respectable Witnesses

Hayward and Dinshaw
Day eighteen: 4 June 1979
Mr Jack Arnold Hayward was a fairly well-known figure in Britain before he took his stand in the witness-box. A millionaire based in the Bahamas, his extreme patriotism had earned him the nick-name "Union Jack" Hayward. The large engineering fortune he inherited from his father, Sir Charles Hayward, had been much increased by development in Freeport, Bahamas. At one time he had been involved in complicated negotiations with Bessell, Thorpe and others to sell his interest in Freeport, but the details of these negotiations did not come out in court. They are set out in the excellent book, *Jeremy Thorpe, A Secret Life*, by three *Sunday Times* journalists, Lewis Chester, Magnus Linklater and David May. No attempt was made in court to impugn Mr Hayward's reputation as a straightforward philanthropist.

This is the story Mr Hayward told:

In 1969, Thorpe was among three West Country MPs sponsoring an appeal to save Lundy Island in the Bristol Channel from development by foreign buyers. Mr Hayward interested himself in the appeal, and eventually bought the island for the nation, paying £150,000. He became friendly with Thorpe, and next year made a gift of £150,000 to the Liberal Party, although not a Liberal himself. In a letter accompanying the cheque, he spoke of their "joint ambition to see you as Prime Minister in five years' time."

In April 1974, he received a letter from Thorpe thanking him for a further present of £50,000 and asking him for yet another gift of the same sum, to be paid in two separate cheques. One for £10,000 was to go to Mr Nadir Dinshaw, in Jersey, who would use it to settle additional election expenses incurred by Thorpe personally during the February 1974 election. Mr Dinshaw, he said, was godfather to his son, Rupert.

Accordingly, Mr Hayward did so. Sprinkled throughout the

correspondence at this time are references to Mr Bessell's dealings with Hayward – he had failed to repay various loans – couched in terms of the greatest revulsion, such as "that bastard Bessell."

On 5 March 1975, Thorpe wrote again asking for a further £10,000 to be paid to Mr Dinshaw. His explanation was that the requirements of the Representation of the People Act made this advisable. Once again, Thorpe volunteered the information that Mr Dinshaw was Rupert's godfather.

Mr Hayward agreed to do so, but took a little time over it. Several nudging letters were received from Thorpe. On 13 September 1975, Thorpe wrote:

> When you can manage the second tranche this would be very welcome. On the strength of your generous promise my Jersey friend has actually advanced the sum to pay off the outstanding election expenses and therefore the payment to the accountant will go straight to him. He's not rushed, but it would be a great thing for me if I could feel that all outstanding election expenses were settled and debts cleared.

On 4 April 1978 he met Thorpe at Thorpe's request, and Thorpe suggested he should put pressure on Mr Bessell by threatening him that if he came to England, Mr Hayward would serve a writ for bankruptcy on him. Thorpe had a theory that if he was made bankrupt, Bessell would not be able to re-enter the United States, where he had a fiancée. Mr Hayward declined to do this.

On 20 April 1978, Mr Hayward wrote to Thorpe:

> I am the last one to shirk a fight or desert my friends, but I do like to know who I am fighting, what it is all about and who my friends are. I am rapidly getting the impression that my friends have not told me the truth and it is also becoming apparent to me that I am being set up as a fall guy and a sucker of the first degree.
>
> All I have done (and God! how I regret it!) was to help the Liberal Party and various Liberals, despite the fact that I am not a member of the party and never was and disagree intensely with a lot of their policies.
>
> I feel a number of innocent people, including myself, have been or are being implicated in these Liberal machinations and I think it is time it stopped and the principals involved came clean.

On 4 May 1978 Mr Hayward wrote again, saying he had received a visit from Detective Chief Superintendent Michael Challes. Mr Challes was asking about these two payments of £10,000. He had forgotten all about them, except that he had loaned them to Thorpe personally during 1974. "Who on earth is Dinshaw?" he asked.

On 14 August Mr Hayward wrote again, complaining that through no fault of his own he had been dragged into the Norman Scott case – "and I do not like it one bit. I have always been proud of my good name and integrity." He asked Thorpe how the two sums of £10,000 were spent, and repeated the question in another letter of 31 August 1978 (after Thorpe had been arrested) asking Thorpe to treat the matter as urgent, but had never received an answer and still did not know how the money was spent. In a telephone conversation when he asked what was happening, Thorpe replied "presumably Dinshaw had panicked," but Mr Hayward never knew what he meant by this.

Mr Hayward cross-examined
If Mr Hayward looked worried when Mr Carman rose to cross-examine, the first question seemed to put him at his ease. His manner when speaking about Thorpe in answer to Mr Taylor's questions had been puzzled and a little resentful. After Mr Carman's first question, it became noticeably warmer.

Carman: "So many names have been bandied about this court I want to make it perfectly clear on behalf of Mr Thorpe that there is no suggestion you have been guilty of any kind of financial or commercial impropriety."

Hayward: "Thank you very much, and thank Mr Thorpe."

Mr Hayward said he had formed a very high opinion of Thorpe over the Lundy Island negotiations, and regarded him as a politician of dedication and enthusiasm.

Later he met Mr Bessell, to whom he had lent £25,000 which had not been repaid. He had also guaranteed a £10,000 overdraft, and the guarantee was called in.

In May 1976 he had found himself pestered by press and television who were trying to discover if he was involved in the Scott affair. He had referred to the two sums of £10,000 as loans, but he remembered later that they had been gifts towards Thorpe's election expenses. He repeated that he had never received any explanation of how this money had been spent – from Thorpe, from his solicitors or in any other way.

Mr Nadir Dinshaw
The next witness, Mr Nadir Dinshaw, was called.

Mr Dinshaw, a Karachi-born businessman, based in Jersey, first met Thorpe on a London Airport bus in 1969, and shortly afterwards was asked to be godfather to Thorpe's son, Rupert. He had been a British national for twenty years and spoke beautiful, educated English. Nobody could doubt that he was a very respectable witness indeed. This is the story he had to tell:

Shortly after the February 1974 election, Thorpe telephoned him and said: "Jack Hayward wants to give me £10,000 for my election expenses – will you take it and hand it over to David Holmes?" Mr Dinshaw agreed to do so provided there was no publicity, which he did not like. He had met Holmes at the Memorial Service for Caroline Thorpe in July 1970. After he had done so, Thorpe telephoned him again and asked if he would do the same with another £10,000 from Mr Hayward, and asked him to keep it confidential. This time Mr Dinshaw felt uneasy, and told Holmes that he was displeased, but Holmes assured him there was no question of publicity. Holmes asked for payment in cash this time, so Mr Dinshaw paid it in small parcels of about £600 a time. He made the payments personally except once, on the last occasion, when he made it through his lawyer. There was some delay about receiving the money from Mr Hayward.

Then in March 1976 Mr Dinshaw and his wife were watching television and learned that Holmes had paid £2,500 to Norman Scott for some letters. When he tackled Holmes on the matter, Holmes denied that there was any connection between the payments.

Shortly after Thorpe's press conference of 27 October 1977, in which he again publicly denied allegations of a homosexual liaison with Scott, Mr Dinshaw had lunch with Thorpe at Boulestin's restaurant in Covent Garden. Thorpe said to him: "That money of Jack Hayward's – what did you do with it?"

"I gave it to David Holmes, of course," said Mr Dinshaw.

"Why?" said Thorpe.

"Because you told me to," said Mr Dinshaw.

Thorpe said, "You could say you'd given it him yourself."

Mr Dinshaw said, "How can I say I've given it him myself – I haven't given it him. My accounts will show it in any case."

Thorpe said, "They won't look into your accounts."

Mr Dinshaw assumed that "they" were the police, and said, "Of course they can, they can look into anybody's account."

Thorpe said, "Only in criminal matters."

"This is a criminal matter," said Mr Dinshaw.

"You could say you received it from Jack Hayward as part of a business deal," said Thorpe.

Mr Dinshaw asked how on earth he could say a thing like that when he had had no business dealings with Mr Hayward and would not recognise him if he walked into the room, although he thought he might have met Mr Hayward at the Caroline Thorpe Memorial Service. Thorpe was distressed by his refusal and Mr Dinshaw felt very sorry for him.

Thorpe said it was very awkward for him as Holmes had asked for some of the money and had been allowed to keep £5,000. Mr Dinshaw told him that he must tell the truth, becase Mr Dinshaw was certain Thorpe was not involved in any kind of criminal conspiracy.

In the course of a long conversation which was painful for both of them, Thorpe suggested it could be very awkward for Mr Dinshaw if he had to explain in court why he had paid the money in cash, particularly with his dislike of publicity. Mr Dinshaw replied it would be something he would simply have to bear.

On 18 April 1978 Thorpe took him for a drive in St James's Park. By now, Mr Dinshaw assumed that the police would be coming to see him, and told Thorpe that he intended to tell them the truth. Thorpe replied that if only he could find £20,000 he could say it was the Hayward money.

Mr Dinshaw said, "Don't be absurd. I gave the money to David Holmes in 1974 and 1975. How can you now say this is that money?"

Thorpe said it would be very awkward – not because he was involved in any conspiracy, which he wasn't, but because of his political career. He was not worried about any conspiracy. He did not know what had happened to the £20,000. Mr Dinshaw said, "None of it?" Thorpe said, "No."

Mr Dinshaw urged him to see his lawyer and tell him the truth. Thorpe said he quite appreciated Mr Dinshaw's position that he must tell the truth, but there was no need for Mr Dinshaw to say more than was necessary – "it will be curtains for me and you will be asked to move on."

Mr Dinshaw considered this a stupid and crude remark. He could not take it seriously, but found it hurtful. He was sorry for Thorpe that he should be frightened enough to make such a remark, but also irritated that Thorpe should think him stupid enough to be influenced by it. By "moving on" Thorpe had meant he would be asked to leave Britain. It was a ludicrous conversation which made Mr Dinshaw "very, very sad, both for myself and for him."

Mr Dinshaw cross-examined
Under cross-examination by Mr Mathew, Mr Dinshaw agreed that

Holmes had paid £2,500 for the letters in February 1974, some time before the arrival of Mr Hayward's first £10,000. He had not understood that the payments to Holmes were a loan, but they might have been.

Mr Carman once again started his cross-examination with an encomium.

Carman: "May I make it absolutely plain publicly on behalf of Mr Thorpe that there is no suggestion of any kind of impropriety by you?"

Mr Dinshaw promptly agreed with counsel that he had always found Thorpe to be a generous, kind and warm-hearted man who was a dedicated and enthusiastic politician. Politics was his life and he breathed it. The thought of losing his political career meant the loss of everything that was valuable to him. This was the dominant theme of his conversation; whenever the question of criminal charges was raised, Thorpe had brushed it aside in irritation.

Dinshaw: "Mr Thorpe has many virtues, but an ability to control his feelings is not one of them."

The trial was adjourned until next day. Mr Carman suggested that the prosecution evidence would be finished by noon, after which he proposed to raise some legal points. *We all rather groaned at this, fearing a repetition of the first two days, when Mr Carman had wasted hours pleading that the evidence of the three chief Crown witnesses should be disallowed. At this stage, we were still keenly looking forward to the evidence of the four defendants, especially Holmes and Thorpe. It seemed that they had many questions to answer, and there was speculation about what they would say.*

As it turned out, the last witness – Chief Superintendent Challes – lasted all the following day and well into the day after. His evidence was to produce what can only be described as a humiliation for Mr Carman which, in the hands of a more unscrupulous prosecutor than Mr Taylor, might have been deployed in powerful support of the Crown argument that Thorpe was a liar.

11

Further Tales of Mr Jeremy Thorpe

Day nineteen: 5 June 1979
After written evidence of an unchallenged, corroborative nature, mostly about the movement of Mr Hayward's £20,000 towards Holmes – the judge advised jurors not to write these things down, as they would be muddled by too much detail – two further unsworn statements by Thorpe were read. The first was published on the front page of the *Sunday Times* under the main headline: "The Lies of Norman Scott – by Jeremy Thorpe." It appeared on 14 March 1976, two days before Newton's trial opened in Exeter. The second was his statement to a press conference at the National Liberal Club on 27 October 1977.

Much had been said – and was still to be said – about the press role in investigating Scott's allegations and offering money to potential witnesses. Very little was ever said about the press's role in keeping the whole matter quiet. Yet it is a fact that for the five years up to the dog-shooting, there had been no mention of Scott's allegations in any national newspaper, despite strenuous efforts by Scott and the journalist Gordon Winter to get them printed. Strong support for Thorpe was to come from the *Sunday Mirror* in its famous leader of 16 May 1976, just after Thorpe's resignation: "After he heard the news of Mr Thorpe's resignation, Mr Scott told reporters that he was so upset he had been sick. It is all decent people in Britain who are sick, Mr Scott. Sick at your behaviour. Ugh!"

Rather tough words, one might think, on a man who had been frightened out of his wits by a gunman who seemed determined to murder him. But by far the most conspicuous among newspapers who, wittingly or unwittingly, joined the cover-up – no doubt for the best motives – was the *Sunday Times*. For that reason, and for various others, I give Thorpe's *Sunday Times* article in full:

The Lies of Norman Scott – by Jeremy Thorpe.

When Norman Scott made his outburst in court I issued a brief statement that I had not seen him for twelve years and that the allegations were baseless. I would have hoped that that assurance would have sufficed, but I am advised that a further refutation in the most categorical and unqualified terms is necessary.

Mr Scott has made the following allegations against me:

(a) the existence of a homosexual relationship with me;
(b) that I stole his national insurance card;
(c) that the Liberal Party, Lord Byers and others have made him from time to time subventions to keep him quiet;
(d) that in the incident of the shot dog, my wife or I had hired a gunman at a five figure sum to kill the dog, or Scott, or both, towards the cost of which the government had contributed;
(e) that the identity of the gunman was variously, my helicopter pilot, or a Liberal worker in the Devon and Cornwall region.
(f) In addition, it is alleged that I was acquainted with or involved in a correspondence between Scott and Bessell and that I knew, or was involved, in the purchase of the Bessell letters from Scott for a sum of £2,500.

All these allegations are totally false. Scott's allegations were investigated – with police assistance – by senior colleagues in the Liberal Party in 1971, when his cross-examination culminated in his flight from the room in an hysterical outburst. My colleagues regarded the allegations as pure moonshine.

They had at that time the correspondence between Bessell and Scott, and have retained copies, and so the suggestion that I would have sought the purchase of the letters for £2,500 is particularly idiotic, since I also knew that the national press had copies of them.

The whole of this tissue of elaborately woven mendacity and malice is based on no more than the fact that I had met Scott in November, 1961, when he called at the House of Commons and sent in a card, the normal approach to an MP, mentioning the name of a man whom I held in high esteem.

He was in a state of great distress, since he asserted plausibly that he was being accused of a crime, the theft of a horse, that he was penniless and the victim of other misfortunes. My sympathy was indeed enlisted and I did help him to find a job.

Scott approached me intermittently from time to time thereafter for further assistance. I introduced him to a few people, particularly to my own mother, who on two occasions put him up for the night. Subsequently I discovered that he was an incorrigible liar – that he invented a story of an aircrash and the death of his father in South America – a gentleman then living peaceably in Kent – and several other pieces of fiction, as a result of which I refused to help him further.

I am informed that I am not the only victim of Scott's accusations – of a similar nature – which have been directed against other public figures.

I hope that this statement will now spare me and my family further harassment and enable me to give my proper attention to the affairs of the Liberal Party and the country.

By the time of the press conference on 27 October 1977, Thorpe's emphasis had shifted on a few points. Where before he had hoped to be left alone, he now said he was pleased that Newton's allegations were to be investigated by the police. Where before he had spoken of intermittent approaches, he now talked of "a close and even affectionate friendship" which developed, while still insisting that "no sexual activity of any kind took place."

Where earlier he had said it was "totally false" to suggest that he had been "acquainted with or involved in a correspondence between Scott and Bessell," he now admitted that he had asked Bessell to help out with the Scott problem, while denying that this amounted to a cover-up.

After repeating the familiar litany of denials, his statement ended with a plea for sympathy, even a bid for admiration, which may give us a clue to his attitude if he had decided to give evidence in his own defence:

"It would be insane to pretend that the re-emergence of this story has not placed an almost intolerable strain on my wife, my family, and on me. Only their steadfast loyalty and the support of many friends known and unknown from all over the country has strengthened my resolve and determination to meet this challenge.

"Consequently I have no intention of resigning (his seat in Parliament) nor have I received a single request to do so from my constituency association."

Thorpe's second and final police statement, given to Mr Challes on 3 June 1978 will be found in full on page 165, where it is produced as part of Mr Challes's evidence.

Mr Challes's evidence

Detective Chief Superintendent Challes was deputy head of the
Somerset and Avon CID at the time of the dog-shooting, which
took place just four hundred yards within his territory. At that time,
he was put in charge of investigations into the actual shooting, while
the background to Scott's allegations was investigated by his opposite number in Devon, Mr Proven Sharpe. Mr Challes took over the
whole investigation in 1977 when Newton was released from prison.

A quiet, imperturbable man whose voice carried the faintest trace
of a Somerset burr, Mr Challes was plainly a dutiful officer whose
greatest concern from the very beginning of the case was to play it
by the rules. It had been an unprecedented investigation with political undertones which made it unique in British criminal history, but
nothing seemed to have worried Mr Challes, whose singleminded
determination and quiet perseverance was more responsible than
anything else for collecting enough evidence to convince the
Director of Public Prosecutions that the defendants should be
charged. Like all the best policemen, he exuded a quiet confidence
that truth and justice would emerge from a fair assessment of the
facts as he presented them. We shall probably never know what he
thought of Mr Justice Cantley's treatment of his evidence, which
had been so meticulously collected over four years.

The first of many documents produced by Mr Challes was a copy
of Deakin's statement to the police. Deakin said that Le Mesurier
had introduced him to Holmes. They told him that an unnamed
friend of Holmes was being blackmailed and asked him if he knew
anyone who could "go along and frighten the chap off." Deakin
could think of nobody at that time, but in February 1975 he met
David Miller, the Cardiff printer, who introduced him to Newton.
Deakin decided Newton was the man. When Newton telephoned
him later, he supplied Holmes's telephone number in Manchester.
In a later statement, Deakin denied meeting Newton at a motorway
services station near Bristol, and denied handing him documents.

Mr Challes went to California to see Mr Bessell and collected
various letters from him in March 1978. Next he went to see Holmes
at his flat in Eaton Place on 3 April, but Holmes answered "No
comment" to all questions of substance put to him, and later handed
him a statement substituting "No comment" for most of the few
questions he had earlier answered.

Mr Challes and Mr Taylor here embarked on a little charade
which had proved a very popular turn at Minehead, with Mr Challes
reading his questions and Mr Taylor reading Holmes's reply –

nearly always "No comment." On this occasion, however, the judge did not seem to like the impression being created, and interrupted.

The judge: "No comment means I do not wish to say anything. It would be quite wrong to interpret the fact that he exercised his option not to answer as an admission."

This interruption, which was later to prove a major refrain of the judge's summing up, rather took the wind out of Mr Taylor's sails. He skipped about five pages of "No comments" from Holmes.

When asked whether he wanted to say anything about the £20,000 he had received from Mr Dinshaw, Holmes replied he did not.

Mr Challes then produced Thorpe's statement on 3 June 1978. I give it here in full:

I have been informed by my solicitors that it has been indicated that the current investigation covers three main areas. The first is whether I had ever been involved in a homosexual relationship with Norman Josiffe, also known as Norman Scott, which might form a motive or a wish on my part to eliminate him, cause him injury, or put him in fear.

The second is whether I had been a party to any conspiracy to kill or injure him or put him in fear. The third, whether I had paid or authorised any payment to one Newton, or any other person, pursuant to or following upon, any such conspiracy, or to Scott in respect of the purchase of certain documents or otherwise.

In October 1977, I made a statement to the press. I now wish to reiterate and confirm as accurate what I said in that statement, save as to certain minor details which are dealt with in the body of this statement and also to add the following:

As to the first allegation, I wish, with all the emphasis I can command to deny that I was at any time engaged in any homosexual relationships with Scott or that I was at any time a party to any homosexual familiarity with him.

I described in my earlier statement, and have here confirmed, the circumstances under which I met Scott. I believed that he was a person who was desperately in need of help and support, in that he was in a suicidal and unbalanced state.

The action which, in the circumstances, I followed was attributable solely to what I saw as my duty, having regard to the conditions under which he approached me; in the event my compassion and kindness towards him was in due course repaid with malevolence and resentment.

Although he never so informed me, I formed the opinion at an early stage on the limited number of occasions I was in his presence, that he was a homosexual and he was becoming too dependent upon me.

Accordingly, I made immediate arrangements for him to be accepted into a family near Tiverton with whom he was to spend Christmas, having explained to them the reasons why I believed he was in need of help.

However, after only a few weeks in their house they decided his highly neurotic and unbalanced state was too disturbing an influence in the house and he was asked to leave.

At about January 1962, Scott was still in an unsettled state and in need of funds to enable him to establish some means of supporting himself. He had informed me that his father had been killed in an air crash in South America and I suggested that it might be possible to obtain some compensation.

Accordingly I requested a solicitor friend to initiate some enquiries. In due course, he informed me the story told by Scott was quite false. In fact, his father was at that time, a hospital porter living in Bexleyheath in Kent, where his mother also lived.

I told him there was nothing further I could do to help. He became highly excited and emotional. The meeting itself lasted no longer than a quarter of an hour. Subsequently, he sought to see me again in 1963 expressing contrition and asking me to allow him to meet me and seek my forgiveness.

I arranged to meet him and did so publicly on the terrace of the House of Commons, at which meeting he again became highly excited and emotional but, before leaving, suggested I owed him some duty to support him financially, which I refuted in forceful terms.

With hindsight I now realise that my proper course would have been to refuse to see him. It was evident from our last meeting that he resented my disinterest in him and was likely to try to cause trouble.

I was on the horns of a dilemma. I foresaw no problem in resisting any demands which he might make upon me and disproving falsehoods which he might offer against me.

However, I suspected that the allegations at which he was hinting, although without the slightest foundation, were such as would involve, as in the event they have, baring my soul in public which could have, however unfairly, serious political implications and repercussions for me and the Liberal Party.

As a result I misguidedly agreed to see him and did so on one further occasion which I think was at my flat. I agreed to this meeting in the belief that it was better to avoid public discussion and that I could convince him that his grievances were wholly unjustified and fanciful.

As to the second allegation I wish, with no less emphasis, entirely to refute any suggestion that I have at any time been a party to any conspiracy to kill or injure Norman Scott, or to put him in fear, or that at any time I had any knowledge of, or believed in the existence of, any such conspiracy.

Quite apart from the fact that any desire or willingness to kill or cause physical harm to any person is wholly alien to my nature, as many would be prepared to confirm, the circumstances which existed at the time when it was subsequently suggested that such a conspiracy may have existed are wholly inconsistent with the pursuit of the alleged objective of such a conspiracy.

As I have mentioned above, there was a period when I was understandably concerned at the political implications which could result from the wild and unfounded allegations which it seemed probable that Norman Scott would publish.

As I have further explained, my disquiet in that connection was in no way attributable to my having in any way been involved in any homosexual relationships with him, but because I foresaw that the mere necessity of truthfully denying such an association might raise, as a matter of public question, my own private matters wholly unconnected with Scott, which in my view I could claim to be private to me alone.

It has been suggested in a recently published book that the time the alleged conspiracy was conceived and embarked upon was in the spring of 1975. By that time Scott had ensured in a variety of ways, including a statement in the course of an inquest in 1973 [the inquest was in fact in May 1972], that his allegations had been widely disseminated and, although fully known by the press and the major political parties, wisely ignored by them.

The worst that Scott could falsely allege had been revealed. Far from this having adversely affected either me or the Liberal Party politically, which had been my fear, the party under my leadership, had increased its vote in two elections in February and October 1974 from two millions to six millions and five and a half millions respectively and I had increased my own majority from 369 to 11,000 and 6,700 respectively.

Against this background it is manifestly ludicrous to suggest either that I any longer considered that any public reliance would be placed upon the utterances of Scott, or that any measures were needed to deal with him, least of all the wholly unthinkable approach of conspiring to achieve his death, injury or otherwise.

It appears that Newton was responsible for causing the death of Scott's dog and may have made an abortive attempt upon the life of Scott. I do not pretend to know the truth of this matter and I can only reassert that not only did I have no need to take any part in any such project, and did not do so, but I had no knowledge whatsoever of it and was not, and would not, have under any circumstances have been willing to allow any such plot to be pursued had any hint of suggestion come to me about it.

Finally, in relation to the third allegation, I wish vigorously to refute any suggestion that at any time I had knowingly been a party, either directly or indirectly, to the payment of any such money whatsoever to Newton or to Scott for the purpose alleged.

The press have reported that the payment of £2,500 was made indirectly to Norman Scott in February 1974, for the delivery of certain letters and documents which had passed between him and others, not including myself.

I understand that it is claimed a sum of £5,000 had been paid to Newton subsequent to the death of Scott's dog after his release from prison and that the second sum had been dispersed from moneys provided by one Jack Hayward.

I had no knowledge whatsoever of the purchase of the letters in question until the early part of 1976 when the fact was first publicly revealed in the national press. I immediately expressed, and continue to express, both my surprise and indeed my horror that any one could have thought it necessary to embark upon such a course.

The letters had already been widely circulated and indeed seen by my parliamentary colleagues in 1971.

I have no personal knowledge whatsoever of any payment to Newton of the sum of £5,000, or otherwise, and at no time made any arrangements for any such payments. It is correct that Mr Hayward paid me personally two sums of £10,000, each of which was to be used by me in any way which I thought appropriate in relation to campaigning expenses.

In fact, by reason of other donations at other times it became unnecessary to have recourse to these sums. There had been grave difficulties at one stage in raising sufficient money for the expenses for the Liberal Party's election campaign and I accordingly resolved that since Mr Hayward had made it quite plain to me that, not being adherent to the Liberal Party, he was not making these money's available to the party but to me personally, I would not cause them to be paid into the Liberal Party fund, where they would be soon defrayed.

I therefore made arrangements for the sum of £20,000 to be deposited with accountants and to be held as an iron reserve against any shortage of funds at any subsequent election. At no time, however, have I ever authorised the use of these funds for any payment of the kind alleged to either Scott or Newton.

I have in consultation with my legal advisers given long and earnest consideration as to whether I should amplify the firm and precise general denial set out above. They are conscious, as I am, of the fact that those who have in the past been minded to put forward false assertions against me have, from time to time, varied the detail of their account in order to adjust it to such hard facts as, from time to time, have emerged.

Having regard to the unusual way in which these current allegations have emerged, there is a real danger that if specific details relating to matters which can be proved are made known at the present time they may, in the course of the investigation, become known to, or be deduced by, those minded to further the allegations with consequent readjustment of their version.

In these circumstances, I have been advised that, whilst it is right and proper that I should re-express the denials which are contained in this statement, it is neither incumbent upon me nor desirable to add anything further.

Thorpe had been present when his solicitor handed Mr Challes this statement at Bath police station on 3 June 1978.

Mr Challes then told of receiving another statement from Deakin and questioning him at Bristol police station. They listened to tape-recordings of a conversation between Deakin and Miller. Deakin repeated his denials of a greater involvement, and said he never gave Newton any details beyond Holmes's telephone number.

Mr Le Mesurier made no attempt whatsoever, answering "Nothing to say" 105 times when interviewed on 6 April 1978.

On 4 August 1978 Mr Challes saw all four at Minehead police station and charged them with conspiracy to murder Norman Scott.

When charged, Le Mesurier, Deakin and Holmes made no reply. Thorpe said, "I hear what you say. I am totally innocent of these charges. I will vigorously challenge them and plead not guilty."

Mr Taylor then moved to what became the major point in police evidence. He referred to Mr Carman's cross-examination of the earlier police witness, Mr Proven Sharpe, in the course of which Mr Carman had said Thorpe expressly requested the Chief Commissioner of Metropolitan Police and the then Home Secretary, Mr Reginald Maudling, to investigate Scott's allegations, and let him know "once and for all if there was any truth or anything further to be investigated." Mr Carman had insisted that there would be documentary evidence of this request.

Taylor: "Have you made enquiries both of the police and of the Home Office and seen documents?"

Challes: "Yes, my lord."

Taylor: "Is there any evidence of any request, either orally or in writing, by Mr Thorpe for an investigation into Norman Scott's allegations?"

Challes: "No, my lord."

Mr Challes cross-examined

This matter would be taken up again when Mr Carman rose to cross-examine but first we had to listen to Mr Mathew on the obsessive subject of the journalists Penrose and Courtiour. (Throughout the whole trial, for some reason or other, Mr Mathew pronounced Courtiour's name "Courteeay" – a habit he had caught from Thorpe's solicitor, Sir David Napley, in Minehead.) Mr Mathew's first question established that Holmes was a man of "impeccable character," ie no previous record.

When Mr Challes flew to California in December 1977, said Mr Mathew, "Lo and behold, there also were Mr Penrose and Mr Courteeay." Mr Challes agreed that the two journalists had travelled in the same plane. He had not expected them to be there. They were also present at his interview with Mr Bessell, on Mr Bessell's insistence. This was unique in his experience and he had not wanted the reporters present, but he had no choice.

The two reporters had also taken him to Holmes's London address on an occasion when he had been unable to find Holmes.

Mathew: "Do you know anything about election expenses?"

Challes: "I don't, no, my lord."

Mathew: "Do you know that the amount is strictly limited by law to £1,075 plus 1p per voter?"

Challes: "Not within my knowledge, my lord."

Mathew: "If a candidate overspends, I believe he may be unseated and fined."

Challes: "Not within my knowledge, my lord."

Mathew's cross-examination was a classic example of suggestion. In fact Holmes never gave any explanation of his dealings with Thorpe's £20,000 "election expenses." Here Mr Mathew was intruding the idea into the jury's mind that it may have been something to do with an election fiddle, without calling any evidence to this effect and without even having his information confirmed by Mr Challes.

When Mr Gareth Williams opened his cross-examination on behalf of Deakin, he did not ask whether or not his client was a man of "impeccable character" – nor as it happens, did Mr Carman for Thorpe, no doubt through an oversight.

The important part of Mr Williams's cross-examination established that Mr Challes had always considered Miller a "potential defendant." *The judge interrupted to say that he intended to ask the jury to consider whether or not they should regard Miller as an accomplice. Evidence of an accomplice is traditionally regarded as unsafe unless it is corroborated. In retrospect, one may doubt the Crown's wisdom in choosing to use Miller as yet another unreliable witness for the prosecution, instead of putting him in the dock with Thorpe, Holmes, Le Mesurier and Deakin. Since the only other evidence against Deakin came from Newton, who was unquestionably an accomplice, this rather reduced the case against Deakin to dust and ashes. One began to appreciate the magnitude of the Crown's task in securing a conviction against any criminal who is not actually caught red-handed by the police, when the prisoner's refusal to give evidence is not allowed to count against him.*

Mr Williams's last question to Mr Challes did not get him anywhere.

Williams: "Did you interview Scott in the presence of Penrose and Courtiour?"

Challes: "No, they were in the vicinity, but we wouldn't let them into the house."

Happening to sit next to Mr Penrose in court at this moment, I received the impression that his memory might have differed from the Chief Superintendent's on this unimportant point, had he been called as a witness. I produce this minor piece of information merely to illustrate the inconsistencies which may arise when two honourable and disinterested witnesses try to remember the same event.

Mr Cowley rose briefly to establish that his client, too, was a man of impeccable character. He said that Le Mesurier had served some six years in the Royal Air Force with an "exceptional" record.

Mr Carman's first questions concerned Mr Challes's dealings with

Penrose and Courtiour. On this occasion, Mr Carman made the explicit suggestion that there might have been "tampering with witnesses."

Challes: "I have not taken any statement from Mr Penrose, Mr Courtiour, or from any other journalist about what witnesses they have interviewed."

At the end of the day, in the absence of the jury, Mr Carman made rather a strange application. He said that last February, London Weekend Television had written to Thorpe asking if he would like to appear on a television programme with the journalists Penrose and Courtiour. Thorpe's lawyers had written back complaining in strong terms to the chairman of London Weekend, Mr John Freeman. They said they wanted to know whom the journalists had interviewed and what payments had been made. Mr Carman thought it right the jury should know who had been seen by the journalists.

Mr Carman was applying for the judge to order Mr Challes to investigate this matter and report to the court. He said that since tampering with witnesses was a criminal matter, this was a proper matter for the police to investigate. The judge was still chuckling to himself about the idea of Thorpe being asked to appear on a television programme with the two journalists. Between chortles he asked Mr Carman why he did not ask the two journalists to give evidence. Mr Carman's answer seemed to suggest that the judge would find them objectionable as witnesses. He insisted that it was Mr Challes's job to investigate any suggestion of tampering with witnesses. The judge managed to control his merriment enough to rule against Mr Carman's application.

The judge: "You must ask Penrose and Courtiour to come and answer questions. I have no objection to them and might even enjoy it. If they perjure themselves, I hope someone will send them to prison."

Of course Mr Carman did not call them as witnesses. He called no witnesses at all having reckoned, perhaps, that the risks of a protracted defence were greater than the possible advantages.

Next Mr Carman turned to the matter which was to dominate the newspaper headlines for the next two days: whether or not Thorpe had asked the Commissioner of Metropolitan Police and the Home Secretary to investigate Scott's allegations. Clearly he had been briefed in the firmest possible way that this request had been made, and thought that Mr Challes was trying to fudge the issue.

It was undoubtedly the case that Thorpe had approached the

Commissioner about one specific allegation which had been attri-
buted to Scott – that he had once turned up with a gun in the House
of Commons – but no request for a general enquiry had ever been
received. On the strength of the one enquiry, Thorpe had elicited a
note from Mr Maudling, the then Home Secretary, which might
have seemed to suggest he had been investigated and was in the
clear, but in fact it referred only to this one specific enquiry about an
incident which had never occurred. Thorpe had used Mr Maudling's
letter to good effect with his Liberal colleagues, and would appear
to have convinced himself of the truth of his claim. Try as he might,
Mr Carman could not shake the Chief Superintendent from the
position that Thorpe had made no such approach.

Carman: "All I want to ask is that in 1971, for whatever reason,
Mr Thorpe was alerting the Home Secretary to the 'anxious'
activities of Norman Scott."

Challes: "I don't accept that the alerting came from Mr Thorpe.
Your suggestion is that Mr Thorpe initiated whatever went on in
1971. I, from my knowledge and examination of the files, don't
accept that."

Mr Carman's last questions were on the matter of the man called
Hetherington. It appeared that the police had first learned about
him in a letter from Thorpe's solicitor, Lord Goodman, to the
Director of Public Prosecutions. Mr Bessell had merely confirmed
the episode when Mr Challes asked him about it.

*The Hetherington mystery was never explained. Plainly Mr
Carman hoped to make more out of it than the prosecution did. They
could scarcely charge Thorpe at this late stage with conspiracy to
murder an unidentified man on the unsupported evidence, once
again, of Mr Bessell. What was most striking was the use the judge
made of it in his summing up.*

When the court rose, Mr Challes was still in the witness-box.

Day twenty: 6 June 1979

The day opened with Mr Challes still in the witness-box. He was at
pains not to gloat when Mr Taylor rose to read a statement which
had finally been agreed with the defence on the vexed question of
whether or not Thorpe had asked the Home Secretary and
Metropolitan Police to investigate Scott's allegation of a homosexual relationship. He would not have been human if one could not
have seen a little gleam of triumph in his eye.

Taylor: "... It is admitted that no request, whether oral or in

writing, was made by Mr Thorpe for an investigation either by the
Home Secretary, Mr Reginald Maudling, or by the Metropolitan
Police, as to the truth of Norman Scott's allegations, save as to the
two points raised in the note of 17 June 1971."

*These two points were a query about the pistol incident in the
House of Commons and a request to know whether the Home Office
possessed any psychiatric reports on Scott.*

*Thorpe's claim to have asked for this investigation was only one
weapon in an arsenal of rebuttal postures, but the prosecution plainly
felt happy to have neutralised it.*

A second admission referred to a draft letter to Lord Byers,
which was rejected because, in fact, Sir John Waldron, the Police
Commissioner, objected to certain words in it. The significance of
the draft letter can be understood from the following letter sent by
Thorpe to Mr Reginald Maudling, then Home Secretary, on 13 July 1971:

My dear Reggie,

I am very grateful to you for your interest and help in the case
of Scott. As far as Byers, Steel and myself are concerned the
matter is closed.

To the intense annoyance of all three of us, Hooson [Liberal
MP for Montomeryshire] – whose motives are not entirely selfless
– is intent to go on rummaging around, seeing if he can't stir up
something. He's already suggested that I should have resigned
from the leadership and possibly Parliament as well!

Frank [Byers] feels the only way to convince him that he is
really muckracking is to set out the facts in a confidential letter
from me to Frank, of which he would keep the letter but which
Hooson should be shown.

The enclosed is the letter which I propose to send Frank.
Before I do so I would want to be certain that it accurately reflects
your own recollection of our exchanges and that of Sir John
Waldron [the Commissioner].

In short I would like to append to my private letter to Frank a
short note from you, and one from Waldron, or one from you on
behalf of both, saying that its contents are a fair summary. No
more is required. Needless to say it would remain in Frank's files
and be treated as totally confidential.

I am sorry to be a bother. But the first lesson in politics is that
no one can ever be as disloyal as one's own colleagues!

Yours ever,
Jeremy.

After the reading of these formal admissions, Mr Carman continued his cross-examination of Mr Challes.

Carman: "Shortly after you interviewed Mr Thorpe, *Private Eye* magazine published an article headed 'the Ditto Man'. Was 'Ditto' the word Thorpe used during the interview to summarise that he had nothing further to add, for reasons he had given earlier?"

Challes: "Yes, my lord. It looks as if that publication had been given an indication of what transpired at the interview. But I am satisfied that it did not come from police sources. It was disturbing not only to your client but also to me."

Lawyers were present at the interview as well as police officers, he said, and gave Mr Carman to understand that the leak had probably come from the office of Sir David Napley, Thorpe's solicitor.

After a few questions in re-examination, Mr Taylor turned to the judge and said, "Well, my lord, that is the case for the Crown." He sat down.

The jury were now sent away while we heard legal submissions. It was proposed they should come back at three o'clock, but once again counsel were not able to restrain themselves to a timetable, and they were sent away for the rest of the day.

Defence submissions

These were to prove a re-run of defence submissions on the first day of the trial, except that whereas on that occasion they were designed to stop the three main Crown witnesses – Bessell, Newton and Scott – on grounds that having accepted money from the press they were not credit-worthy, the arguments were now addressed to stopping the whole trial, there being no case to answer, on the same grounds. Here, stripped of most rhetorical flourishes and judicial interruptions, are the bare bones of their submission.

Mr Mathew for Holmes

The evidence is so unreliable that any verdict of guilty would be unsafe. Evidence of conspiracy to kill against Holmes relies on two witnesses: Newton and Bessell. Of these two, Bessell's evidence against Holmes on this charge is limited to Holmes's alleged admission in California. It is not the judge's job to decide who is lying, but he may decide whether a witness is credit-worthy, and he must advise on the danger of convicting on the uncorroborated evidence of an accomplice. Newton was not only an accomplice, he was also a perjurer – by his own admission, at Exeter Crown Court, and in the witness-box at the Old Bailey (over the American traffic accident

and other matters). In addition to having lied in the witness-box –
the judge was invited to remember his attitude there – Newton was
tainted by a financial interest. Finally, said Mr Mathew, he had lied
about the gun jamming.

The judge: "I would think that if the gun really jammed, that
would help the prosecution. It indicates an intention to kill."

Mathew: "In my submission, the jury must decide the gun *did* jam
and therefore Newton was lying. He is therefore an unsafe witness.
Is the jury going to be allowed to say yes, we believe the witness on
this point, but not on that one?"

The only possible corroboration of Newton's and Bessell's unsafe
evidence, said Mr Mathew, was the tape-recording where there was
reference to a "conspiracy to bloody murder." But that was inconclusive. Miller should be treated as an accomplice and so, said Mr
Mathew, should Mr Bessell.

Bessell agreed he had lied on many occasions. How can the
Crown put forward evidence in such scandalous circumstances?

The judge: "Ha, ha, I must agree that nobody seems interested in
justice, only money. Ha, ha."

*Suddenly – irrelevantly – one noticed that Mr Mathew had a
surprisingly common accent as he ended his address.*

Mathew: "If I be right about this, m'lord, in my submission they
should not be allowed to corroborate each other."

Mr Williams for Deakin

There was no corroboration of Newton's evidence against Deakin
on the murder aspect. The only corroborative evidence against
Deakin at all came from Miller, a co-conspirator who had been
described as such by the Crown. Of that evidence, the only part
against Deakin from Miller was supporting Newton's claim of having made a telephone call from Heathrow, and Miller's evidence on
that point was not conclusive. To leave Deakin to the jury on
Newton's uncorroborated evidence would result in an unsafe
conviction.

Mr Cowley for Le Mesurier

The conspiracy, if there was one, ended on Porlock Hill. All evidence against Le Mesurier on the murder charge related to events
after that incident. *Ergo* Le Mesurier could not have been a
member of the conspiracy. Evidence against him is irrelevant,
therefore inadmissible, so any conviction would be unsafe.

Mr Carman for Thorpe
The second charge, of incitement, should be dismissed out of hand since it relied only on Mr Bessell's evidence. The law's definitions of exhortation or suggestion did not include humorous badinage. (The judge ruled against this application out of hand, pointing out that humour was only on one side, according to the evidence.)

On the second charge, of conspiracy, there were six named conspirators: the four defendants, Newton and Miller. The only evidence against Thorpe related to what passed between him and Holmes. There was no evidence connecting him with any of the other four. The only evidence against Thorpe on this point was circumstantial rather than direct.

It was in the course of bickering with Mr Carman about whether this consideration justified him in stopping the trial – whether, that is, the jury could be trusted to assess the truth of Mr Bessell's evidence – that the judge first produced his notable remark: "Remember, I have the last word."

12

The Defence

The defence opened with a minor bombshell. Many journalists had not yet arrived in court when Mr Mathew stood up to open his defence of Holmes.

Mathew: "My lord, on behalf of Mr Holmes I call no evidence."

He sat down again. The few journalists in the press benches at that unearthly hour of half past ten in the morning looked at each other stupidly. Then the truth dawned. Holmes, who had so much to explain, was not going to give evidence or take the oath in his own defence. After a pause of about ten seconds while everybody worked it out, there was a noisy scramble for the door which drowned the voice of Mr Williams calling his first and only witness for the defence, George Deakin.

Red-haired and pasty-faced, Deakin was not the most beautiful of the four defendants, but he was the only one to give evidence. He spoke in a surprisingly deep voice for such a small man. Under examination from his counsel, Gareth Williams QC, this is the story Deakin told:

A friend introduced Deakin to Le Mesurier who recommended Holmes to him for advice on tax, currency and house-buying matters. Deakin had never been a homosexual and had no connection with the Liberal Party – in fact he voted Conservative. He was trying to find a legal way of avoiding the dollar premiums to buy a house overseas and Holmes produced a scheme involving the export of antiques. At the end of their last meeting, Le Mesurier said that a friend of Holmes was having trouble with a blackmailer; that a woman had already committed suicide and a three-year-old child's life was threatened. Deakin assumed it was Holmes's own wife and child and said, "Why don't you go to the police?"

Homes replied, "It is one of those situations where you can't."

Deakin was never on close social or personal terms with Holmes and did not realise he was a bachelor. Le Mesurier, whom he described as "a jovial fellow and a bit loud – if he was in the same room, you knew he was there," became a drinking-friend. Le Mesurier asked him if he knew anyone to frighten the blackmailer off. Deakin suspected they wanted to put the fear of God into the blackmailer, threatening him with violence without actually using violence. Neither Holmes nor Le Mesurier ever asked him to hire someone to kill Scott. If they had, he would have refused, he said. Deakin replied, "I'll see what I can do."

In about October 1974, Deakin mentioned the matter to Miller. Miller said he knew someone who would do anything for a "laugh and giggle." Holmes was persistently asking him on the telephone if he had found anyone to frighten the blackmailer. He never went to Barnstaple with Holmes.

At the Showman's Dinner in Blackpool on 26 February 1975, Miller introduced him to Newton, whom he had not previously met, saying, "This is the boy for you problem."

Deakin replied, "It's not my bloody problem."

No money was discussed, but when Newton asked how much he would be paid "for the frightening job," Deakin replied, "I don't expect they would want you to do it for nothing."

Later Newton got drunk and Deakin took him home. Three days later Newton telephoned and Deakin gave him Holmes's telephone number in Manchester, later giving him Holmes's other telephone in London and Dent.

The judge: "Dent?"

Deakin: "Dent, my lord. DENT."

Williams: "DENT."

The judge: "Where's that?"

Williams: "I don't, my lord."

Deakin: "I don't know."

Deakin met Newton once later, at Miller's business premises in Cardiff, but did not wish to engage him in much conversation because he suspected Newton had designs on his wife. He never met him at Aust, never gave him photographs of Scott, had no further contact with Le Mesurier until after December 1975, no contact with Holmes after putting Newton in touch with him, and received no telephone call from Newton at Heathrow Airport in 1975 after the dog-shooting. He first heard of the dog-shooting from Miller, who also told him of Scott's sexual allegations about Thorpe and another Person, named on Newton's pink paper. Miller also told him of prominent politicians and high-ranking people engaged in hushing it up. Le Mesurier had later confirmed this on the telephone, naming Harold Wilson, the Prime Minster, Lord Goodman . . .

The judge: "Thomas Cobley? We keeping getting these names and everybody gets wildly excited although it's hearsay upon hearsay upon hearsay."

Deakin told his solicitor – a friend – who told him to keep his head down and say nothing. He had seen Le Mesurier once or twice, but all his information came from Miller. When he told Miller he would deny everything he was referring to press enquiries. The press had been most troublesome, parking outside his home for five days. (The judge here interrupted to say something, being apparently overcome by laughter.)

Later, he had made a voluntary statement to the police. It was on his initiative that reporting restrictions had been lifted at the Minehead committal proceedings. Similarly, he had chosen to give evidence despite his legal right to say nothing.

"I am here because I have nothing to hide," he said.

Deakin cross-examined

We did not know it at the time, but this was to be our only opportunity to see Mr Taylor in the role of cross-examiner. His mild, understanding manner had never left him when he was examining his own witnesses even when – as with Newton's insistence that he was only pretending the gun had jammed, or Miller's insistence that he knew only of a conspiracy to frighten – he must have felt intensely irritated by them. Now a new Mr Taylor emerged, still polite, but firm, and with occasional hints of righteous exasperation. In his final speech, Mr Taylor was to suggest that the case against Deakin was not, perhaps, as firm as it might have been against the other three defendants, nor did Mr Taylor oppose Deakin's application for costs. But one would not have guessed that he had any indulgent feelings towards Deakin now. Perhaps he already knew – or had guessed – that neither Thorpe nor Le Mesurier would give evidence, and this would be his only chance.

Mr Taylor's first ploy was to hint, however delicately, that Deakin moved in crooked circles. Deakin, for his part, kept reiterating how compassionate he felt towards this three-year-old child whom he believed to be threatened.

Taylor: "You thought you were being asked to assist because through the business that you were involved in, you may well be in contact with someone who might give this sort of assistance?"

Deakin: "That was their impression but it was wrong . . . I

suppose they thought I had more chance than Le Mesurier or a merchant banker would."

Frequently, Mr Taylor found himself stumbling against this three-year-old child, about whom Deakin seemed to feel an almost hysterical sentimentality.

Taylor: "Did you intend to follow this up, or do nothing about it?"

Deakin: "Both."

Taylor: "?*!!"

Deakin: "I was thinking of this three-year-old child. I had only been told that a woman had committed suicide and they were threatening the life of a three-year-old child."

Mr Taylor kept pressing him on the point that, by his account, Deakin had never even so much as asked what the blackmail was all about, or who was involved. Deakin gave as good as he got.

Taylor: "It was Holmes who said it was one of those cases where you couldn't go to the police?"

Deakin: "Yes."

Taylor: "Weren't you interested in what it was all about?"

Deakin: "No. I didn't want to know, so I didn't ask."

Taylor: "You might have got involved yourself?"

Deakin: "I have."

Taylor: "There are various ways, aren't there, of frightening someone? You might threaten to give some information, or threaten someone's family . . . ?"

Deakin: "Shooting a dog is one."

Taylor: "What the police couldn't do to a blackmailer, you agree, would be to go and kill him?"

Deakin: "I agree."

The more Mr Taylor pressed him on the degree of his involvement in the conspiracy, the more firmly Deakin denied that he had done anything beyond putting Newton in touch with Holmes. He strongly denied that Newton had said to him, "I hear you want someone bumped off. I am your man." Taylor put it to him that Holmes knew very well where Scott was living and was most unlikely to confuse Barnstaple with Dunstable, whereas Deakin had made this mistake, by a slip of the tongue, in evidence that very morning. *But one had the impression that Mr Taylor's subtlety was being wasted on Deakin.* He countered with another sturdy denial.

Deakin: "I didn't think I had done anything wrong. I thought I was helping someone in relation to a blackmailer."

It was 4.25 pm when Deakin stood down. Everybody assumed

that the trial would be adjourned until next morning, with Le Mesurier in the box, to be followed by any defence witnesses Mr Cowley might have up his sleeve, and then Thorpe. But the dramas of the day were not yet over. In quick succession, we heard from Mr Cowley and Mr Carman.

Cowley: "I call no evidence."

Carman: "My lord, on behalf of Mr Jeremy Thorpe, I call no evidence."

Once again, it took people some time to realise what had happened, particularly those who had missed the morning's drama.

Looking not in the least bit put out – I am convinced he had been informed that morning – Mr Taylor jumped to his feet and asked the judge for an adjournment until Monday, 11 June. This would give the prosecution time to prepare its closing address to the jury.

The judge looked slightly surprised but rather amused that neither Thorpe nor any of the other defendants were going into the witness-box. *I had a horrible suspicion, watching him, that one of his reasons for being amused was that the world's press would be denied the drama of Thorpe's appearance. Certainly there were groans and curses among the journalists and book-writers afterwards. Things were said about Thorpe and his colleagues which had been better left unsaid. No doubt there was someone from Kingsley, Napley and Company, taking it all down.*

The judge: "That is a good idea for all of us."

13

Closing Addresses: the Crown

Day twenty-two: 11 June 1979
Before Mr Taylor could begin his closing address, which was to last
two days, the jury had some questions to ask the judge. The first was
on a point of fact – the date of the arrival of Scott's letters from
Switzerland. The second asked whether the jury should disregard
the Van de Vater letters.

This was quite an interesting point, since the judge, in an angry
moment – "that's just a bit of dirt thrown in" – had more or less
directed them to do so while Scott was giving evidence. Mr Taylor
later told them that the only significance of these letters, as far as he
was concerned, was for the light they threw on Scott's mental attitude
at the time of his first approach to Thorpe in the House of Commons –
Scott knew that Thorpe was a man of homosexual tendencies and, it
had been suggested by the defence, wanted to have a homosexual
affair with him.

The judge, however, seemed to put a different light on the letters. In
a ruminative tone, he said he thought it odd that Scott should steal
someone's letters if he wasn't a blackmailer. *Later, Mr Taylor was to*
point out that there wasn't the slightest suggestion that Scott had
blackmailed Vater over these letters, although that was not to stop the
judge making the same point in his summing up. In fact, any sugges-
tion that Scott was a blackmailer rather strengthened the motive, but
the judge gave priority throughout to expressing his abhorrence of the
four main Crown witnesses. The fact that Scott might have been a
blackmailer gave another reason for discountenancing the whole
prosecution case.

Next the jury note said: "We would like more information about
dates and interviews with Penrose and Courtiour."

This suggested the jury were approaching their task as private
enquiry agents. The judge slapped them down:

The judge: "The Crown has closed its case and after Deakin's
evidence on Thursday the defence are not going to call any more

evidence. So if you want to know any more the answer is, 'You never will . . . the curtains are down and you must decide the case on what you have heard.' "

In reply to quibbles from Mr Carman, the judge once again produced his ominous remark: "Remember, I have the last word." *It crossed my mind that on this second occasion the judge not only derived comfort from the reflexion, but he seemed to be inviting the defence to derive comfort from it too. But perhaps my impression was mistaken, and I was imagining things.*

Finally, the jury wrote this: "We were promised a bundle of agreed facts. Can we have them?"

This question suggested an attentive conscientious jury, even an intelligent one. Presumably the bundle of agreed facts was produced. Mr Taylor proceeded to list about sixty of them in the course of his closing address.

Mr Taylor's closing address: a sad duty

Two days was too long to spend on the job. The best of these closing addresses came from Mr Williams, and it was also one of the shortest. Parts of Mr Taylor's speech were beautiful, parts were highly effective, but it should have been quarter the length and had more venom in it. No speech which lasts two days can end by breeding anything but confusion and resentment in its hearers. His opening passages, which occupied the headlines in every British newspaper next day, established the major confusion in Mr Taylor's approach which, one could now see, had plagued the whole presentation. Put at its simplest, Mr Taylor was too much of a gentleman. If the jurors noticed any difference between his approach and that of Mr Carman or Mr Williams, they probably wrote it down to weakness. Mr Taylor was bound by the convention which makes prosecuting counsel "ministers of justice," rather than advocates of one side. To someone unfamilar with this convention, it seemed that Mr Taylor's gentlemanliness was his fatal flaw. This is how he opened his address to the jury:

"You have heard some four weeks of evidence on behalf of the Crown in this trial and on Thursday last you heard Mr Deakin's account. Now as you stand back and look at this case as a whole, two facts lie at the root of it.

"Both of them are clear and unchallenged. Mr Thorpe in 1961 was a bachelor with homosexual tendencies. He was also a young Member of Parliament with the highest and most determined ambitions to get to the top.

"It is the working out over the years, and the conflict of these two traits of character that are the key, and the only key, to what followed.

"The tragedy of this case on any view is that Mr Thorpe has been surrounded and in the end his career blighted by the Scott affair. His story is a tragedy of truly Greek or Shakespearian proportions – the slow but inevitable destruction of a man by the stamp of one defect."

It seemed curious that Mr Taylor should cast Thorpe as a heroic character when there had been no evidence on this point. The English do not traditionally regard politicians as heroic, and probably few people would have thought of regarding him as a hero if he had not been charged with conspiracy and incitement to murder. He had had an opportunity to display such heroic qualities as he might possess in the witness-box and had declined to avail himself of it, but Mr Taylor was too gentlemanly, and played too much by the rules, to attempt to take advantage of that. All the jury had seen was a pale face in the dock.

The evidence did not suggest that homosexuality was Thorpe's only defect, nor did Mr Taylor call other evidence to illustrate the scope of these admitted "homosexual tendencies." The court had heard quite enough in evidence to make it odd that he should be identified now as a classical hero destroyed by the stamp of one defect. Other defects which had been suggested were an extraordinarily cavalier attitude to normal commercial properties – over the Hayward property deal – ruthless manipulation of other people, meanness, selfishness as a lover and a readiness to lie, twist and bluff which, in anybody but a party politician, would be considered truly breathtaking.

My point is not that there was any moral obligation on the part of Mr Taylor to present Thorpe as a squalid and unscrupulous opportunist who had finally met his come-uppance. My point is simply that he made his job as prosecutor more difficult by producing, at this late stage and in the teeth of all the evidence, the image of a classical hero beset by the Furies as the result of one defect. Instead of asking the jury to act as society's watchdog to punish a sordid and reprehensible crime, he was asking the jury to cast itself as an avenging Nemesis – blind to pity, servant of distant and inscrutable gods – and complete the destruction of a classical hero. Of course, this is one interpretation of the prosecution's job, but I am not sure it is the most effective one, and I rather fear it may have been placing too great a burden on any jury of predominantly working-class Londoners.

Mr Taylor's next passage may seem to reduce the effect of his great rhetorical flight about Thorpe, but the impression had already been created: it might be a painful and unwelcome one, but it was nevertheless the duty of the jury to convict Thorpe if (and only if) they decided the case against him had been established. *A less scrupulous prosecutor, as I say, might have hinted improperly that it was the jury's happy privilege to act for society in this matter.* The other three defendants, said Mr Taylor, were men of less renown. They were before the court because of their involvement in the hiring of Newton as Thorpe's hit man.

"It is now clear beyond dispute is it not, that each of them did play a part in that hiring. Not only are these three charged with a serious crime but because of the fame of the fourth defendant the case has attracted the widest publicity to which they are not used. To them and to those close to them, just as for Thorpe, this is a sad and tragic case.

"I start with this not for effect, but because it would be inhuman if one did not feel sympathy for the defendants – maybe not in large measure, and perhaps not particularly for Thorpe. But sympathy can have no part in your deliberations as a jury . . . the jury must decide whether in each defendant's case the Crown has discharged the burden of proving guilt. Sympathy, though you may feel it, has to be put aside when considering your verdicts."

Perhaps it was as well that Mr Taylor did not plan this passage for effect. If he had paused to consider the effect of asking a jury to put aside all feelings of sympathy, he might have realised that it would have precisely the opposite one. A more aggressive prosecutor might have urged them to keep some rein on their understandable feelings of anger and contempt.

But the worst trap he fell into here was in accepting the defence – and judge's – representation of the burden of proof, as if proof were some abstruse intellectual game played according to complicated rules which a jury could only partially understand – rather than simply a matter of convincing the jurors beyond reasonable doubt that the defendants did it.

Coming after the encomium to Thorpe as a classical tragic hero destroyed by the stamp of one defect, this suggestion that the jury might feel greater sympathy for the other defendants than for Thorpe would do nothing to reduce Thorpe's chances of acquittal, and could only have increased the other defendants' chances.

Next, Mr Taylor dealt with the gravity of the charges:

"The fact that the murder attempt was bungled does not detract from its gravity. It cannot be excused or overlooked because no human being was, in fact, harmed, or because it was a long time ago, or because the defendants, perhaps especially Mr Thorpe, have already suffered much anguish.

"If Mr Scott had been killed, the atmosphere of this trial would have been very different . . . it would have been a grim affair."

Once again, it seemed to me that Mr Taylor had miscalculated, or misunderstood human nature. It is no good enlisting people's indignation over a hypothetical outcome. The point surely was that attempted murder is of itself an exceptionally unpleasant business and one that society, for its own protection, quite rightly discourages. So, he might have added, is violence against the person.

Next, Mr Taylor launched himself into what I thought was a very sporting defence of press activities throughout the case. He did not, of course, mention the part played by those sections of the press which decided that Thorpe should be protected, even after the events on Porlock Hill. It would be quite wrong, said Mr Taylor, if the jury returned verdicts of not guilty, because the press had muddied the waters or made fair trial difficult or impossible.

His witnesses, he said, had been blackguarded in the most forceful terms.

"They have been called liars, accomplished liars, practised liars – every epithet that is in the vocabulary. Perjury, drug addiction, mental illness, greed and sheer wickedness are all sticks that have been used to beat various witnesses."

All these matters were outside the scope of the case, said Mr Taylor – *rather hopefully, I thought.* Furthermore, all four of his main witnesses (Bessell, Scott, Newton and Miller) had been involved in pecuniary arrangements with the press or media. But all the jury had to ask themselves was, is it true? The mere fact that a man sold his story to the press did not mean that it was false.

This was all right so far as it went, but it ignored the important point that all four witnesses stood to gain much more money if there was a conviction. Mr Taylor should surely have dealt with this, perhaps to suggest it made the encouraging point (in his submission) that truth was a more valuable commodity than fantasy. Or he could have manfully agreed that it might seem to weaken their evidence, but only if the jury decided they were all lying on the essential points.

The witnesses were not a closely knit group who could put their heads together to concoct a wicked story, said Mr Taylor. One was in California, another working horses in Devon, while Newton and Miller were plainly at loggerheads. In some cases, their stories did not even agree. Newton and Scott were hardly bosom companions after the shooting incident. There was no suggestion of collusion. The defence would blame the evil machinations of Penrose and Courtiour, but in fact it was simply the case that the evidence dovetailed.

This struck me as rather a weak answer to defence claims that Penrose and Courtiour had co-ordinated the story. Mr Taylor might have pointed out that the defence had called no evidence to support this claim, although it could perfectly well have called both journalists. In fact, the judge was to make this point in his summing up.

Next Mr Taylor launched on his great list of facts which were either unchallenged or proved by documents. Others present counted sixty-one of them eventually. The important ones at this stage were that Thorpe in 1961 was a bachelor with homosexual tendencies; that he gave Scott money, wrote him affectionate letters; that Holmes had paid £2,500 to recover letters from Scott; that Thorpe had arranged for £20,000 to be paid to Holmes; that Holmes and Le Mesurier asked Deakin to find someone; that Newton took Scott and shot his dog without harming Scott; that Holmes met Newton and discussed his defence; that Le Mesurier arranged through Miller to meet and pay Newton £5,000; that Thorpe tried to persuade Mr Dinshaw to give different accounts of the money; and that he tried to persuade Mr Hayward to put pressure on Mr Bessell not to come to England.

These agreed facts, said Mr Taylor, were undisputed. *He might have added that it was agreed that Holmes met Newton before the shooting; and that Holmes and Thorpe were very close friends.*

Next, Mr Taylor dealt with the suggestion that the murder conspiracy was a matter of light-hearted banter. But the jury had only to look at the motive, and at what happened later, to know whether the incitement was a joke or serious.

Three of the defendants had admitted an agreement to frighten, said Mr Taylor. *This, in my own estimate, was by far the most important admission of the whole trial, but Mr Taylor dealt with it more from the angle of the challenge this admission presented to the charge of conspiracy to murder than from the point of view that such an admission carried three-quarters of the prosecution case with it: motive, opportunity, agreement on criminal intent.*

Mr Taylor then proceeded to waste a great deal of time in establishing motive, as if the existence of a homosexual relationship was crucial to the murder conspiracy, when the existence of a criminal conspiracy of some sort had already been accepted by three of the conspirators. *In the event it probably did not matter because the jury decided that it had not been satisfactorily proved that the conspiracy was to murder, but at the time I thought he should have spent more effort arguing Thorpe's connection with the conspiracy which had been admitted, less time on alleging the homosexual relationship.*

With the benefit of hindsight one can see he should have spent far more time on establishing, or trying to establish, the lethal nature of the compact.

Next Mr Taylor took the jury through the various untruths which had been established and agreed in Thorpe's defence postures. Through his counsel Mr Carman, Thorpe had said he expressly requested Sir John Waldron, the former Police Commissioner and Mr Reginald Maudling, the Home Secretary, to investigate the matter. "It all looked very businesslike, frank, forthcoming and very impressive, did it not, until the jury learned it just was not true. Thorpe did not ask these authorities to investigate the matter. Only when Chief Superintendent Michael Challes revealed this in evidence did the defence concede it.

"This is important, I submit, because it gives some insight into the way Thorpe worked. I am sorry to have to put it this way, but it comes to this – trying to fix the record."

Once again, Mr Taylor was striking this apologetic note. He later went on to list other occasions on which Thorpe had tried to fix the record and whitewash his own behaviour. Next day he was going to drop the apologetic tone a little and close his address in a fine state of indignation, saying how Thorpe had "lied, lied and lied again" over the money given to him by Hayward. But by then, in my judgment, it was too late. We should have had this at the beginning of the address, as well as at the end. If only Mr Gareth Williams had been prosecuting and Mr Taylor had been defending Thorpe we would have had a battle to remember. As it was there were moments during Mr Williams's excellent closing address on behalf of Deakin when I received the impression that this might have been the case.

Mr Taylor closed his morning's address with a summary of the reasons for believing that Thorpe had a homosexual relationship with Scott.

"The defence have said that there was no homosexual relationship with Scott, but three other concessions have been made. These are that Thorpe did have homosexual tendencies; that he did have what he described in his 1977 statement to the press as a "close and affectionate relationship" with Scott; and that Mr Scott wanted to have a relationship with Mr Thorpe. These facts simply will not lie down together, other than on the basis of the account given by Mr Scott. You may think that is the truth of it, and it was a really powerful motive in causing Mr Thorpe to act as he did, with progressive attempts to deal with Mr Scott over the years – until in the end killing seemed to him in his obsessed state of mind the only way of dealing with it."

After lunch, the four defendants jumped up from the steps into the dock like rabbits, Thorpe bowed deeply to the judge – *the first sign that his old histrionic presence was still alive.*

Mr Taylor took the jury slowly through the attempts to silence Scott: Mr Bessell's efforts to frighten him in Dublin by naming the Home Secretary, Sir Frank Soskice; offers of help; removing letters from the suitcase; the retainer paid to Scott when Thorpe became leader of the Liberal Party; payments to set him up as a model – "there is no suggestion that Bessell had motives of his own for paying Scott."

At one stage, Thorpe had said that if ever it became known he was a homosexual he would take his own life. "If you believe that, then that is some measure as to how seriously Thorpe took both his politics and the seriousness of this threat to it. Do you think for one moment that at that stage Mr Thorpe would be joking in light-hearted banter about Mr Scott?"

Of course, if the jury believed Mr Bessell, Thorpe was guilty anyway. There was no need to add circumstantial details culled from Mr Bessell's evidence which supported its main theme. But every time Mr Taylor introduced that conditional he was – perhaps uncon- sciously – intruding an element of doubt in the jury's mind. I proceed at such length with Mr Taylor's speech because it seemed to me, for all its elegance, honesty and undoubted sincerity, a model of how prosecuting counsel should not address a jury in modern times, when jurors are drawn from every section of society and are often of limited intelligence, limited powers of concentration and limited affection for the police.

"Why would Mr Bessell fabricate his allegations of the incite- ment to kill in 1969, the admission in 1976 and the plot to hire Newton? If his allegations are invented, he must be the most diabol- ical man who ever lived. It would be unhappy enough for someone to give true evidence against former friends, but if the evidence is false and fabricated it would make Shakespeare's Iago and even Judas himself seem mildly disloyal."

After this elegant flight, Mr Taylor moved on – *much too fast, in my opinion* – to discuss the suggestion that Mr Bessell was a drug addict, suffering from delusions. *He should have stuck on this earlier point, which illustrates the mistake of asking rhetorical questions. The listeners' immediate reaction is to answer: "Because he stands to gain £25,000 if Thorpe is convicted." This consideration would make Bessell no less of a grotesque monster, but it should have been dealt with here, and not left for the jury to discover for themselves. Mr*

*Taylor should have dwelled on the extreme unlikelihood of anyone
hoping to get away with such a far-fetched way of making money.
Unfortunately for Mr Taylor, a predominantly working-class jury
nurtured on television detective serials may have found such suggestions all too familiar, but Mr Taylor should have tried to separate
fantasy from life in the jury's mind at this point.*

Having disposed of the drug question, pointing out that while on
the drug Mandrax Mr Bessell was "apparently a trusted colleague,"
Mr Taylor dealt with revenge as a possible motive. Finally, Mr
Taylor arrived at the money motive – *too late, in my view, since it
would already have fixed itself in the jurors' minds as their own
conclusion. Mr Taylor tried to minimise the sum involved, suggesting
it was only a third of £50,000, and this was a mistake, since to a
working man or woman £16,666.66 belongs no less to the realms of
fantasy than £50,000, even if he is prepared to do the arithmetic. Mr
Taylor would probably be receiving something closer to the larger sum
(less tax) for his fee in the case, but not the jury.*

Was it really likely, asked Mr Taylor, that Mr Bessell would come
to court knowing that every attempt would be made to destroy him
for a small sum of money?

"I ask you to consider this – is that something a man does, because
in the end a man who has lied and been discredited comes to a point
where he wants to tell the truth?"

*Even here, the rhetorical device of "I ask you to consider this" distances
the speaker from his audience and puts a conscious element of persuasion
into the argument – one which people instinctively react against.*

At this point, Mr Taylor suggested a possible reason for Mr
Bessell's willingness to testify: "Bessell knows he's not going to
have an old age. Perhaps he gave evidence because even a man who
has told lies wants to tell the truth."

*It was a manful point, but should have been developed at greater
length if it was going to overcome the jury's inbuilt scepticism where
money was concerned, and the further battering Mr Bessell was going
to receive in the defence speeches. Better to have left the question of
Mr Bessell's true motive alone.*

On the question of immunity, Mr Taylor pointed out that there
was no suggestion Mr Bessell was an accomplice; on the question of
having Pencourt present at his first interview with the police, Mr
Taylor made the interesting observation that Mr Bessell had no
reason to suppose at that stage that the police were interested in
anything but a cover-up. Nobody had been to see him at the time of
Newton's trial in 1976, and it was only when Newton spilled the

beans on his release from prison that the police showed any interest. Bessell knew the Pencourt journalists were interested in exposure, and their presence was a safeguard.

"As soon as I see Mr Challes, I knew he was a bird of a different feather. A straightforward, honest West Countryman, doing his job without fear or favour. But in the light of what had been suppressed in 1976, wasn't it understandable that he was alarmed?"

Mr Taylor took the jury through the correspondence between Thorpe and Mr Bessell on the attempt to defraud Jack Hayward of £250,000, arguing that Thorpe knew all about it all along. Once again, he said that Thorpe was "scheming and deviously planning to adjust the record . . . I am sorry to say this, but the deviousness of Mr Thorpe rings through this case again and again." He had been devious with Mr Hayward and Mr Bessell, writing letters to Mr Hayward denouncing "that bastard Bessell" at the same time as he was writing letters to Bessell in the most cordial terms.

Mr Taylor ended for the day with a summary of the evidence on the incitement charge, and one realised with a shock that while urging us not to take the charges in isolation he had in fact been addressing himself to the incitement charge all day:

"Either Mr Bessell made this up wickedly or it is true. There is really no other alternative about this."

Day twenty-three: 12 June 1979
Mr Taylor's closing address continued
On the second day of his closing address, Mr Taylor devoted himself to the conspiracy charge. He opened by pointing out that it did not matter to the murder conspiracy charge whether Newton went on Exmoor intending to kill Scott or bungle it; a conspiracy offence was complete once there was agreement to do something unlawful.

There were three points to be borne in mind: the first was that Newton went on to the moor with a loaded gun; secondly he went as the result of an agreement at least with Holmes; thirdly the jury must ask themselves what he had agreed to do, and who was a party to it apart from Holmes. There was direct evidence from Deakin of the meeting between himself, Le Mesurier and Holmes at which the question of finding somebody to do something was discussed.

Clearly there was an agreement between Newton and Holmes to do something. Mr Bessell said Holmes told him it was to kill Scott. Newton said the same. They both named £5,000 as the figure eventually paid. The two had never met.

Holmes and Deakin maintains that it was a conspiracy to frighten, Le Mesurier claimed that he only came into the conspiracy at the pay-off. There was positive evidence from Deakin that Le Mesurier had been in it right from the beginning.

The conspirators had tried to frighten Scott, to buy him, to steal his documents, but he still presented a threat. There was nothing left to do but kill him. Two appointments were made at hotels – they were a bad place to frighten people, quite a good place for killing them – and "you might think £10,000 is a big sum for anyone to pay just to go and frighten someone."

Newton was an accomplice and, in law, it would be dangerous to convict on Newton's evidence alone. But Mr Bessell was not an accomplice and his evidence corroborated what Newton had said.

Where Newton's evidence was concerned, Mr Taylor plainly regarded himself as on dangerous ground:

"You will be told by the defence that Newton is an unmitigated liar, but would you expect a hit man to give evidence like the Archbishop of Canterbury? . . . You may make an allowance for the fact that he is not a very cultivated man. It is the substance of his evidence that counts rather than the insolence of manner that surrounded it."

Mr Taylor then proceeded to cast doubt on the substance of it, suggesting that Newton was telling lies when he said he pretended the gun had jammed; and that he really intended to kill Scott all along. *The defence made merry hell with this passage from Mr Taylor's speech, but poor Mr Taylor had a hopeless witness in Newton and it is hard to see what else he could have said. All his other evidence pointed to the fact that the gun* had *jammed.*

Next he turned to the curious feature of the bogus letter sent to Holmes purporting to be from Newton in prison. Le Mesurier later turned up with this letter, asking Miller to authenticate Newton's signature. In face the letter had been concocted by the journalist Barrie Penrose, which was an unacceptable thing to do, said Mr Taylor, but it did establish the connection between Holmes and Le Mesurier.

Miller was an accomplice, said Mr Taylor, and his evidence would require corroboration, but it was useful in some respects. *Mr Taylor did not really elaborate on the respects in which it was useful: one had the impression that he must have heartily regretted putting Miller in the witness-box rather than in the dock. But it was Miller who had taken Newton to the pay-off.*

The money was crucial because it linked all the defendants. There was unchallenged evidence that Mr Hayward's first payment procured by Thorpe had gone to reduce Holmes's over-draft. Holmes was not in a position to spend £2,500 on the letters in 1974 and a further £5,000 to pay off Newton in 1977. He told Mr Proven Sharpe he had never met Scott and didn't know Newton, which enabled the Exeter trial to proceed on a basis of no con-spiracy – that the shooting was "Newton's frolic on his own."

Both the money and the tapes linked Holmes to the conspiracy, the tapes providing some corroboration of conspiracy to murder.

Where Deakin was concerned, Newton's evidence of having told him about the dog-shooting was corroborated by Miller, although denied by Deakin.

"The jury might think they can rely on something Newton and Miller really agree about," said Mr Taylor with a valiant attempt at humour in his adversity. "After all, they have not put their heads together. They are at loggerheads."

The last twenty-five minutes were devoted to a blistering attack on Thorpe. *It was fine, stirring stuff, but from the point of view of convincing the jury I could not help feeling we should have had it earlier.* First, he took us through the Dinshaw-Hayward episode, pointing out that both were men of integrity. Thorpe had misled Mr Hayward time and again, and when Mr Dinshaw threatened to tell the truth about the money Thorpe had instructed him to send to Holmes, Thorpe had threatened that Dinshaw would have to leave the country. *This episode, more than any other in the whole squalid case, appeared to make Mr Taylor really angry. Whether it was because Mr Dinshaw was a respectable witness, or because he was a Pakistani by birth and therefore required especially polite treatment, it started Mr Taylor off in the first and only denunciation of Thorpe's behaviour he was to deliver.*

"That, however groping an attempt, was an attempt by Mr Thorpe to pervert the course of justice," he began. Thorpe had given several conflicting accounts of what he had done with the money. He had never given Mr Hayward an explanation.

"It is a measure of Thorpe's preparedness to go to any lengths to avoid being exposed, and you may think it is not irrelevant to consider that when you are considering whether he would really go to the lengths of taking a life."

Mr Taylor referred to the celebrated *Sunday Times* headline of 14 March 1976: "The Lies of Norman Scott – by Jeremy Thorpe." His June 1978 statement to the police should be headed, "The Lies of Jeremy Thorpe – by Jeremy Thorpe," said Mr Taylor, in a nice phrase. Mr Thorpe had "lied, lied and lied again," he said, but the biggest whopper of all was when he said he had deposited Mr Hayward's £20,000 with accountants as an iron reserve against future elections.

After this magnificent display of indignation – *directed, it may be noted, against lying rather than against such crimes as attempted murder, conspiracy or incitement to murder* – Mr Taylor practically invited the jury to let George Deakin off. He was the only one of the four to have given evidence, Mr Taylor pointed out. If he was not allowed to count it against the others that they had declined to give evidence, he seemed quite prepared to count it in Deakin's favour that he had done so. The only real evidence against Deakin came from Newton, said Mr Taylor, forgetting for the moment his previous reference to Miller's evidence. If the jury came to the conclusion that they could not convict him on the evidence given by Newton, then the proper verdict would be one of not guilty.

He said he thought he had made out a good case against all four, but if the jury had any doubts, they should acquit.

"All the Crown asks you to do is to return true verdicts in accordance with your oaths."

There can be no doubt that Mr Taylor had done his best, and a very valiant best, too. I don't think his form of advocacy was particularly well adjusted to a London jury – it might and perhaps should have impressed the judge, but the judge made it plain, long before Mr Taylor started, that he had other things in mind.

To the extent that he was responsible for the framing of the charges, Mr Taylor must share the blame for an unsuccessful prosecution. At least two, possibly three, of the defendants would seem to be admitting the lesser crime of conspiracy to frighten. If he had taken that charge as well he might have been able to concentrate on the more serious charges to better effect. I think he – or rather the DPP – was wrong to put Miller in the witness-box rather than in the dock – a larger group in the dock might have added plausibility to the idea of a conspiracy. As it was, he was gravely handicapped by having two hopeless witnesses in Newton and Miller, and handicapped also by the judge's attitude to Mr Bessell and Scott.

Perhaps the mildness of his tone in everything except the one matter of Thorpe lying is attributable to feelings of discouragement and fear that he would lose, anyway. But it was a sturdy effort for all that, and one had the impression that no private citizen would ever suffer an injustice at his hands. He had very little opportunity to practise his skills in cross-examination, two of his witnesses were useless, but he did his best.

14

Closing Addresses: the Defence

Day twenty-four: 13 June 1979
Mr Mathew
Mr Mathew opened on a note of high indignation with an attack on the evidence of Mr Bessell and a strong defence of his client's unimpeachable character which was only slightly damaged when he admitted, later on in his speech, that his client had undoubtedly been part of a conspiracy to frighten Scott and had hired the ruffian Newton for this purpose. Perhaps I should explain here what was never satisfactorily explained in court, that in criminal parlance the expression "to frighten" or "put the frighteners on" someone is understood to include a considerable degree of physical violence – whether razor-slashing or breaking some bones. It is not used in the colloquial sense of giving a mild shock, or promoting a sense of foreboding – "I'm frightened that it is going to rain." The burden of Mr Mathew's speech – as, indeed, that of the judge – was that it would be a disgraceful thing for someone of Holmes's irreproachable character to be convicted on the evidence of anyone so disreputable as Mr Bessell, let alone Newton. Neither seemed to consider that Holmes's respectability had been in any way impaired by this admission that he had been part of a criminal conspiracy to harm a member of the public who was seen as a political embarrassment.

But Mr Mathew's indignation seemed genuine enough. Just occasionally the suspicion crossed my mind not only that he was hamming it up but that he wished us to know he was hamming it up. But perhaps I am attributing a greater degree of sensitivity to this expert and professional advocate than it would be proper for him to claim.

The first reference was to Mr Bessell's "double your money" arrangement with the *Sunday Telegraph*, whereby he would receive £50,000 for his story on a conviction, £25,000 on acquittal.

"I wonder whether the scales of justice held by that figure on the dome at the top of this court is [sic] still trembling, having heard the startling admission from the witness Mr Peter Bessell," he began. *At the time, I thought one could object to this opening sentence on several grounds – that scales are plural and do not have ears, that if he really wanted to know whether they were still trembling he could perfectly well have gone outside and looked. But I also began to suspect that the exaggeratedly high-flown oratory was deliberate.*

"The premeditated and planned taking of another's life is a most terrible crime. It is the ultimate offence because it offends against the fundamental laws of God and civilised people. It is with conspiring to commit such an offence that David Holmes is charged – a man of whom you, as members of the jury, have seen a lot but heard little.

"He is a man of unimpeachable character. He works as a financial consultant in Manchester, and he is a prominent member of the Liberal Party, having at one time been its deputy treasurer. Nobody has even suggested of him before that he carried out or even contemplated the merest act of violence against another.

"He now stands accused of conspiracy to murder on the evidence of two people who are self-confessed liars and perjurers and who have accepted that their behaviour in this case has been deceitful, devious and dishonest. They have received immunities – one of them so wide and all embracing as to be unique in the annals of English law . . .

"They have suffered what can only be described as the Machiavellian attentions of two journalists whose names have dogged us from first to last during the saga of these unhappy events.

"The two witnesses have very large financial interests not only in the case generally but actually in its outcome, the jury's verdicts . . ."

Mr Mathew was to repeat these points over and over again in ever more violent language. The reason for this approach became clear when he dealt with his client's refusal to give evidence: it was not just that the evidence against him was questionable, but it was so tainted, so obviously to be dismissed out of hand, that there was no useful purpose in answering it.

"Why should a man, subject no doubt to his own pressures, worries, inhibitions and possibly weaknesses, and maybe misgivings as to his own conduct – which, though they are not in any way possibly relevant to the offences with which he is charged, may nevertheless do him no credit – why should he submit himself to the ordeal of the witness-box? . . . Why should he, unless, of course, the evidence is such that it requires him to do so?

"Perhaps it is unusual for a defendant not to give evidence. But this is a very unusual case, brought on the evidence of very unusual witnesses, and, you may think, therefore, that a very unusual course is justified."

Mr Mathew suggested that special circumstances might apply which Holmes could not describe without going into the witness-box and which his counsel could not mention on his behalf. He was confident, he said, that the judge would direct the jury that it would be utterly wrong for them to regard Holmes's silence as contributing in any way towards guilt.

Nor, of course, was his confidence in the judge misplaced. But on this point, it seemed to me, legal practice departed from the rules of common-sense. Holmes had exercised his right of silence not only in court but also throughout his police interrogation, relaxing it only once during his initial interview with Mr Proven Sharpe when he untruthfully said he had never met Newton. To invite the jury to disregard this was asking them to subordinate their reasoning faculties to some elaborate and arbitrary set of rules governing the nature of proof; in other words they were not being asked whether they thought beyond reasonable doubt that Holmes and the others had conspired to murder Scott. They were being asked to umpire a game called "Proof" in which the players from time to time informed them of the rules.

"Through me, what Mr Holmes is saying to you is this: 'I am not guilty of this offence. You have not proved through the evidence that I am, because the evidence you have brought defies belief. Therefore, there is no need, because there is no evidence, for me to deny the charge.' "

Once again, Mr Mathew ran through the reasons for regarding Newton and Mr Bessell as unreliable witnesses. *One wondered if, in their boredom over this endless repetition, the jury might not start trying to find reasons for regarding them as reliable.*

Newton had perjured himself at Exeter; was an accomplice; was trying to sell his story; had a clear motive for perjuring himself again. Mr Bessell had agreed there was a credibility problem, he had agreed . . . all Mr Bessell's self-flagellation was recalled, his devious business proposals to Mr Hayward, his immunity, his "double your money" arrangement with the *Sunday Telegraph* . . .

A more interesting passage, which took up a large part of his morning address, concerned the journalists Penrose and Courtiour.

What had previously been hinted at was now made explicit. Without having called any evidence on the point, Mr Mathew was suggesting that Penrose and Courtiour had deliberately orchestrated the evidence between Mr Bessell and Newton with a view to the commercial possibilities of their book. *Nobody was in a position to argue the point, of course, but one rather admired Mr Mathew's nerve here. He was asking the jury to accept not only that Mr Bessell had concocted the story of a murder conspiracy with a view to writing a book about it and making money after Thorpe's conviction, but also to accept that Penrose and Courtiour were similarly concerned to secure a conviction although their book came out before Thorpe and Holmes were even arrested.* But his next question was the most breathtaking of all:

"Why have we not seen Messrs Penrose and Courtiour? Why has the Crown not put them in the witness-box? You are entitled to ask yourselves why."

Even the judge baulked at this, pointing out in the course of his summing up that he had excluded the two journalists from large parts of the trial on a defence application, assuming the defence proposed to call them. Mr Taylor had made it clear from the beginning that he had no intention of calling them – indeed they could have had no evidence to offer on anything which had happened before May 1976 when they were called in by the former Prime Minister, Sir Harold Wilson, to investigate the matter. By then, the conspiracy – if there had been a conspiracy – was over.

Mr Mathew proceeded to take the jury through the various stages of Pencourt's investigation into the Thorpe case, intimating that at every stage they were not concerned to discover the truth so much as to orchestrate an untruthful charge against Holmes and Thorpe for the purpose of making money: "You may think that the behaviour and clear interest of these two journalists explain a great deal about the case," he concluded ominously. He told them that the journalists had made £100,000 from their book, *although there had been no evidence on this point, but he neglected to mention that the book had been published before the prosecution was started, or that, under those circumstances, evidence of a criminal conspiracy to frighten against a prominent politician was just as sensational, and rather easier to believe, than evidence of conspiracy to murder.*

It was an oddly unsatisfactory passage in the defence case for Holmes, and rather stole the thunder – so dramatically had it been made – from what was surely the strongest point of the defence, in so far as it hung on the distinction between a conspiracy to kill and

*conspiracy to frighten. This was that on his own admission in the Old·
Bailey (although he had seemed to deny it at Minehead) Newton had
asked Mr Kuttner, of the* Evening News: *"Suppose I was only sent to
put the frighteners on him. How would that look?" Newton did have
an explanation of sorts for his question, but in Mr Mathew's hands it
need have looked no more convincing than his insistence that the gun
had not jammed – or than anything else that Newton said. But Mr
Mathew rather threw away this valid point, I thought, by his
insistence on the bogus one.*

In the afternoon, having spent the first part of the day impressing
the jury with his client's unimpeachable reputation, Mr Mathew
started by conceding the existence of a conspiracy to frighten Scott,
and his client's part in it, and concentrated on denying that it was a
conspiracy to kill.

His first target was Newton's preposterous story of having gone to
the Royal Garden Hotel in Kensington with a coal chisel hidden in a
bunch of flowers to kill Scott. The chief reason for disbelieving this
story was that Scott, in evidence, said he never agreed to go to the
Royal Garden Hotel. Other implausibilities in Newton's account
were as easily explained by his incompetence as by the suggestion
that he was lying, but this one stood out as a lie. Even the Crown had
insisted that one part of Newton's story was a lie – where Newton
insisted that he had only been pretending that his gun had jammed.

"How can they invite you to accept parts of his evidence and in
the next breath say that you may think he is lying in another part?
How are you to know which part to believe?"

*It did not require great skill on Mr Mathew's part to point out that
Newton was a hopeless witness and his evidence to all intents and
purposes worthless, but he devoted about twenty minutes to repeating
this obvious fact, nevertheless.*

Next he suggested – *again without evidence having been called on
the point* – that the second £10,000 from Mr Hayward might have
been spent by Holmes on illicit election expenses by Thorpe. This
would explain Thorpe's behaviour and his attempts to persuade Mr
Dinshaw to hide them: "If these moneys were, in fact, for some
illicit under counter election expenses, that could explain a great
deal of this part of the evidence."

*But I did not understand why, once a conspiracy to frighten was
admitted, Mr Mathew should need to find further explanation for the
payments – why, in fact, it was necessary to invent further criminal
activities on the part of Thorpe and Holmes when the payments had
already been explained. No doubt this passage of the defence, with its*

ingenious explanation about the money, belonged to some earlier draft before Mr Mathew had decided to admit the existence of a conspiracy to frighten. At Minehead he had merely admitted to the possibility of a prima facie *case on this score.*

By the end of the afternoon, Mr Mathew's client Holmes was not cutting such a pretty figure as he had done at the beginning of the day. I found I had to keep pinching myself to avoid the suspicion that Mr Mathew did not want his client to win.

"This case can never have a happy ending, whatever your verdict may be, because the scars are too deep and will remain," he concluded. "But there can be a fast and fair ending to the agonies which, albeit brought on by himself, must have been suffered by Mr Holmes in recent times."

Poor sod, I thought. Surely Mr Mathew could have summoned up a little more enthusiasm than that. But then I had thought the same, to a lesser degree, at the beginning of Mr Taylor's closing address for the prosecution. It was as if neither barrister really wanted to win. But perhaps that is the way top-flight barristers are expected to behave.

Day twenty-five: 14 June 1979
Mr Williams

Nobody could level the same charge against Mr Gareth Williams. His determination to see his client all right was only matched, it would seem, by his determination to assist the prosecution in the case against the other three. His was a most remarkable speech, and a welcome change from the others. One could not help wondering about the extent to which it was inspired by gratitude for Mr Taylor's closing remarks about his client Deakin. To receive an accurate impression, one should read it aloud in a musical, high-pitched, Welsh lilt, occasionally dropping to a venomous monotone when the names of Thorpe or Holmes come up.

"To begin with, I would like to say that bearing in mind Thorpe's position and connections, the bringing of this prosecution was an act of courage and discrimination by the Director of Public Prosecutions and prosecuting counsel. This case has upheld the rule of law, so it can be seen that even the mighty in this land are in the end subject to the same ventilation as the most obscure.

"You will recall Mr Peter Taylor's analogy of this trial as a Greek or Shakespearian tragedy. They have their tragedies, also in humbler places, and if on this evidence you were minded to convict Mr Deakin, it would be wrong. It would be a tragedy in a small town."

There was a strong element of class antagonism in the comparison between his client and two of the other defendants, Thorpe and Holmes, but stronger than this was the disdain to be put into comparisons of their honesty, their courage, their manliness.

"Mr Deakin's case is not the same as the other defendants, as you may recall Mr Taylor saying in his closing speech for the Crown. I would say in view of the evidence that you would be perfectly entitled and logically consistent to convict the other three defendants and acquit George Deakin.

"Again, this is not to harm the other defendants if you were minded to decide that Mr Holmes deceived, misled and lied, that Mr Bessell had been deceived by Mr Thorpe and Mr Holmes on the Barnes letter, you would be entitled to think that one or other of those defendants used people as if they were marionettes. If Mr Holmes got hold of Mr Deakin, is it not a possibility if not a probability, that they would use Mr Deakin in the same way?"

He said the jury might have thought, after hearing the evidence of Mr Bessell, that it sometimes disclosed quite disgraceful conduct on the part of Thorpe and Holmes, but none of that had anything to do with George Deakin. Compared with Thorpe and Holmes, who. were highly educated, Deakin left school at fifteen and made his own way in life.

"But you don't need to be highly educated to give your evidence. All you need is determination to meet the case against you and, you may think, treat the jury and the case with respect . . . Deakin alone treated you with respect and gave you his explanation, although he knew he would be cross-examined hard."

It was the next passage which marked, so far as I could see, the only sign in the whole trial that the jury might be prepared to take an independent line from the judge. The judge scowled horribly and ground his teeth in the way that elderly gentlemen are allowed to do, but I saw three or four members of the jury grin broadly as Mr Williams continued in his cheeky, provocative Welsh voice.

"Mr Deakin does not have powerful friends in high places. Mr Deakin does not write letters to the Home Secretary starting 'Dear Reggie . . .' so far as we know. Mr Deakin does not seem to be on close and affectionate terms with the Commissioner of the Metropolitan Police."

Before dealing with the evidence against him, Mr Williams continued at some length on the subject of how helpful Mr Deakin had been to the police, how from the very beginning he had been consistent and straightforward in his account: "None of that proves

that Mr Deakin is not guilty, but it is a pretty good test in his case."
Whether consciously or not, Mr Williams was appealing to a strong sympathy in the courtroom. Deakin may not have made a very good impression in the witness-box, but we were so grateful to have heard some evidence from the defence, anything which was not the interminable voices of Messrs Mathew and Carman, that I have no doubt the entire press contingent would have voted for Deakin's acquittal on these grounds alone.

On the case against Deakin Mr Williams pointed out – as Mr Taylor had done – that it relied pretty well entirely on the evidence of Newton. This enabled him to launch himself into a knockabout turn on the general subject of chicken-brains: "If it wasn't so desperately serious for Mr Deakin – until you acquit him – it would be farcical."

Mr Williams made one point of such sublime silliness that I found myself beginning to doubt that he was quite as much convinced by his client's purity as he seemed. He asked why Newton had not tape-recorded the alleged meeting in which he claimed Deakin hired him to kill.

"Don't you think that greedy little man, if he thought there was any benefit in it, would have taped George Deakin? He did not do so because Deakin was on the periphery."

Deakin may indeed have been on the periphery, but this did not prevent people taping him later on. At that stage the greedy little man did not know there was any benefit to be gained – it was not until Scott started mentioning names to him in Barnstaple. But even this was acceptable when compared to the splendid non sequitur *with which Mr Williams concluded his oration:*

"As I say again, George Deakin was until this trial, just an obscure businessman in Wales. He might be despised by some people in high places. Someone who could be used, someone of no account – a tool. Someone who left school at fifteen. It would be wrong to think of convicting him.

"There is a hymn which people sometimes sing in Wales: '*Rwyn gweld o bell y dydd yn dod*' which may be translated into English: 'I see from afar off the day which is coming . . .'

"Mr Deakin has waited a long time since 1977 and his day will come with your verdict of not guilty."

If it had been appropriate, I feel that the whole court would have burst into applause when Mr Williams sat down. It would not be true to say there was scarcely a dry eye. Everybody was laughing. But then Mr Williams had been playing it for laughs – confident, perhaps, that

his client would get off after Mr Taylor's generous admission that the
case against him was perhaps less satisfactory than those against the
other three defendants.

But Mr Williams was the only one of the counsel with any apparent
appeal for the jury, and the only one who did not appear intimidated
by the judge's obsessive urge to treat Thorpe as a visiting dignitary. I
vowed that if ever I found myself before a jury on a criminal charge, I
would hire Mr Williams as my counsel.

Mr Cowley

Mr Cowley had not spoken much in the course of the trial and he did
not say much now. Perhaps this was in deference to the wishes of his
client, the loud fellow Le Mesurier. But the case for Le Mesurier
was fairly straightforward, and did not require any elaborate
character assassination of Crown witnesses. He had tried a little
character assassination on the witness Colin Lambert, the old
soldier who had once worked for Le Mesurier, but accepted the
judge's ruling that it was not necessary, and did not return to it now.

There was Deakin's evidence of Le Mesurier's casually mentioning a blackmail problem to him on one occasion, he said, but
otherwise the only evidence to connect his client with the conspiracy
referred to events after the dog-shooting when the conspiracy was
at an end.

"There is not one iota of evidence to connect him with anything in
between," said Mr Cowley in his loud, grating voice. The tapes
showed his client's lack of knowledge of what was going on.

"Even Mr Newton said he did not regard Le Mesurier as one of
the conspirators," said Mr Cowley. It was odd, I thought, that
anyone should use Newton as an authority at this late stage. Certainly, Mr Taylor seemed reluctant to do so.

"As my learned friend, Mr Gareth Jones [sic] said, you've got to
look at the case in three ways," he droned. First, there was the
conspiracy to frighten. Then there was conspiracy to murder. Then
there was conspiracy to frighten which developed into a conspiracy
to murder. Mr Cowley hoped that the jury would opt for the first,
but if they opted for the third there was no evidence against his
client on that one, either.

One possible motive for his client's involvement in the conspiracy
was gratitude to Mr Holmes for having introduced him to a pools
winner called Gibbs who invested a large sum of money in Le
Mesurier's carpet business. But there was no suggestion that Le
Mesurier had had any advantage out of Holmes's help.

Mr Le Mesurier had an impeccable previous character, with an excellent record of six years' service in the Royal Air Force.

"Is he the sort of man that you think is going to be engaged in a scheme to kill somebody he does not know and has never met and has nothing to do with?"

Mr Cowley sat down in a general atmosphere of gloom. The truth was that nobody cared very much whether his client was guilty or not. The trial had lost much of its interest since the announcement that Thorpe would not give evidence. Now we were all impatient for it to end and to know the verdict – with perhaps a certain curiosity about which side the judge would take on various small matters of interpretation which had been left to his discretion. We all knew pretty well what the defence lawyers would say in their closing addresses. We had heard Mr Carman make the same, or nearly the same speech twice before in the absence of the jury. There was something almost approaching a groan when the small, red-faced QC from Manchester stood up to make his final plea for Thorpe.

Mr Carman

In fact, Mr Carman's posture had subtly altered throughout the trial. Where his earlier addresses seemed calculated to appeal to an indignation that anybody of such unassailable character as his client should be affronted by scurrilous charges from such disreputable quarters, Mr Carman's final address to the jury was essentially an appeal for pity. Whatever his client had done (and he continued to deny most of it) he had been punished: his career was in ruins, his public life was finished. That, at any rate, was the theme of the first day's address. A lion set upon by jackals and hyenas, Thorpe had been brought to the ground by them.

"Privately he is a man with a life that has had more than its fair share of grief and agony. Nature so fashioned him that at the time he had the misfortune to meet Norman Scott, he was a man with homosexual tendencies . . . You will recognise from the evidence that a political life and political future are now irrevocably and irreversibly denied to him."

Mr Carman gave a sort of blanket absolution to all the "distinguished names in the public life of this country" who had been mentioned. "There is not, I say at once, a shred of credible evidence of the slightest impropriety on the part of any one of them, save and in so far as innuendo and smear emerge from certain squalid witnesses called by the Crown."

The jury had been rightly reminded that all were equal before the law.

"Mr Jeremy Thorpe does not wish any advantage or disadvantage. He is now in your sole charge and he is content with that position. But inevitably because of the prominence he has achieved in the public life of this country, the case has centred to an extent on the life and times of Jeremy Thorpe – his frailties, his weaknesses have been exposed remorselessly to the public gaze."

Mr Taylor had asked the jury to put aside all sympathy in considering their verdict – a foolish request, as I remarked at the time. Mr Carman now proceeded to cash in:

"I would respectfully agree with that . . . but although you rightly put aside sympathy, you do not divest yourself of proper compassion and common humanity in assessing the man.

"In the political life of this country it is all too evident that Mr Thorpe made an important, a significant contribution, a politician, the evidence reveals, of distinction with the qualities of ability, enthusiasm and dedication. The political scene would be poorer without men of that kind and calibre."

However, the judgment that "a political life and political future are now irreversibly denied to him" was only applicable to the first day of Mr Carman's address. Next morning, having presumably thought about the matter overnight, Mr Carman suggested that the trial need not necessarily be a complete end to Thorpe's public life, if he was found not guilty.

"At his age, if your conscience and your oath permit you to say not guilty, there may still be a place somewhere in the public life and public service of this country for a man of his talents."

Still urging the jury to put aside all sympathy while not divesting themselves of proper compassion or common humanity, Mr Carman reminded them of the untimely death of Thorpe's first wife and paid tribute to his second wife Marion, the former Lady Harewood, "whose constant presence in this court speaks eloquently for itself."

According to the Sunday Times *team who interviewed one or more members of the jury, this plea had a profound effect on at least one juror, who decided that Marion had suffered enough and advanced this as a major reason for acquittal.*

Mr Carman ended this passage rather disconcertingly with this assessment of Thorpe's character: "He is human like us all. We learn, do we not, that idols sometimes have feet of clay?"

At this stage of the trial Mr Carman placed less emphasis than

formerly on the suggestion that Thorpe's proposals to Mr Bessell –
if made at all – were made in jocular spirit.

"He is a man with a sense of humour, capable of great wit, and
certainly a man to whom comedy was never absent for very long in
his life. But tragedy has replaced it in large measure."

Next Mr Carman moved into the now routine attack on the press,
prefaced by the stereotyped avowal which I have heard so often on
the lips of nearly every barrister, judge and politician who has any
dealing with the press.

"I shall yield to no one in my admiration of the British press and
the vital part they play in the administration of justice in this
country. Very often they assist the administration of justice.
However . . ."

There was a small section of the press, said Mr Carman, which fell
seriously below the high standards the press normally sets itself. It
included on this occasion the *Sunday Telegraph*, the *Evening News*
and the two journalists Penrose and Courtiour.

"They never actually emerged into the daylight of the court or the
witness-box but always lurked in the murky shadows," said Mr
Carman, *without actually mentioning that it was he who had sent
them out of the daylight of the court into the murky shadows; or that it
was he who had neglected to call them as witnesses after the judge had
all but ordered him to do so.*

They had been present at an interview between Scott and Mr
Challes; later they had gone out horse-riding with Scott.

"Scott claimed friendship with one of them in the witness-box. I
am tempted to say birds of a feather . . ."

They had also co-operated with Mr Bessell in the preparation of
their book.

"There is a role for investigative journalism provided appropriate
ethical standards are maintained. But where you get, as in this case –
Mr Taylor's word for it – 'tinkering' with the evidence, I would
prefer to say 'fabrication' of the evidence, by Penrose and
Courtiour, it shows the length to which these two men were prepared to go to launch this prosecution to their financial advantage."

*Once again Mr Carman did not see fit to mention that the book by
Penrose and Courtiour – whose name he still pronounced, on the
twenty-fifth day of the trial, as if it had been spelled Courteeay – was
published* before *the prosecution was launched. One would like to
think that Mr Carman, in retrospect, felt ashamed of this disreputable
passage. In every other way, his closing address was a model of good
sense and powerful argument.*

He went on to treat of the need for hard, reliable evidence on which to convict. Scott, Newton and Mr Bessell's evidence was not reliable, Mr Hayward's and Mr Dinshaw's was not sufficiently incriminating. The proper test to apply was the standard required by law for "hard, fast, reliable, safe evidence," said Mr Carman. This was plainly quite a different thing from being certain beyond reasonable doubt that a defendant was guilty.

Mr Carman was at pains to point out – *and quite reasonably after the immense production which Mr Taylor had made of the issue* – that Thorpe was not charged with having had a homosexual relationship with Scott, although he denied it.

"May I be permitted to make a general comment on the question of Mr Thorpe's admitted homosexual tendencies at that time? We live, I hope, in a civilised society, in a tolerant society. There are people who have propensities which we personally may not understand. To them we have to extend tolerance, sympathy and compassion. Homosexual activity of any kind was, of course, contrary to the criminal law of this country until the late 1960s. Times have changed, Parliament, reflecting public opinion, changed the law."

Homosexuality, he said, was at the periphery of the case, not at the heart of it, for a very good reason.

"Whether there was or was not a homosexual relationship, the motive for Mr Thorpe to take part in any unlawful activity against Norman Scott was the same, whether the relationship existed or not." This was because Scott constituted a threat either way. It was an obvious point to make, and I do not know why Mr Taylor was not prepared to accept it. But Mr Carman went on just the same to list all the reasons for supposing that the relationship never existed. Scott was a liar and a hysteric – "sad, mad or bad or a combination of all three, I care not" – who had invented a relationship with Thorpe even by his own account before it had existed.

"There is no doubt that Mr Thorpe formed a degree of affection for this young man. He tried to help him . . . and wasn't Jeremy Thorpe being used by this inveterate liar, a social climber and scrounger?" The "Bunnies" letter, he said, contained no hard evidence whatever of any physical sexual relationship.

With great skill, Mr Carman managed to turn Thorpe's refusal to go into the witness-box into a further indictment of the press.

"Those who stood to gain financially might be the most bitterly disappointed of all," he said.

"It is a right invested by law that a defendant can stay silent. Everyone suspected or accused of a crime is entitled at the beginning and at every stage until the end of his trial to the right to say: 'Ask me no questions. I shall answer none.'

"We are not here to entertain the public or provide journalists with further copy. We are here for a much more serious purpose, to determine whether these charges are made out."

A careless or unreflective listener might have inferred that Thorpe's refusal to give evidence was inspired by a desire to assist the jury in this matter.

Mr Carman proceeded to the familiar litany of abuse against Mr Bessell as a reliable witness on the incitement charge.

"Mr Bessell may go down at the end of this case as the Judas Iscariot of British politics of the twentieth century because he has three things in common: one, he seeks to betray a friend; two, he seeks to betray him for money; and three, he seeks to betray a man who, I submit, is innocent of the charges laid against him.

"If, by your verdict, you say not guilty, that may be the final epitaph of Mr Bessell."

Apart from Mr Bessell, the Crown relied on Newton to provide evidence of a conspiracy to murder – Newton, whom the Crown itself sought to discredit on the question of what happened that night on Porlock Moor.

Mr Carman said he was tempted to reopen the Christmas pantomime of Newton's evidence about the coal chisel and the bouquet of flowers, but he would resist the temptation and call half time on his speech. The trial adjourned.

Day twenty-six: 15 June 1979
Mr Carman concluded

On the last day of his closing address, Mr Carman struck a more tentative note than before. His speech lacked any great coherence, being more a collection of unrelated points which he now realised, as an afterthought, might be troubling the jury. Having deliberately left it open for the jury to decide either way whether there had been a homosexual relationship or not, he now examined what was meant by guilt. This was not so much a matter of whether the defendants had done the things of which they were accused, but of whether the prosecution had proved they had done it to the very strict standard of proof required by law. The law was a wonderful thing to rattle at the jury because, if they wanted to obey it, they would have to accept what it was from their elders and betters.

"You must not suppose that a not guilty verdict is some sort of certificate of innocence awarded by the jury. In law, it means that the prosecution has failed to make out the case."

In other words, acquittal required no more than an extended Bessell-bash. But first Mr Carman exerted himself to put the most favourable light possible on his own admission that Thorpe had *not* asked Mr Maudling, the Home Secretary, or Sir John Waldron, the Metropolitan Commissioner, to investigate Scott's allegations. Was it not remarkable enough, he asked blithely, that Thorpe had been prepared to approach Maudling and Waldron at all? The whole correspondence reflected more to Thorpe's credit than to his discredit, he suggested.

Next he dealt with Holmes's purchase of Scott's letters for £2,500.

"It has not been satisfactorily proved that the letters were purchased with Mr Thorpe's knowledge. And if he did that without Jeremy Thorpe's knowledge, that may be the key to whether he did anything else without Jeremy Thorpe's knowledge."

This was the first time Mr Carman had put forward the "Thomas à Becket" explanation suggested by Newton in a tape earlier on. The objection to it, of course, was that Henry II did not send large sums of money to the four knights after Becket's murder to reimburse them for any incidental expenses. Mr Carman addressed himself next to the problem of the £20,000 which Thorpe had arranged to be sent to Holmes, in two batches, about this time.

On this point, Mr Carman's remarks added up to a resounding "No comment." He was not even prepared to suggest, as Mr Mathew had suggested, that the money had been used for illicit election purposes. The prosecution, said Mr Carman, claimed that the money, although requested for election expenses, had been used to finance the conspiracy.

"I'm not going to solve for you the mystery of this money. You can spend a long time trying to work it out, and come up with six different answers. The Crown has to prove it is referable to guilt. That is one possibility, but there are many others the prosecution has not explored."

For a moment, it seemed as if Mr Carman was conceding the point. One admired his nerve, but how could he hope to get away with suggesting that it was the prosecution's job, rather than the defence's, to suggest alternative ways for the money to have been spent? To a lay observer this seemed incredible, but it is apparently established in legal practice. He must have known that the judge was going to let him get away with what seemed to be semantic jugglery, treating words

like "proof" and "guilt" as if they were somehow removed, for legal
purposes, from the normal processes of human reasoning. Another
judge might well have pointed out that the fact of these payments by
Thorpe to Holmes at a time when Holmes was financing the con-
spiracy might not have provided conclusive proof in itself but cer-
tainly established some corroborative probability (in default of any
other explanation) that Thorpe was helping to finance the conspiracy.
It seemed a dangerous gamble for Mr Carman to take when the only
solid benefit would be to save Thorpe from admitting to illicit election
activities. By any reckoning, it was an extraordinarily cavalier way to
dismiss one of the prosecution's more solid pieces of corroborative
evidence.

After this Mr Carman reverted to the familiar noises of a ritual
Bessell-bash. Then a brief reference to Thorpe's treatment of Mr
Dinshaw, about which Mr Taylor had grown so indignant. This
momentary lapse of good manners – when Thorpe had threatened
Mr Dinshaw with exportation if he revealed how he had sent the
money to Holmes on Thorpe's instructions – was to be explained by
the fact that Thorpe was "clearly desperately worried and concerned" about the money at that time. Mr Carman was not, of
course, going to explain *why* Thorpe was desperately worried and
concerned. We might spend a long time time trying to solve the
mystery and come up with six different answers . . .

"I don't run away from that. That is regrettable," said Mr
Carman.

Finally, he retracted his suggestion of the day before that
Thorpe's political career was irrevocably finished. There may still
be a place somewhere . . .

"This case has been fought and considered against the backcloth
of British politics. It is important to remind you of your rights in this
case.

"You have the right as citizens to vote in elections. But you have a
much more important right and a much greater responsibility to
vote guilty or not guilty. Mr Thorpe has spent twenty years in British
politics and obtained thousands and thousands of votes in his
favour. Now the most precious twelve votes of all come from you. In
accordance with your conscience, I say to you, on behalf of Jeremy
Thorpe this prosecution has not been made out. Let this prosecution fold its tent and quietly creep away."

That ended the defence of Jeremy Thorpe. The last sentence was in
continuation of an extended metaphor first introduced by Mr Taylor,
which I have not bothered to pursue. For all his qualified suggestion

that Thorpe might one day return to public service, Mr Carman ended on a much less strident note than we had heard from him at the beginning of the trial. "I say to you on behalf of Jeremy Thorpe, this prosecution has not been made out" is not quite such a rabble-rousing cry as "Jeremy Thorpe is innocent."

The judge adjourned the trial until Monday, 18 June when, he said, "we will all have a clean start." The weekend also gave him an opportunity to compose his summing up. This was to run for two days, with a few sentences added on the Wednesday. Pondering the matter myself during this interlude, I drew up what seemed the direction which any summing up must take. It seemed to me that, with the traditional cautions about uncorroborated evidence from accomplices and the value to be given to the concept of "reasonable doubt," there was no need for the summing up to take more than twenty minutes. That, in my experience, is the longest period which most people are prepared to spend concentrating on the words of a single speaker. What the judge actually said in his summing up may be found in Chapter 16. Here, in the interlude provided by a June weekend, is my own.

15

Interlude

16 and 17 June 1979
A layman's summary of the evidence
The dog is dead. That is the first unchallenged fact. The second is that there has been a criminal conspiracy to harm Scott. The third is that Thorpe had a motive for joining such a conspiracy.

Once those three unchallenged facts are established, we may disregard the details of Scott's evidence as irrelevant. It does not matter if he was buggered by Thorpe, or how often, if he is truthful or if he is a liar. The motive exists, and that is the only relevance.

Before considering whether the conspiracy was to murder or to frighten I would suggest the jury first consider whether all four were members of a criminal conspiracy. Next they should decide whether it was a conspiracy to frighten or to kill. If it was a conspiracy to frighten, the indictment fails, but if the jury decide there was a conspiracy to murder, they should next ask themselves whether it was always a conspiracy to murder, or whether it became one at a later stage of the conspiracy. If it became a conspiracy to murder at a later stage, the jury should finally ask themselves whether all the four defendants were still members of this conspiracy.

On the first point, of whether all four defendants were members of the conspiracy to harm Scott, we have Mr Mathew's admission, on behalf of his client, that Holmes was part of such a conspiracy. We have Deakin's evidence in the witness-box that he put Newton in touch with Holmes for the purpose of advancing the conspiracy, which makes him a member of it, although the extent of his involvement thereafter is questioned. We have Deakin's evidence, which was unchallenged by Mr Cowley, that Le Mesurier introduced him to Holmes for the purpose of assisting the conspiracy. This would make him a member of it, although once again the extent of his subsequent involvement is disputed.

Which only leaves Thorpe. Circumstantially, we can see that he had a motive for belonging to such a conspiracy, that the conspiracy was entirely concocted for his benefit, and that at some time after

Holmes started paying for the conspiracy, he arranged for large sums of money to be paid to Holmes. That is unchallenged. We also have the direct evidence of Mr Bessell, who has been represented by the defences as a liar and scoundrel, inspired by revenge. Mr Bessell's evidence is unequivocal, if it is believed. The jury must ask themselves whether Mr Bessell is telling the truth or whether he is lying. The defence have suggested that he is lying for the purpose of pecuniary advantage. That he will receive pecuniary advantage if he is believed is not disputed. The jury might reflect that he composed his *aide-mémoire* setting out the substance of his evidence against Thorpe in 1976 before the second police enquiry had started. If his motive was primarily commercial, he must have reckoned to concoct this false accusation which the defence have described as being of a wild and implausible nature against a public figure of unblemished reputation, persuade the police to prosecute and a court to convict and then collect his money. The jury must decide whether the likelihood of this is such as to create a reasonable doubt in their minds.

On the question of whether the conspiracy was one to murder or one to frighten, we have the unequivocal evidence of Newton that he was hired by Holmes and Deakin to kill Scott, but the jury may well decide that the evidence of Newton should be treated with the utmost suspicion. On the fact of Newton's being an accomplice, which is unchallenged, the jury should require corroboration of his evidence; on the fact of his having perjured himself at Exeter, which is agreed, they should treat his account with care; on the fact of his having misled this court about his experiences in America on evidence which, although untested, was supplied by the prosecution to the defence, they should treat anything he says with caution; on the fact that the prosecution itself claims he is lying on oath in his account of the scene on Porlock Moor – whether his gun jammed or not – they might reasonably decide to treat his evidence as completely worthless. The only solid fact to emerge from his period in the witness-box may be that he is an unprincipled and mercenary figure who was hired by Holmes to harm Scott, but prosecution and defence (for Holmes) both agree that Newton was lying when he said he pretended that his gun jammed. If the jury agree, they may decide that this provides powerful circumstantial reason for accepting that his intention was to kill, and he is lying to save face, however belatedly.

Further circumstantial support for this comes from the fact that many other methods of silencing Scott had been tried – including frightening him – and all had failed. But the only direct evidence on this point comes from Mr Bessell. His evidence, again, is unequivocal. Once again, the jury must decide whether Mr Bessell is telling diabolical lies for the purpose of gain or revenge, or whether he is telling the truth. On the point of whether the conspiracy was to murder or to cause lesser harm the jury might ask themselves whether it has been established that there was less money to be gained by revealing the plot by a distinguished politician to intimidate and put in terror – if it was true – than there was to be made by revealing a plot to murder, if it was false.

What the jury must decide is whether the four defendants did what they are accused of doing, or whether they did not. If they have doubt, and it is reasonable doubt, they must acquit. The crime of which the four defendants are accused is a vicious and cowardly one, and the jury must not for a moment entertain the thought that it was justified because Scott had proved himself so vexatious a threat to Thorpe's political career, or threatened his domestic tranquillity. If the jury are convinced beyond reasonable doubt that the defendants are guilty – which means no more and no less than that they did what they are accused of doing – then they must convict, and convict in the happy knowledge that they are doing their duty as citizens in face of a conspiracy which would be made worse, not better, by the fact that its aim might have been to protect a figure in political life whom large numbers of people trusted for his apparent honesty.

On the question of whether the conspiracy started as a plot to frighten and later became a plot to murder, we have only the evidence of Deakin to suggest that this might be the case, but we have only the evidence of Newton to suggest that it is not. The other three defendants have chosen not to speak, as it is their perfect right to do. This should not be seen as necessarily indicating guilt, but it would be quite wrong for the jury to try and guess what they would have said if they had given evidence. They have chosen this course of action with its advantage to them, that they do not have to face cross-examination, and its disadvantage, that we shall never know what alternative version of events they might have proposed, had they chosen to do so.

On the question of whether to prefer Deakin's or Newton's word for the nature of the conspiracy at its outset, the jury might bear in mind that Newton has been shown – and accepted by the prosecution – to be an unreliable witness, whereas Deakin's account had been consistent throughout. The prosecution itself invited the jury to consider whether the case against Deakin might be less satisfactory than it is against the other defendants. If the jury feel that the circumstances create reasonable doubt in the case of Mr Deakin, they should acquit.

Where Holmes and Thorpe are concerned, this suggestion has not been advanced. Holmes was plainly a member of the conspiracy to frighten at every stage, by his counsel's own admission, and we have the evidence of Mr Bessell, with which I have already dealt, that Thorpe's intention throughout was to apply the final solution. If the possibility of a changing conspiracy is applied to Le Mesurier, we have against it the evidence of Mr Colin Lambert, who described Le Mesurier as talking of a conspiracy to shoot Scott, and the circumstantial fact, which is unchallenged, of Le Mesurier having arranged Newton's payment at the end of the day. Le Mesurier has chosen not to give evidence, and the jury must not try to guess at what he would have said if he had, but must decide on the evidence before them whether or not Le Mesurier played his part in a conspiracy to kill Scott.

So on the conspiracy charge, I suggest the jury first decide whether all four defendants were members of the agreed conspiracy to harm Scott; then whether it was, in fact, a conspiracy to murder, rather than frighten him; finally whether the conspiracy might have changed course at some stage from one to the other and, if so, whether all four followed it on its course to an attempted murder.

On the incitement charge against Thorpe we have only the uncorroborated evidence of Mr Bessell. If Mr Bessell is lying, it has been suggested that this might be for pecuniary advantage but it might also be out of revenge because Thorpe exposed his disreputable business activities to the *Sunday Times*. Until that moment, Mr Bessell had been a supporter of Thorpe, by his own account prepared to lie and cover up for him. Revenge may be a motive for lying, it may also be a motive for telling the truth. If Thorpe had chosen to give evidence, the jury could have decided which they believed. As it is, they can only decide whether or not they believe Mr Bessell. Mr Carman suggested as one reason for Thorpe's decision not to give evidence that there is no case for him to answer. That is a matter which is exclusively for the jury to decide.

16

The Judge's Summing Up

Day twenty-seven: 18 June 1979
Sir Joseph Cantley OBE, the Honourable Mr Justice Cantley
Defendants' good reputation
"This is a very serious charge and a rather bizarre and surprising case. It is right for you to pause and consider whether it is likely that such persons would do the things these persons are said to have done. But if, however unlikely you would otherwise have thought, you are ultimately convinced by the evidence that they did, then, however sadly, you will have to convict.

"The four accused are men of hitherto unblemished reputation. Mr Thorpe is a Privy Councillor, a former leader of the Liberal Party and a national figure with a very distinguished public record.

"What is the effect of the defendants' character in a criminal trial? Normally it has its most important effect when the defendant goes into the witness-box and gives evidence, because the jury is then reminded that they have been listening to the evidence of a man of good character, and give it the attention which a man of good character deserves . . .

"You would pay more attention to the evidence of a bishop than a burglar . . .

"In this case, three of the accused have not gone into the witness-box. This does not mean that their good character should be ignored . . ."

In discussing the "hitherto unblemished reputation" of the four defendants, the judge, who had only heard evidence of good character on two of them from the police, would not have been permitted to mention that one had a criminal record; or that another's business activities had been severely criticised by a Department of Trade enquiry. Nor did he suggest at this stage that various revelations in the course of the trial – unexplained by the defendants – might have produced a blemish or two: that Thorpe had lied in a police statement about £20,000 solicited under false pretences from Hayward, that

Holmes had lied to the police when he claimed never to have met Newton, had engaged in a criminal conspiracy to harm Scott; that Deakin had, on his own admission, been part of that conspiracy, albeit a small one; that Le Mesurier had been part of that conspiracy and had also, by agreeing to hand over the money to Newton, conspired to pervert the course of justice. None of these considerations was to be held against the "hitherto unblemished reputation" of the four defendants.

Refusal to give evidence no sign of guilt

The judge next discussed the effect of not going into the witness-box.

"This is a neutral fact. It adds nothing to the prosecution's case and adds nothing to the defence. The burden of proof is on the prosecution and if the evidence called by the prosecution does not, by itself, make the jury feel sure that the charge has been proved, the defendant is entitled to be acquitted . . .

"You must not speculate on the reason why the defendants have decided not to give evidence. There might be many reasons other than guilt for not giving evidence. You must not say, on looking at the evidence, that you would have had some doubt except that the defendant has not gone into the witness-box.

"That is the wrong approach. If members of the jury have a reasonable doubt, the prosecution has failed to prove its case and you should acquit."

Further reasons for acquitting the defendants

Next, he dealt with the nature of a conspiracy.

"If, for example, Mr Le Mesurier joined what he thought was a conspiracy to frighten somebody and then found out in October 1975 that the real object was murder, the mere fact he helped after that to hush it up would not make him a member of the conspiracy to murder.

"It would make him a member of another conspiracy of which he is not charged – that would be a conspiracy to defeat justice . . .

"A conspiracy to frighten somebody is a criminal conspiracy, but the defendants are not charged with that. You have to consider only whether they conspired to murder somebody. Unless you are sure that was the object of the conspiracy, they must all be acquitted on the first count."

Prosecution evidence tainted
The judge said he would now deal with the tainting of evidence.
"You have seen it illustrated in this case. It has happened: the
pursuit not of justice but of profit has tampered with the quality of
important evidence. I could not help thinking at one point that if
there had been really enterprising and competitive media in those
days, Judas Iscariot might have thought the thirty pieces of silver the
least of his rewards."

*The relevance of this passage might seem obscure, until one
remembers that Mr Carman, in a flight of rhetoric, had described Mr
Bessell as the "Judas Iscariot of British politics."*

What should the jury do when they find a witness has a financial
interest of his own which might tempt him to tell lies?

"We can only play for safety . . . we must look at his evidence
with distrust if that is the conclusion we have come to about him and
treat it as dangerous to act upon his evidence unless we find good
reasons elsewhere to believe it to be true.

"We should look for some untainted evidence from elsewhere
which tends to confirm what he is saying."

*This passage must have come as the cruellest blow to the police and
prosecution side. The judge was effectively instructing the jury to
disregard Mr Bessell's evidence unless it was corroborated, just as if
Mr Bessell had been an accomplice, although, as he later admitted,
Mr Bessell was not an accomplice. With that instruction, he destroyed
three-quarters of the Crown case against Thorpe – if the jury heeded
him. As this was still the first half-hour of the summing up, there
seemed every possibility that the jury were taking it in and would
remember it.*

The reasons for the Sunday Telegraph's *"double your money"
contract with Mr Bessell have been adequately explained. Just as the
libel laws had prevented any newspaper from printing Mr Bessell's
story before the trial, so they would prevent it afterwards in the event
of an acquittal. The* Sunday Telegraph *in typical penny-pinching
way, was merely introducing an insurance that it would not spend too
much money on an unprintable story. This quirk of the British libel
laws was not only going to preserve Thorpe's unblemished reputation
before conviction, it was also going to make conviction virtually
impossible.*

Bad or immoral behaviour not relevant
The judge referred to a reminder in Mr Carman's closing address to
the jury that this was not a "court of morals."

"I'm not quite sure what a court of morals is, but this is not one of those . . . The fact that a man may have behaved badly is no reason why he should be convicted of another offence with which he is not charged."

Peter Bessell: humbug with a record

The judge now embarked on a review of the evidence which he said he hoped would be less coloured than the accounts they had been hearing up to now. First he would deal with Mr Bessell's evidence.

"You will have seen that Mr Bessell is plainly a very intelligent, very articulate man. He must have impressed the electors of Cornwall very much. He told us he was a lay preacher at the same time as being, as he put it, sexually promiscuous. And therefore a humbug."

The only evidence on the incitement charge was that given by Bessell of a conversation in the House of Commons. But when he told the story to Penrose and Courtiour three years earlier, he had said it took place somewhere else. However, if the jury accepted the evidence and came to the conclusion that Thorpe was serious, that would be incitement to murder.

Various minor parts of Mr Bessell's evidence were corroborated, said the judge, but these did not bear on what Thorpe was alleged to have said on this occasion. In fact none of Mr Bessell's incriminating allegations was corroborated. According to Mr Bessell, Holmes admitted to him that he had hired the pilot to kill Scott, but tape-recordings made after this alleged admission were of "cordial conversations." In one curious passage, he said, Mr Bessell said of Holmes that he was a "good and faithful servant to our friend," going on to describe him as a "respectable private citizen."

"I say that was a curious moment, to say of a man who has told you he is trying to murder someone – 'you are after all a respectable private citizen.' Either it goes against Mr Bessell's credibility or it shows that he is broadminded to an unusual extent."

I do not know whether the judge was being deliberately obtuse here, or whether he had genuinely not understood the point of Mr Bessell's remark that Holmes was, after all, a respectable private citizen. The point was surely that Holmes, as a man of unblemished reputation, was most unlikely to be suspected of murdering any male models, and therefore had a right not to have his home invaded by the press; moreover, Holmes was a private citizen in a sense that Mr Bessell was not, having been an MP. It was surely no odder that Mr Bessell should describe Holmes as a respectable private citizen at that time than that the judge should describe him as a man of unblemished reputation after hearing Holmes's own counsel agree that he had been part of a criminal conspiracy to put Scott in terror. But it was an extra drop of bat's blood in the cauldron.

After lunch, the judge returned to the attack. Mr Bessell had "quite a record," he said, before detailing some of the attacks which had been made on him. Later, he referred to Bessell's current earnings, which had been put at £2,500 a year.

"I do not know how that compares with the national average wage, but I would have thought it was under average, and certainly would not be accepted pay at British Leyland."

The purpose of this observation was not clear. If the judge intended to suggest that Mr Bessell was desperate for money, it should have been mentioned that Mr Bessell also had a rich wife, or at any rate a rich father-in-law.

Next the judge turned to consider whether Mr Bessell's evidence might have been affected by his dealings with Barrie Penrose and Roger Courtiour. He did not seem particularly impressed by Mr Mathew's and Mr Carman's onslaughts on the good name of the two journalists.

"They are mystery men as far as we are concerned. Every time Mr Carman has mentioned them you could detect the faint smell of brimstone. Both Mr Carman and Mr Mathew referred in rather a menacing way to the fact that neither has appeared in the witness-box.

"It is not their fault. I excluded the pair from court during some of the evidence – no doubt to their commercial dismay – because I had been told they might be giving evidence. We don't know what they could have said about themselves if someone had given them the opportunity. And we don't to this day know how to pronounce the name of the junior partner, Mr Courtiour."

It was heartwarming to learn that the judge had no hard feelings towards the pair after they had been hustled out of court, reviled and treated as a general football between defence counsel and the judge for nearly six weeks.

Next the judge discussed Mr Bessell's "deplorable contract" with the *Sunday Telegraph*, which, he said, he mentioned only to give it unfavourable publicity. Fortunately for the *Sunday Telegraph*, he said, the "double your money" agreement was reached only after Mr Bessell's evidence had been finalised – or "crystallised" – in his *aide-mémoire*, otherwise, "I should be considering what further action should have been taken by me when this case was over."

But if this consideration let the Sunday Telegraph *off the worst of its hooks, it did not appear to have much effect on the judge's estimate of Mr Bessell's evidence.* A few minutes earlier, he had said:

"So although his evidence may have crystallised by the time of the *aide-mémoire* in that it hasn't varied since then it is said, there is some evidence that he may have had publication of an adequately sensational book in mind before the *aide-mémoire* came."

I am not sure to what evidence the judge was referring. It could only have come from Mr Bessell, since neither Penrose nor Courtiour had spoken, and search Mr Bessell's evidence as hard as I can I find no reference to any intention to write an "adequately sensational book" before he began work on the aide-mémoire. *The judge was determined that Mr Bessell's evidence should be given minimum weight, but this drop of bat's blood would appear to be no more than a bit of dirt thrown in.*

The judge then turned to the Hetherington incident, where Mr Bessell had got a date wrong, and suggested this implied the whole story was a lie. For reasons best known to himself, he chose to take a surprisingly lenient view of this "lie."

"These are matters which question Mr Bessell's credibility, but the fact that a man tells a lie in a case does not mean he is telling lies all the time. That is the snakes and ladders approach to litigation. You cannot say a witness is disqualified and down the snake he goes if he is caught out in one lie.

"If you think that before he even crystallised his evidence he was actuated by a wish to make as much money as he could by publishing a book, then you should view his evidence with suspicion and be slow to act on it unless it is supported by other evidence."

In fact there was no evidence that the Hetherington story was a lie, merely that Mr Bessell had got a date wrong. The prosecution might have taken heart from the fact that here the judge was merely urging the jury to view Mr Bessell's evidence with suspicion and be slow to act on it without corroboration whereas at the beginning of his summing up he had said it would be dangerous to act on it without corroboration. But I doubt whether Mr Taylor noticed.

Next the judge went through all those parts of Mr Bessell's evidence which were corroborated, pointing out that all the most important parts rested on Mr Bessell's word alone. *After this protracted and damaging list the judge slipped in a little sentence which, if the jury were extremely alert, might seem to contradict everything he had said about Mr Bessell's evidence earlier:*

"When I say you must look at Bessell's evidence with suspicion it does not mean you cannot believe it if there is no corroboration."

One may doubt whether anybody paid any attention to this, after he had stated the opposite so often and so forcibly. But it is there, on the record, in case anybody accuses him of not having said it.

The judge then turned to Mr Bessell's evidence against Mr Holmes. Mr Bessell had said that Holmes admitted to him that he had hired Newton to kill Scott. "But whether there is any evidence capable of corroborating that I will deal with later."

Back to the need for corroboration. That ended the judge's attack on Mr Bessell for the day. It had been as deliberate and as prolonged a destruction of one witness as anyone was likely to hear. Whether it was justified, or whether it was an abuse of judicial power, is something which would have to be decided between Joseph Cantley and his Maker. No doubt the tenor and direction of the judge's summing up represented his honest opinion of the witness, but without Mr Bessell the Crown had no case on the charge of conspiracy or incitement to murder. The only other substantial witness on the first point was Newton, whose evidence might reasonably be regarded as worthless by any conscientious jury. And there was no other witness of any sort on the second. All that remained to be seen was whether the jury would follow the judge's direction.

Norman Scott: liar, fraud, sponger, crook

The judge next turned to Scott's evidence. It was not important whether Norman Scott had a homosexual relationship with Thorpe or not, as the judge pointed out. The motive was there in either case. In fact the disputed part of Scott's evidence was entirely irrelevant. But that did not stop the judge entering with relish into the task of destroying him and so, obliquely, discrediting the prosecution case.

"I now turn to the evidence of Mr Norman Scott. You will remember him well – a hysterical, warped personality, accomplished sponger and very skilful at exciting and exploiting sympathy."

On the "Bunnies" letter of February 1962 (it was dated 1961, which would have made Scott a minor at the time of the alleged offence, but Mr Taylor accepted that this might have been in error for 1962) the judge had this to say:

"All I can say is that this is capable of corroborating some homosexual relationship between the two – but not necessarily. It is for the jury to decide whether or not. You may take a different view ... It is capable of corroborating a homosexual relationship. I do not mean that it necessarily corroborates buggery, which is what is alleged to have happened. A man may write to a girl he liked and say

'I miss you,' but that would not be capable of suggesting that they had had sexual intercourse. It indicates affection, perhaps, but we must not assume that affection necessarily implies buggery, no more than a letter to a girl you hope to see or perhaps marry is able to imply sexual intercourse. 'I miss you' – I would not write that to a man, but I might have written something like that to a girl."

After mentioning Scott's "very nasty" letter to Thorpe's mother and various other aspects of his evidence, which he tended to discount in so far as they related to the charges before the court, the judge turned to the general question of Scott's credibility. He pointed out that while Scott was in a psychiatric clinic (*I think he got this slightly wrong – it was while Scott was staying with a couple in Enstone, Oxfordshire, between visits to the clinic*) having had only three minutes' conversation with Thorpe at Vater's stables, he was boasting that he had had a homosexual relationship with Thorpe. Scott now admitted there was no truth in this, but "if he was prepared to say that when there was no foundation for it, then to what extent can you rely at any rate on the full detail of what he is saying?"

What was the relevance of the alleged relationship?

"The only relevance to our case is whether or not Mr Thorpe had a motive for wanting Scott to disappear. That is all. We are not here to decide whether he had a homosexual relationship or not. Even if you conclude there was no homosexual relationship of the nature that Mr Scott described, it would not be an end to the matter. It is not decisive whether there was a relationship or not. It is not one of the things we have to decide. We have to decide, looking at the whole of the evidence, if Mr Thorpe had a motive which would really go so far as to impel him to the conspiracy for getting rid of Scott."

From this lofty and significant point, the judge turned to the lies and sexual adventures of Norman Scott. He had pretended to be a relative of Lord Eldon. "He has told many lies to improve his image." He had told many amazing lies. He knew Thorpe had homosexual tendencies, and according to Mr Carman, went to the House of Commons hoping to make something out of these tendencies. He had lived with a rich homosexual and a widow. He agreed that he had fraudulently pledged other people's credit (*was this a reference to his buying a shirt on Thorpe's account?*) and was at one time suspected of stealing silver from a house where he was living in Dublin although he denied this.

"He is a crook," said the judge.

Mr Scott also admitted to stealing letters from Vater.

"He said they were from Mr Thorpe," said the judge. "We have not seen them, but let's assume they were. What did he keep them for? Why was he upset when he lost them and do you agree with Mr Bessell that he is not a blackmailer?

"He is a fraud. He is a sponger. He is a whiner. He is a parasite. "But of course, he could still be telling the truth. It is a question of belief."

In case the jury doubted this last sentence, the judge repeated it: "You must not think that because I am not concealing my opinion of Mr Scott I am suggesting that you should not believe him. That is not for me. I am not expressing any opinion."

If the jury believed that the judge was not expressing any opinion they would have believed anything.

Finally, the judge turned to the money that Scott had made or might be going to make from the case, although Scott had denied that he was going ahead with his book on the subject. If Scott was believed, he said, it proved that there was a homosexual relationship: "It proves he successfully exploited the relationship for some time and it proves, I suggest, his hatred of Mr Thorpe." It also proved, said the judge, that he moved into Thorpe's constituency before Christmas 1973, where he drank in local pubs and talked of his relationship with Thorpe – as the prosecution suggested presenting a constant danger to Thorpe's reputation.

The judge had just turned to Newton's evidence, and was pointing out how dangerous it was to convict on the uncorroborated evidence of an accomplice, when he decided it was time to adjourn for the day.

Day twenty-eight: 19 June 1979
Mr Justice Cantley continued
Newton: accomplice, perjurer and chump
It was on the second day of his summing up that the judge warmed to the humorous possibilities of the narrative. This was especially apparent after lunch, when it was sometimes difficult to follow the drift of his argument through the private chuckles and wheezing noises which accompanied his observations. A summary may give a wrong impression of whatever emphasis the judge may have intended, but this intention was by no means clear. At one point he seemed to be urging the jury to decide that it was, indeed, a conspiracy to kill – subject to the reservation that if they had the slightest reasonable doubt on this score they should acquit all four

defendants – at the next he seemed to be urging them that the evidence against each of the four individually was too flimsy and disreputable to entertain. From the muddle of his observations three important directions remained: that disreputable or tainted evidence created doubt, that if they had the slightest doubt they should acquit, that the only evidence in this case which was neither disreputable nor tainted was peripheral to the main charges.

First he took the jury through Newton's evidence. What had struck the judge most about Newton was his extraordinary incompetence, whether as frightener or murderer.

After the Royal Garden Hotel fiasco, with coal chisel and bunch of flowers, Newton hired a bright yellow car to accost Scott in Barnstaple, where it drew so much attention that one woman took its number. He then offered to buy Scott's letters, without either the money or authority to do so. This again showed Newton as a "highly incompetent performer with all his self-advertisement."

"He did not think things through very carefully," commented the judge.

Newton claimed he planned to try and frighten Scott into being a bundle of nerves. He thought of a plan to lure him into a lonely place and pretend to shoot him. He claimed the idea to frighten was his alone. He would pretend the gun had jammed. When he went to carry it out he picked up his girl-friend's car to take Scott on to Exmoor. "But what a chump the man is. To frighten or to murder – that is no way to go about it!"

The judge next listed four reasons for believing the gun had genuinely jammed, despite Newton's claim that he was only pretending: a firearms expert testified that it had jammed four times in twenty-seven shots when he tested it; the man who supplied the gun told the court that Newton had complained of the jamming; David Miller said he saw a round jammed under the firing pin on the night of the shooting; Newton, at Exeter, had said the gun jammed, along with his fabricated story of having been blackmailed.

"The relevance of that for the purposes of this case is that he is capable of inventing an entirely false story."

The judge quite plainly thought the gun had jammed, and was not prepared to shirk the implication of this.

After Newton's release from prison he received £5,000 in cash from Le Mesurier, who also gave him an air ticket to Rhodesia where he was trying to find a job. Newton said he took tapes in order to protect himself, but the judge suggested they would also corroborate a "sensational story which could be published for large sums of money."

In cross-examination Newton agreed that he had lied often and for his own purposes. At Exeter, he had committed perjury himself and suborned a witness to commit perjury on his behalf. He agreed he was now trying to sell his story.

"He is resolved to milk the case as hard as he can. He told us so. He has already been paid £10,950 for interviews with newspapers and television, plus the £5,000 from Holmes. I doubt whether he has paid any income tax."

One would not have thought there was any need to blacken Newton's character still further for the jury to see that Newton's evidence was suspect, even worthless. The judge had not heard a jot or tittle of evidence to suggest that Newton, in addition to this other crimes, was a tax evader; most of the £5,000 he received from Le Mesurier had been recovered by the police, and was produced as an exhibit in court; and the total of £10,950 was far less than Newton would have earned in three years as a commercial pilot.

But the most interesting aspect of this passage was where the judge referred – almost inadvertently – to the £5,000 as having come from Holmes. Obviously he thought it had, and it was a reasonable inference that it had, but the prosecution had not been able, in fact, to establish any link between the £20,000 given to Holmes by Mr Dinshaw – £9,500 of it in cash – and the £5,000 cash given by Le Mesurier to Deakin. As counsel and judge alike were at pains to point out, the burden of proof rested at every stage on the prosecution.

The judge then discussed Newton's story of having been offered £100,000 by the *Evening News* on the basis that Newton said it was a conspiracy to murder rather than to frighten. Mr Justice Cantley tended to disbelieve these figures, but pointed out that Newton agreed he had been peddling his story around: "He agreed that everything he has is for sale. He also agreed that he had the clearest possible motive for perjuring himself in these proceedings . . . One had to look at his evidence with great care, not only because he is an accomplice . . . but also because he has the clearest possible motives for making a sensational story." The tape of a conversation between Holmes and Newton where reference is made to a "conspiracy to bloody . . . murder" might provide some corroboration, said the judge, if the jury chose to take it that way. Having warned them against accepting Newton's uncorroborated evidence, the judge then listed the things which Newton proved if the jury believed him:

that Deakin briefed him to kill Scott at a meeting at Aust Motorway Service Station – this was uncorroborated and contradicted by Miller; that Holmes hired him to murder Scott for £10,000 – uncorroborated, although there was no dispute that the meeting took place. Against Le Mesurier, Newton produced tapes to confirm the payment of £5,000. Another tape suggested that Le Mesurier might have been the person who originally thought up the solution to the Scott problem.

Next, the judge turned to David Miller's evidence. This supported Deakin's claim that when he introduced Deakin to Newton it was as someone who would frighten for money. It also suggested that Le Mesurier was an intermediary for Holmes.

Miller was "the last of the dubious commercial witnesses." It was up to the jury to decide whether they could believe these witnesses.

Mr Jack Hayward and Mr Nadir Dinshaw, the Jersey businessman, by contrast, were "nice respectable witnesses." The judge traced the timetable of payments, to Scott and Newton, relating them to the £20,000 received from Mr Hayward by Mr Dinshaw and handed over to Holmes.

After lunch, as I say, it seemed to me that the judge's observations lacked their earlier precision. One must remember that he was an elderly gentleman who had been talking now for a day and a half. But it is hard to see what the jury can have made of his comments on Deakin's evidence which, he said, did help the other witnesses, although not conclusively, for this reason:

"If you're hiring a man who is willing to frighten someone else for money, he's the sort of man who might be prepared to do a murder for you. On the other hand, it's a bit risky to hire someone to frighten and then ask him to do a murder for you, because if he says no, he might go away and tell somebody."

His thoughts on Thorpe seemed of an even more random nature. The judge would not read Thorpe's statement as the jury already had a copy. A statement was not the same thing as evidence, except to the extent that it contains admissions.

"But if a statement is made by a defendant in which he merely makes denials of the allegations against him or gives his reasons why he says the allegations are untrue, the statement is no evidence of what he says is true."

Where there were admissions, the jury should look carefully at qualifications in them. Thorpe had admitted there was an affectionate relationship between him and Scott (in his press statement of October 1977) but he went on to say there was no homosexual behaviour. On the other hand, the statement was not to be taken as an equivalent of evidence on oath.

The judge then gave general advice to the jury on how they should approach the task of reaching a verdict.

The first question they should ask themselves was whether there was a conspiracy to kill. If they were not sure there was a conspiracy to kill, that was an end to the matter, and all defendants should be acquitted on the conspiracy charge.

If they decided, on the other hand that there was a conspiracy to murder, they should then go on to consider separately whether each of the defendants was a member of it.

On the first point, of whether it was a conspiracy to murder or to frighten, he suggested that it might be a useful exercise for them to assume there was a conspiracy to frighten and see how it fitted in with the evidence.

"That there was a conspiracy of some sort with Newton I don't think is disputed. I don't think Newton went on the moor with Scott just on some frolic of his own, or for some eccentric reason of his own."

When the judge had finished chuckling to himself over this sally, he tried fitting the evidence to the idea of a conspiracy to frighten. *If the jury were listening closely to his more or less random observations on the point, they might have been excused for concluding that his lordship did not honestly think that the theory of a conspiracy to frighten fitted the evidence at all.*

"It has been suggested on behalf of Holmes and Le Mesurier that they might be in difficulties – heh! heh! – if charged with conspiracy to frighten but they never conspired with anyone to murder. Let us assume there was a conspiracy to frighten. You have to ask yourselves questions like this: would giving Scott a big fright serve to silence him?

"What would conspirators of ordinary intelligence expect Scott to do if thoroughly frightened?

"You have seen Scott for yourselves. He is a spineless neurotic character, addicted to hysteria and self-advertisement, rushing to others for help whenever he felt it would do any good. Would he be expected to keep quiet if thoroughly frightened? Or would conspirators of reasonable intelligence expect him to be silenced by being thoroughly frightened?

"The answer might be Yes, No, or Don't know. If the latter, the jury should pass on."

Neither the question, nor the way in which it was put, suggested that a "Don't know" answer was likely, but the judge was plainly enjoying himself too much to resist the temptation of putting the same question twice again.

"If, as Newton and Scott say, there were two attempts to lure Scott into a hotel – one in Kensington, the other in Bristol – how would conspirators of ordinary intelligence expect that to work out?

"You get him there and give him a thorough fright. What happens next? What could you expect Scott to do next?"

The third point at which to apply this assumption of conspiracy to frighten was on the deserted moor, where Newton took Scott with a loaded pistol and live ammunition.

"Suppose he thoroughly frightens Scott by trying to shoot him – either by pretending the gun was jammed or by shooting at him but deliberately missing him – he would not give him a lift back in the car after that. He would be left on the moor.

"What happens next? Does Scott say he had better not say anything or had better not mention names? Would people who knew Scott expect him really to keep quiet?"

Finally, he suggested the jury should consider whether the gun really did jam on the moor. Was it a pretence, or if the gun jammed was that the reason why the whole thing failed?

At this point the judge decided he had gone far enough. Nobody listening to the last passage could have doubted that the judge was inviting the jury to decide that there had been a conspiracy to murder, and that it had involved Holmes and Le Mesurier. Thorpe's name had not been mentioned, and when the judge came round to it later it was equally plain he was not going to encourage the jury to convict Thorpe of anything. But having gone a long way towards advising them that on the first question – whether it was a conspiracy to kill or to frighten – they should decide it was a conspiracy to kill, he now backpedalled furiously. It was simply a question of which part the jury remembered more vividly.

He reminded them that in deciding these questions they should remember where the burden of proof lay.

"You must be *sure* it was a conspiracy to murder before you convict anybody. If you are left wondering which it was, then the Crown have not proved a conspiracy to murder. You are not being asked to decide whether it was a conspiracy to frighten. The question is: are you sure it was a conspiracy to murder.

"If you think it was a conspiracy to frighten, that is an end of it. If you don't know which it was, you cannot convict on a conspiracy to murder. If you *think* it was but are not sure, then you cannot convict of conspiracy to murder."

Deakin and Miller both testified that at any rate in the beginning, it had been a conspiracy to frighten. And there was also the fact that at the end all that had happened was that Scott was thoroughly frightened.

"So you could say: there you are, the proof of the pudding is in the eating. They asked for a man to frighten somebody, and look what happened, he was frightened."

Nothing seemed to have been thought out, whichever it was, said the judge, although "it could be argued that if the intention was to murder then even a conceited bungler like Newton might have been stimulated to take a little more care to avoid detection."

That ended discussion of whether it had been a conspiracy to frighten or to murder. *At one point in the judge's rambling discourse it seemed there could be no doubt that he was unconvinced by defence suggestions of a conspiracy to frighten. In the sense that a summing up can be said to be directed towards a particular conclusion, this section was directed towards a conviction, at any rate of Holmes and Le Mesurier. Then came the sudden about-turn: no conviction was possible except under circumstances of utter certainty, and doubt might be introduced by various, slightly far-fetched considerations.*

The only explanation which occurs to me for this remarkable about-turn is that the judge suddenly noticed that his rambling discourse was heading in the wrong direction. He may also have reflected that a jury might have been reluctant to convict Le Mesurier and Holmes while acquitting Thorpe.

The judge next summarised the case against each defendant.

Holmes agreed he was part of a conspiracy, but only to frighten. He paid Scott £2,500 in February 1974 at a time when he was short of money. Holmes actually admitted to Mr Bessell that he hired Newton to kill Scott, but only "if you accept the evidence of Mr Bessell." Mr Bessell had a financial interest in conviction. Newton, also, said that Holmes had hired him to kill Scott – "if you believe Mr Newton." Newton was an accomplice and it would be dangerous to accept his evidence in corroboration. Otherwise, there was only the telephone conversation to corroborate, when Holmes said, "Just fine. You may rely on that," in answer to Newton saying he should keep quiet since there was a possibility of a charge of conspiracy to murder. The jury had to consider whether this statement implicated Holmes. "If you came to that conclusion, it is capable of corroborating the evidence of Newton – even Newton."

Against Deakin, who, he said, was probably the type of man whose taste ran to a cocktail bar in his living room, there was no corroboration of Newton's evidence whatever; indeed Newton's evidence was contradicted by Miller.

Le Mesurier's counsel invited the jury to decide he never knew it was a conspiracy to murder until it was abandoned. Against him was the evidence of Colin Lambert, the old soldier who worked for Le Mesurier. He said Le Mesurier told him: "We should have hired someone like you because the chap who went to do the shooting was an idiot." The judge drew attention to his use of "we" in this context, but went on to suggest that Le Mesurier might have been trying to make out he had a bigger part in something than he actually had.

Where Thorpe was concerned, the evidence against him was "almost entirely circumstantial." There was the question of motive. Motive was not always relevant, he said. "But motive and absence of motive may, in a particular case, be relevant. In this case, motive, although it is not conclusive – far from it – is not irrelevant in the case against Mr Thorpe. It is a matter you can take into account." From 1965 onwards, Scott had been telling his story to anyone who would listen: "It was the kind of story people are so ready to believe these days, even if it wasn't true.

"You had the opportunity of seeing Scott in the witness-box and you can see his vindictive attitude. Scott has said 'I pity him', but he doesn't – he hates him, whether with justification or not is a different matter.

"And so in 1974, he was coming on. He was a leader and he was a very successful leader. And yet this wretched Scott is still in his constituency with his file and his grievance and his story and his visits to public houses and so on."

It would be quite wrong to suggest that the natural reaction would be to kill Scott. "But it would be in his interest if Scott stopped spreading this scandal, and he would also be greatly benefitted if one way or another Scott was silenced."

There was not a great deal of other evidence against Thorpe, said the judge. *He had not yet mentioned the chief evidence against him. He now proceeded to do so, almost as an afterthought, as if there was little importance to be attached to it.*

"There is Mr Bessell. If you accept his evidence – and I warned you about the danger in Bessell – then he established that in 1969 Mr Thorpe said of Scott, 'We've got to get rid of him.'

"He followed that – if you believe it – with an attempt at persuading Mr Holmes to kill Scott. That is the charge of incitement."

Next he dealt with the evidence from Mr Hayward that Thorpe had tried to persuade him to frighten off Mr Bessell from coming to England in 1978. Perhaps Thorpe was nervous of homosexual revelations, said the judge. Nobody denied that two sums of £10,000 were handed over to Holmes, and the prosecution had suggested they were raised to finance the conspiracy. But the jury had never been told what the money was for. Thorpe had produced a number of explanations about it and they could not all be true.

"If, in the end, the only inference you can draw from the evidence about the money is that Mr Thorpe obtained it by telling lies to Mr Hayward, that does not add anything to the prosecution case. The fact that a man obtains money by deceit does not amount to any sort of proof that the man was a member of a conspiracy to murder somebody else."

At this point, I thought the judge was going too far, and the jury would react against him. They might have missed his comments at the beginning, where he was dealing with Holmes and advanced Newton as possibly corroborating Mr Bessell rather than the other way round. They may have missed the fudging of his earlier statement that Mr Bessell's evidence did not need corroborating. They may have accepted his cavalier treatment of the evidence against Le Mesurier as suggesting no more than that Le Mesurier was boasting of having committed a crime he did not commit. But to dismiss the evidence of Mr Hayward and Mr Dinshaw as having no relevance to the conspiracy charge struck me as pushing his luck. In the course of doing so, the judge invited them to accept that Thorpe was a liar. Why, in that case, did the judge seem so extraordinarily anxious – and prepared to stand so much of the prosecution case on its head – in order to see him off the charges he faced? Perhaps he was reluctant to sentence a public figure, perhaps he felt sympathy for Thorpe over the persecution by Scott. We shall probably never know. But if the jury could see the summing up as no more and no less than an extension of Mr Carman's speech for the defence they might easily decide not to be spoon-fed to this extent. Or so I thought. But I did not have the judge's long experience of British juries, or of how malleable they are when treated with consideration and courtesy.

The judge ended with a further reason for acquitting Thorpe, even if it meant sending Holmes to prison. He reminded the jury that Mr Carman had asked them to consider whether, even if

Holmes was a member of a conspiracy to murder, it followed that
Thorpe was in it, too.

"I do not know what motives you could think of for Mr Holmes
doing all this by himself," said the judge. Mr Bessell had said
Holmes was very loyal and devoted to the Liberal Party.

"I am not a political animal so I cannot understand that but it is
obvious that some people are very loyal to political parties.

"If you are wondering whether perhaps Holmes did it himself and
Thorpe did not know, it follows the case against Thorpe is not
proved."

Leaving that thought in their heads, the judge proposed to
adjourn until the next day. First, he had suggested they ask themselves whether perhaps Holmes did it by himself, then he said that if
they were wondering whether this was the case they should acquit
Thorpe. *The introduction of this new element of "wonder" seemed to
offer an interesting extension of the familiar doctrine of reasonable
doubt.*

There, as I say, the judge would have left it, but Mr Carman
foolishly decided to push his luck still further. Jumping to his feet he
told the judge that there was no evidence at all that if there was a
conspiracy to frighten, it ever became more serious.

*Nor, of course, there was. It was a device by which the jury were
given the option of acquitting Deakin and/or Le Mesurier while
convicting Thorpe and Holmes – a way of saying they believed Mr
Bessell, disbelieved Newton. The prosecution seemed ready to accept
it as a device for acquitting Deakin. The judge, however, was not
going to be pushed around. Despite the fact that they were both on the
same side – or perhaps because of it – he seemed to find Mr Carman
strangely irritating, and certainly wasn't going to take any lessons
from the tiny Lancashire man on how to conduct Thorpe's defence.*

"I am going to leave that to the jury," he said. It was true there
was no evidence of a change of course in the conspiracy, but then a
"conspiracy charge is never supported by minutes of the meeting of
the conspirators." *This, I thought, was rather a dangerous admission
from the point of view of the defence. If the judge had made it earlier
and in a more general context it might have shown the prosecution
case in a more favourable light than either Mr Carman or the judge
really wanted.* The court adjourned.

Day twenty-nine: 20 June 1979
Next morning the judge was as good as his word, and spent only a

few minutes on the means by which the jury were to reach their verdict for an acquittal. First, they should consider the conspiracy charge to which all four defendants had pleaded not guilty:

"You should ask yourselves if you are sure there was a conspiracy to murder Norman Scott. Put it that way because that is the correct way to apply the burden of proof, which is on the prosecution. If the answer to that is "No we are not sure," that is an end to it, because if there was no conspiracy, none of the accused can be guilty of it.

"If the answer is 'Yes, we are sure,' then you should proceed conscientiously to examine the evidence against each of the defendants in turn. If you find a doubt about any of the accused, he is entitled to be acquitted."

He went on to deal with the second charge of incitement, against Thorpe alone.

"Again you must ask yourself if you are sure that early in 1969 Thorpe seriously and genuinely tried to persuade Holmes to murder Mr Scott. If you are completely sure, you will convict, but if there is any reasonable doubt you will acquit."

He warned them that he expected a unanimous verdict, and would not accept anything less. Then, with a smile and a wave, he said: "You may go now. Take as long as you like. There is no hurry. We shall wait for you."

17

Verdict, Aftermath and Epilogue

The jury was out all the day. At nightfall, they were taken to a secret hotel, unable to talk to anyone except a court official to say whether or not they had reached a unanimous verdict. The four defendants were taken to Brixton Prison for the night. Three of them were shut up in circumstances of considerable privation in a cell with two other prisoners, one of them apparently an aggressive Negro who had been convicted of manslaughter. Thorpe, however, found himself afflicted by an upset stomach, and was taken to the prison hospital, where conditions were less austere. The prison authorities were reluctant to reveal whether it was normal to take people to hospital suffering from a stomach upset.

Next day, again, the jury deliberated throughout the morning and throughout the long afternoon. Various accounts have been given of how their deliberations went – one version, based on an interview with a single juror, appeared in the *New Statesman* of 27 July 1979. It was written by Peter Chippindale and David Leigh, the two *Guardian* journalists who had been covering the case for many months and who published their own account of the committal proceedings in Minehead, *The Thorpe Committal*. A second version appears in the excellently readable, if slightly rushed, background to the case by three *Sunday Times* journalists, Lewis Chester, Magnus Linklater and David May, *Jeremy Thorpe, A Secret Life*. Both are agreed that a majority soon settled for acquittal on the first point (that there had been no conspiracy for murder), and that they decided, after the judge's remarks about pecuniary interest, that Mr Bessell's evidence could not be accepted unless it was corroborated. This inevitably meant acquittal on the second charge. They disagree on the details, and I have nothing first-hand to add to their accounts.

That night, once again, the four defendants were taken to Brixton prison. Once again, Thorpe found that his stomach was upset, and was taken to the prison hospital. That afternoon, after lunch – the defendants ate well, on smoked salmon, beef and wine supplied by Clement Freud, a Liberal MP with business interests in the restaurant and hotel trade – the jury returned for Celia Kettle-Williams, the foreman, to make her contribution to the history of our times, acquitting all four defendants on all charges.

The time was just after half-past two, and the jury had been out for fifty-two hours. The trial had lasted six weeks. No sooner had the verdicts been announced than there was a stampede for the door, which gave the judge an opportunity to end the trial as he had begun it, threatening journalists with the power of the court. "Keep still, stand still or regret it," he snapped.

One by one, counsel stood up to make their applications for costs. Mr Mathew, for Mr Holmes, said that his client had been prepared to admit the lesser charge of conspiracy to frighten throughout. The Crown was to blame for this long and expensive trial because it had chosen to prefer the graver charge. The judge said he would have to consider whether Mr Holmes had brought it on his head by his reluctance to help the police. Mr Williams, for Mr Deakin, said the proceedings were no fault of Deakin, who had volunteered statements, never changed his story and given evidence. Mr Cowley asked for a £100 contribution back which Mr Le Mesurier had paid towards his costs. Mr Carman decided against making any application on behalf of Mr Thorpe.

Carman: "No adverse inference must be drawn from the fact that I do not make any application in respect of his costs in the case. But, at the risk of reiteration, that does not involve any admission of any kind of legal culpability."

The judge: "You are saying that it was a matter properly investigated?"

Carman: "Properly investigated and, if I may say so, now properly decided."

The judge granted costs to Mr Deakin, refused them to Mr Holmes and Mr Le Mesurier.

After the verdicts became known, many statements were issued. Mr David Steel, the new leader of the Liberal Party, seemed in no hurry to welcome Mr Thorpe back to the fold:

> The news of Jeremy Thorpe's acquittal has come as a great relief to the large number of his friends and colleagues within Parliament and outside it. The ordeal, which both he and Marion have faced with such characteristic courage, has, in the words of his counsel, destroyed his parliamentary career. Nothing, however, can take away the great contribution he has made to the

political life of this country in general, and to the Liberal Party in particular, whatever misjudgements he may have made. I hope that after a suitable period of rest and recuperation he may find many avenues where his great talents may be used.

Sir Harold Wilson, the former Prime Minister, had no comment to make. Mr Alf Parsons, former chairman of the North Devon Liberals, said, "I am thoroughly delighted. I have known all along that Jeremy was innocent of the charges against him. If there is a nomination for 'Woman of the Year' I would like to nominate Mrs Thorpe."

Mr Thorpe issued a statement through his solicitor, Sir David Napley: "I have always maintained that I was innocent of the charges brought against me. The verdict of the jury, after a prolonged and careful investigation by them, I regard as totally fair, just and a complete vindication . . ."

Sir David Napley added, "Kindness and humanity require that he should be left alone for a while." Later we learned that he was drinking champagne at his wife's house in Orme Square, Paddington, after an hour and a half closeted with his legal advisers. His stomach upset appeared to have resolved itself.

Norman Scott said he was not in the least bit surprised by the result. A mighty cheer went up from the crowd outside the Old Bailey when Mr Thorpe eventually emerged. Andrew Newton, on hearing the verdict, said, "I am not too wrapped up in that judge."

Lord Goodman issued a statement:

"In view of the observations from the learned judge and leading counsel relating to the individuals whose names were brought into the case without being parties or witnesses, it would be quite unnecessary for any further statement to be made by me except to reaffirm that there is not a scintilla of truth in any of the allegations that have been aired."

The Press Council announced it would urgently consider the ethical issues raised by the trial. The Director of Public Prosecutions justified his action in bringing the prosecution by the length of time the jury had taken to decide on an acquittal.

The *Daily Star* produced a moving tribute to Mr Thorpe in his moment of triumph:

Jeremy Thorpe, ex-leader of the Liberal Party and passionate democrat, was fired by the belief that right would triumph in the end. It was his unswerving belief in himself, and the unshakeable knowledge that he was innocent, that made Mr Thorpe a mighty man. After Norman Scott's first courtroom allegation, Mr Thorpe spent three years in the public pillory. It all began many years before with a chance meeting and a few words of kindness for a weak, lonely boy . . .

Jeremy Thorpe, the man with the film-star charm, once dreamed of the political peaks he planned to scale. He wished to be remembered as a statesman of stature and courage, of vision and of truth. He expected to achieve that at Westminster. *He may well have achieved it in the dock of the Old Bailey.*

Other press comment was more reserved. All newspapers agreed that on the uncontested evidence alone, Mr Thorpe's political career was finished. All over Fleet Street one heard the noise of tearing paper as "background" stories, written in the expectation that the defendants would be convicted, were torn up. London Weekend Television, which had commissioned the journalists Penrose and Courtiour to prepare a huge two-hour documentary – over a year's work, costing a rumoured £250,000 – decided not to show it. The BBC, which had had a unit engaged on the job even longer, shredded its film.

Elsewhere, faint sounds of derision could be heard. *Private Eye* produced a Special Acquittal Souvenir issue, with the picture of a triumphant Jeremy Thorpe under the bubble: "Buggers can't be losers." A punk group, Rex Barker and the Ricochets, produced a 45 rpm record, "Jeremy is Innocent." It consisted of the refrain, "Jeremy, Jeremy," interrupted by a barking dog and gun fire. Peter Cook, the grand old man of British satire, produced a twelve-inch long-playing record devoted to a parody of Mr Justice Cantley's summing up.

But in one quarter, at least, there was no derision. At the tiny eleventh-century church of Bratton Fleming on Exmoor – a good twenty miles from the spot where Rinka was shot to death and in the heart of Thorpe's constituency – the Sunday of 1 July 1979 was devoted to a "Thanksgiving Service for Marion and Jeremy Thorpe," attended by Mr and Mrs Thorpe and Mr Thorpe's young son, Rupert. A largish collection of the world's press and a handful of villagers heard the incumbent, the Reverend John Hornby, announce of Mr Thorpe: "Countless thousands of people in North Devon rise up and call him Blessed!"

Mr Hornby, who doubled as Rural Dean and Chairman of the village Liberals Association, invited the congregation of seventy-five to pray that Mr Thorpe would be re-adopted by the Liberal Party as their candidate for the next General Election.

At least one person present felt that the service was designed to celebrate a resurrection. When the Archdeacon of Barnstaple, the Venerable Ronald Herniman, later criticised the service as being in bad taste, Mr Hornby replied that his critics were the sort of people who "would probably have been disappointed if Jesus Christ had not been crucified."

It was a very English occasion, and a suitable ending to the Jeremy Thorpe story. "By common consent, Jeremy has been the best MP North Devon has ever had and ever could have," said Mr Hornby. He prayed that God would "drive out from human hearts the Evils of Suspicion, Hatred and most of all the Self-Righteousness of all those concerned in the recent trial at the Old Bailey."

He offered prayers for the "deliverance of Jeremy, Marion, Rupert and their families from the recent ordeal through which they have now come." The grace of God had upheld them through the long, dark tunnel.

For the first lesson, Mr John Gregory, grey-haired, quiet-looking chairman of the North Devon Liberal Party, read from the Apocrypha, Ecclesiasticus XLIV:1 "Let us now praise famous men." The second lesson, read by Councillor Douglas Potter, chairman of the North Devon District Council, was St Luke's account of the birth of Christ. Mr Hornby chose as the text for his sermon the passage from Luke I:37: "For with God nothing shall be impossible."

"God is so fantastic in His making things possible which He wishes to happen. No wonder we have the opportunity to give thanks to God for the ministry of his servant Jeremy in North Devon. My dears, don't you think if it had been you or I in Jeremy's or Marion's shoes, that we'd be either round the bend or in the madhouse, or had a couple of coronaries long since with all they've been through in the last year?

"The darkness is now past and the True Light shines! This is the day which the Lord hath made! Now is the day of our salvation! Thanks be to God, for with God nothing is impossible!"